M000275203

The Politics of Park Design

The Politics of Park Design

A History of Urban Parks in America

Galen Cranz

The MIT Press
Cambridge, Massachusetts
London, England

This book was set in VIP Trump by Graphic Composition, Inc., and printed and bound by Halliday Lithograph in the United States of America.

Library of Congress Cataloging in Publication Data

Cranz, Galen.
The politics of park design.

Bibliography: p.
Includes index.
1. Parks—United States—History. 2. Parks—Design and construction—Political aspects—United States. 3. City planning—United States. I. Title. II. Title: Urban parks in America.
SB482.A4C73 1982 363.6'8'0973 82-8929
ISBN 0-262-03086-1 AACR2

Contents

II THE POLITICS OF PARK DESIGN

Preface

In the summer of 1969 I designed playgrounds for Chicago's Neighborhood Improvement and Beautification (NIB) Program, which was part of the federally funded open-space program. My job was to convert vacant lots into temporary playgrounds—they would stand as long as their owners did not want the land for other purposes. I soon learned that I needed to understand the ultimate purpose of parks in order to design these playgrounds. Looking for guides for action, I began to pay attention to what people and professionals felt were the purposes of parks and open space.

Among the variety of views no single one dominated. Inconclusive debate about the oldest and largest parks, the great nineteenth-century pleasure grounds, epitomized the confusing situation. These older urban parks were under attack. They had already developed a reputation as barren no-man's-lands, unsafe for use day or night, and now hippies, radicals, and war resisters were using them as rallying grounds. The association of parks with deviants, already established by beggars, winos, and bums, was intensified. Because these parks lay unused and dangerous, some people suggested that they be sold for other, more pressing uses, such as housing and schools, which would simultaneously generate revenues for ailing municipal budgets. To those worried about losing open spaces for future generations, others suggested keeping the land in the public domain and leasing it to developers. The objection was that, once buildings were constructed, tearing them down would be hard to justify. Still another possibility was trading sections of the large parks for lots within densely built areas of the city, so that a checkerboard of open and built space would replace the large concentration of park land. Critics responded that only large amounts of land could create the psychological sense of being in nature. But people could now drive to regional or national forests, which suggested that cities had no need for this simulation within their borders. The rejoinder was that children from poor families without cars could not afford to get to the countryside, so the need for an experience of nature within the city was as real now as when the parks were created. In general the costs of trading large parks for small ones were not well enough understood for anyone to champion the idea seriously as a risk worth taking.

Irresolution about how to treat parks from the past was symptomatic of contemporary uncertainty about the meaning of parks. When I looked to present-day examples of park construction and supervision, I found confusion and failure more often than revelation. The precedent set by the urban designers during the previous two years of Chicago's NIB program was no help; they had done little more than drop a Bunker Hill climber, a swing, and a slide—all ready-made, standard playground equipment from a catalog—onto the site. These playgrounds had been wrecked within a matter of days after the work crews left the sites, leading me to speculate that people felt insulted by these superficial tokens of recreational service.

The NIB designers had few other models available to them, either from architecture schools, which tend to overlook outdoor recreation design, or from practicing professionals, who had established this scattershot approach in the first place. Contemporary park and recreation designers would typically include berms and curved paths to suggest a naturalistic landscape, gymnastic equipment to accommodate vigorous physical activity, tennis courts to meet demand,

and free-form modular timber sets to stimulate a child's imagination. Each of these elements has come from a different park type, evolved at a different stage in urban park history, but, rather than differentiate these elements and group them into coherent patterns, designers proceed as if they hope that a smattering of each type will increase their probability of success.

When I turned to professional writing about park design and to legal and bureaucratic practice, definition was also lacking. I discovered that the purpose of municipal parks became problematic not long after parks became institutionalized as a governmental service. In contrast some planners looked wistfully to preindustrial towns where the green spaces had well-defined purposes, were a distinctive component of the original townscape, and hence resonated aesthetically with their urban surroundings. In contemporary practice the word "park" applied to an almost indiscriminate range of properties, from children's playgrounds, neighborhood playfields, golf, bathing, and camping areas, athletic fields to zoological and botanical gardens, arboretums, landscaped ovals, triangles, and other small segments of street grid, neighborhood parks, downtown squares, scenic outlets, waterfront, and land reservations. The common purpose uniting this collection was not obvious.

A sociologist might be expected to turn to popular opinion to find a set of guidelines for park design, or to observe actual park usage to induce design principles. Such an empirical user-needs approach is one tactic for shaping design but obviated in this case by the very confusion and apathy that alerted me to the problem in the first place. Moreover this kind of empiricism simply adds up what individuals want or do, without reference to what parks can or should do for groups, neighborhoods, cities, and society as a whole.

Turning from behavior to contemporary cultural symbolism as a way to induce purpose fares no better, for today parks mean greenery, grass, and trees, and the park is an innocuous symbol that everybody favors except bad people. Thus in Kurosawa's movie about the heroism of a dying

Japanese bureaucrat, only gangsters want a bar rather than a playground on an open site. While American parks are now associated with danger—American film-makers for the last ten years have used parks as symbols not just of tranquility and innocence but also of fear and foreboding—people do not think that the parks themselves are fearsome. Rather they blame external intrusion, and never for a moment do they think that the institution of the park itself might invite conflict because of the ambiguity of the norms for its proper use. Academic attempts to identify any widely agreed-upon idea about the purpose of city parks have fared no better than professional, activist, or lay efforts.

In response to this widespread confusion, and because of my own confusion about what should be done with my vacant lots, I decided to investigate the history of urban parks in the United States. At some point, I thought, taxpayers must have had clear-cut notions about what parks could accomplish; at least when parks were first created, they must have agreed about the wisdom of creating them and articulated some explicit goals for them. I sensed that the choices made in those early years would have an appreciable effect on how people defined and planned parks today, and I hoped to be able to anticipate the trajectory set by prior social conditions. Thus I began a long journey into the past, where I discovered not just one set of ideas about the role of city parks but four distinct constellations. Without a historical, comparative method I would not have been able to discover this evolution. This book is the story of what I learned and an attempt to fill part of the unexplained gap regarding the role of city parks within American social structure and the intellectual and moral life of the culture.

Despite my commitment to a historical method, this study differs from ordinary narrative history in several ways. More like a sociologist than a historian, I sought general trends, often at the expense of the full particulars leading to and stemming from specific events. That is to say, particular points in time were not as important as understanding the forces that shaped the movement. The concern for the movement as a whole required a distinctively interdisciplinary study that weaves together concepts and methods from architecture, landscape architecture, social history, and sociology. This in turn meant that shifting the lens of analysis has been more important than presenting a straightforward chronology. The structure of the book reflects that process of successive inquiry in which ideal types are created, located within social structure, and their cultural function assessed. The device of constructing ideal types from the historical record is associated with Weberian sociology, but its broad outlines recur in many areas. Even Hellenistic Greek sculpture is a composite of the ideal features of human form, rather than a realistic, literal representation of any particular person. This study is more concerned with the construction of models and the internal logic of the type itself than an ordinary narrative history would be.

This study differs not only from historical narratives in general but also from the existing scholarship on parks. It is the first history of the first 130 years of the American park movement in one account, not restricted to one city, one region, or one period. Other studies have looked at one dimension—usually the aesthetic or recreation as a social service—or restrict a fuller analysis to only one city or region or to only one period in time.

In keeping with social research methods, I treated three urban park systems—those of New York, Chicago, and San Francisco—as case studies. Together with occasional comparisons with other American towns and an overview of the urban park movement across the nation, they lead to generalization about the nature of the American park movement as a whole. This is possible because the development of American urban parks has been remarkably homogeneous.

New York is an important case because Central Park was the first public park developed in the context of what became the urban park movement, and the city continued to pioneer in many aspects of park planning. Chicago is significant because the reform park was developed to its fullest there: among park administrations Chicago became famous for the first and highest development of the field house, a distinctive physical prototype with a new philosophy of social programming. San Francisco completes the triad with a western case, and one in which similarities to the others is not simply the result of Frederick Law Olmsted's personal tastes and ideals, as it might be argued with the early parks in the many other cities where he worked.

Parks themselves are still important today in different ways, emphatically not just part of the parenthetical history of gardens or landscape design. From the point of view of understanding society they are an excellent example of how social forces shape and are shaped by the physical world. Social, economic, political, and psychological processes influenced park location, size, shape, composition, and equipment and landscaping. Once these features were fixed, they both limited and stimulated the options available for human interaction.

City parks are also important for the role they played and continue to play in urbanization. They are part of the rise of modern institutions—the successive attempts to gain control over the social and physical consequences of urbanization in the context of industrial capitalism. Their past and potential use in the processes of creating social, psychological, and political order, of planning and controlling land use, and of shaping civic form and beauty make them important today. The earliest park spokesmen, like Andrew Jackson Downing and Frederick Law Olmsted, believed that park environments could exert a civilizing influence on working-class men, and today policy-makers still acknowledge the physical configuration of the park as an active culture-bearing medium in people's lives, both materially and intellectually.

A host of people have helped me write this book. Financial aid has come from Princeton University's Committee on Research in the Humanities and Social Sciences, the Institute of Planning and Urban Development and its director Mel Webber at the University of California at Berkeley, the Regents Humanities Fellowship of the University of California, and the Department of Architecture and its chair Joseph Esherick. With this support, I was able to hire fine research assistants: Tom Seebohm, Mark Knoerr, and Marcie Adelsohn. Nancy Layton, Marjorie Dobkin, and Tonia Chao were especially helpful assistants. Carolyn Francis and David Fagundes helped verify the manuscript. Two typists bore the largest share of manuscript preparation: Dorothy Heydt and Marcie McGaugh. Working with my editor, John Taylor, both strengthened and lightened the manuscript before it went to the MIT Press, where skillful editors improved the manuscript yet again. Thanks also to Gerald Suttles, Richard Wade, Albert Fein, David Matza, Charles McLaughlin, Norma Evenson, John Pock and Mark Mack—who read or commented on selected chapters. The librarians at the Chicago Historical Society, the University of Chicago, the New York Public Library, the Museum of the City of New York, the University of Washington Library, Seattle Historical Society, University of California, and the San Francisco Public Library have helped me find the documents, newspapers, and photographs important to this study.

I

HISTORICAL OVERVIEW OF PARK USAGE

1

The Pleasure Ground: 1850–1900

Transcending the City

In the conventional opposition of city and country, the country has always stood for simplicity, health, peace and quiet, and the stability of personal, family, and community relations while the cities have always had their critics. The case against them has remained roughly the same: they are too big, too built up, too crowded, diseased, polluted, artificial, overly commercial, corrupting, and stressful. Industrialization, technological innovation, rapid growth, and increased migration up through the 1850s had made American cities especially vulnerable to criticisms. The effects of these developments were particularly great in the newer American cities, because many of them, like San Francisco, had been little more than settlements in the memory of some of their inhabitants, and tradition and established order had little influence on them. Thus a San Francisco *Herald* editorial of 1854 compared the "half-graded, half-planked, and thoroughly swampy streets" of San Francisco to the "beautiful squares, noble avenues, and tasteful promenades of Eastern States and European countries, devoted to parades, meetings, and holidays," and this was a frequent note.[1] Americans attributed the apparent tradition and order elsewhere to the refining effects of parks and art.

The parks that Americans built to improve their cities derived not from European urban models but from an anti-urban ideal that dwelt on the traditional prescription for

The tranquil sheet of water, ambiguous shoreline, and use of trees to modulate space express the pastoral ideal of the pleasure ground. Jackson Park, Chicago, 1880s. Courtesy Chicago Historical Society.

relief from the evils of the city—to escape to the country. The new American parks thus were conceived as great pleasure grounds meant to be pieces of the country, with fresh air, meadows, lakes, and sunshine right in the city. Park proponents argued that the presence of these green expanses could do much to alleviate the problems of city life. Throughout the late nineteenth century their writings, beyond complaining about specific pressures of the American urban explosion, stressed the intrinsic drawbacks of urban life to which they viewed the parks as an antidote. For example, *Scribner's Monthly* in 1873 decried the loss of space in Hudson River Villages, including New York City, before the creation of Central Park:

> There is actually no stroll possible! The hateful railroad . . . cut off all access to the river-shore, private "places" run down close to the railroad, and, if one climbs the hill to the highway, he finds that fences, walls, hedges, and close huddling houses cut him off from all but a few tantalizing glimpses of the landscape he would enjoy. . . . [For a while the Croton aqueduct was open, but soon people put up fences across it.] Only one [property owner left] the aqueduct-walk free . . . the rest have done what they could to shut off the villagers from their one poor chance of recreation.[2]

Similarly, an article on Central Park published in *Harper's New Monthly* in 1879 feared that without it "the great necessities of commerce would swallow up the whole of Manhattan Island and leave no breathing room for its inhabitants."[3] Such worries about the acute situation of unbridled growth, indoor work, mass communication, and intensification of business life, as well as the loss of breathing space and glimpses of landscape heightened the positive qualities taken for granted in the country. The notion of a park was endorsed as if it were a check on the encroachment of the city rather than as a feature of the city itself.

In a general sense these habits of thought are romantic. Before the country was romanticized thus, it meant the farm and village and environs, rural social and economic life. Its vistas and breathing space might include fences and closely clustered houses. But by mid-century the simple

Even before Chicago's Humboldt Park was completely landscaped, painters pursued the ideal of enjoyment. Undated. Courtesy Chicago Historical Society.

benefits of the country had come to be popularly associated with nature itself, whatever nature was unimproved by man—woods, plains, mountains, lakes. These associations, though inherited from European romanticism, gained currency in America largely through transcendentalist influence. For Emerson and his followers, nature—attunement with it, contemplation of it, immersion in it—was thought to train the spirit. The softened popular version of the transcendentalist ideals attributed virtues to things found in nature like trees and meadows that could be transplanted or duplicated by human ingenuity and paved the way for park propaganda and park design theory.

Unstructured Pleasures

Recreationists from the 1940s onward have typically characterized the early parks as organized around passive use. A summary of the activities that appeared on the pleasure ground shows that by 1895 they were not so much passive as unstructured: racing, galloping and jumping, polo playing, bicycle riding, merry-go-round, toboggan sliding, coasting on rinks, watching shows such as circuses and shooting matches, tennis and croquet, baseball and lacrosse, military maneuvers, and mass meetings.[4] Even the earliest pleasure grounds promoted spontaneous activities organized by families and church groups rather than by paid play leaders. Children were expected to romp, adults to row, ride horseback, and walk, men and boys to play vigorously at sport. The spectators at these picturesque events were expected to be mentally alert in their appreciation of them. Their pleasures were of a different order from those of, say, the modern-day stadium spectator.

Pleasure ground activities were almost exclusively outdoor activities because of the number of hours, shocking at the time, during which people found themselves indoors, in particular working under artificial light. Park commissioners would emphasize outdoor sports not so much an accommodation of popular recreation as a compensation for the widening split between work and leisure. Both clerical and factory workers' powers of reasoning, ability to deduce cause from effect, memorize, and categorize had all been used actively in the city. A stretch of nature in the city would not merely give respite to the tired worker but also stimulate and exercise the unused part of his mind. Today we might argue that Frederick Law Olmsted and his followers were attempting to stimulate the right hemisphere of the brain, and its powers for perception of space, volume, kinesthetic sequence, sound, and music.[5] Writing about New York, Olmsted made explicit the importance of this counteraction; he conceived of the park not only as an open area exempt from the urban environ but as "a class of opposite conditions," a visual antithesis to gridded streets and rectangular houses.

From the "class of opposite conditions," would arise the notion of "aesthetic colony."[6] Rules applied in the park differed from those employed outside. For this reason attempts to promote park values any where else in the city were typically met with indifference or resistance. Advertising dramatizes the point: although no one objected to the banishment of signs from parks, property owners chastized city officials for taking the same attitude toward streets.[7]

Ideal Activities

With pleasure grounds designed to facilitate activities that provided exercise, instruction, and psychic restoration, sports supplied the exercise once offered by work but lost in factory production, certain amusements aroused the cultural awareness of the masses, and appreciation of scenery stimulated the psyche to wholeness. Park officials especially promoted walking as an exercise compatible with psychic renewal. In this spirit they built pleasant paths amid agreeable surroundings and treated the promenade as a major pastime. *Harper's* told New Yorkers that they would understand Central Park much more thoroughly if they would abandon their carriages and explore it on foot where shady, winding paths allow them to "saunter at will, resting . . . at intervals on the rustic seats which are placed at every shaded turn."[8] As late as 1893 the San Francisco park commissioners could justify plans for a new forest by deciding that it would stimulate pedestrianism.

Parks were equally available to those on horseback, in a carriage, or on foot, whichever best suited the inclination or means of an individual.[9] Park commissioners in most cities sold rides in phaetons, popular among the less fortunate. During the 1860s rich New Yorkers turned out their fashionable carriages for a Sunday trot around the ten miles of road in Central Park—a Currier and Ives lithograph depicts this scene. Park boulevards and drives offered some of the best roads in town, and particular drives and certain days of the week were designated for steed racing by owners of fine equipment and horses.

Watching the procession of horses and carriages—and the people—became a recreation in its own right:

First comes a man on horseback. His arms are spread out like the cropped wings of a barnyard fowl attempting to fly. He rises briskly up and down in the saddle to the motion of an awkward-gaited horse. He is a clerk in an English insurance office, and labors under the delusion that he cuts a good figure on horseback. A sedate-looking German corner groceryman comes next. He is giving his family a Sunday airing in the wagonette which he uses for delivering his goods on weekdays. Then there comes a crowd of more stylish rigs. As a rule the real swell set do not turn out on Sundays, but some of them are here this afternoon . . . [the] President of the Police Commission leads the procession with a magnificently equipped four-in-hands. Nothing more stylish can be seen in Central Park, New York, or Hyde Park, London, during the season . . .

Next comes a swell stranger . . . with a four-in-hands from the stables of Thomas Kelly and Sons, the California-Street liverymen. This turn-out is as perfect in all its appointments and details as any private equipage could be . . . a fast-stepping trotter . . . is driven by a handsome blonde who is accompanied by a female friend. The blond is one of the mysteries of the city—a mystery of a type that is to be found in all great cities. She lives with her husband in a swagger hotel . . . they both live well and never seem short of money. . . . Young Doppelkroutz . . . is a grocer's clerk with a salary of $30 per month and board. He is only two years out from Germany, and is anxious to show people that he is a blood. . . . One might watch this procession with interest and amusement all the afternoon, for it never ceases.[10]

Ideally, people would spend an entire day in the park, selecting some portion of it and spending the time there with friends and books, watching squirrels and birds, listening to music, picnicking, playing croquet, boating, watching their children at play, and so on. Spending a day in the park required creature comforts, refreshment stands, comfort stations, and other support structures, even though they were not entirely in keeping with the outdoor ideal of the pleasure garden. Some of these constructions such as lamps, benches, and settees, offered places of rest, the amenities from which to enjoy military reviews and social promenades. Comfort stations roused some ambivalence; for example, railway companies, not the Park Department, constructed the toilets at the rail terminus in Golden Gate Park. Drinking fountains were provided both for horses and humans, though the latter were supplied less as a creature comfort than as a reform device intended to compete with saloons for the working man's lunch hour. As such, a mineral water concession in Central Park could turn the American social invitation to come and take a drink into a harmless indulgence: "Cold water won't do, and milk is not the thing, either: these sparkling waters answer the purpose, and gratify, besides, that incomprehensible liking . . . for taking quack medicines."[11]

All park departments sponsored music, though not all kinds. Administrators excluded German polkas—"oompah" music—on the grounds that they were undignified, overly stimulating, and associated with dancing. By contrast classical music was edifying, though the demand for popular music led to a compromise: light music composed of popular versions of more classical tunes.[12]

In anticipation of the importance of concerts, planners in all three cities designed roadways to include places for carriages to stop and listen. San Franciscans noted with satis-

The ideal of spending a day in the pleasure ground required conveniences, but surprisingly some planners were reluctant to install restaurants and toilets because they smacked of routine urban life and had potential for licentiousness. Lewis Miller Collection, Museum of the City of New York.

The ideal of spending a day stopped at residence and even recreational camping, except during emergencies like the San Francisco earthquake of 1906, or barracking soldiers during World War II. Courtesy the Bancroft Library, University of California, Berkeley.

faction that park concerts were popular enough to have become established as a public necessity.[13]

Skating was both a vigorous sport and a winter form of airing. In 1873 *Scribner's Monthly* observed, "No sooner had the commissioners established the Winter Skating Pond than 'rinks,' as they were called, were built in the city [of New York] itself, and in the villages in the immediate vicinity, and every owner of a duck pond saw his way to fortune by putting up a shanty on its edge and sending out the tidings of a new skating place."[14] Ice skating became so popular in New York City that the commissioners and horse-car companies would take pains to let the skating public know when the ice was in good condition. From the day after Christmas until the twenty-third of February, trolleys carried white flags if the ice was strong enough for skating.[15] The sport spread to Chicago, where park management flooded small lakes and maintained the ice.

In the 1890s vigorous athletics took an increasingly large place in park programming. Baseball was the most popular, then football and lacrosse. Baseball had been played since the end of the Civil War, but parks did not accommodate it until the 1890s. Similarly, bicyclists were resisted for some time, but by the 1890s New Yorkers, Chicagoans, and San Franciscans could ride bicycles or velocipedes on paths constructed specifically for them. Even motorcycle races joined Chicago's repertoire of acceptable activities in 1895 when Lincoln and Jackson Parks both hosted them.

Enjoyment

Commercial activities smacked of the city to which the pleasure ground was an antidote, so park guardians fought them. San Francisco papers feared the possibility of the park's being turned into a "shop where all sorts of business and games may be carried on," and *Harper's Weekly* resisted the idea that "every man with a project, from a peanut stand to a zoological garden . . . should have a place in the Central Park."[16] Similarly, commissioners forbade advertising: "where people go for the express object of avoiding offensive objects and appeals to the attention, displays that intend to arrest the attention are clearly public nuisances."[17] When a steel company donated a fence to Golden Gate Park and asked that a sign acknowledge their donation, the commissioners were willing to remove the fence along with the sign if that was necessary to keep the parks as a pleasure ground, not an advertising medium.[18] Even athletic associations announcing activities could not post a sign.[19]

Not all exclusions were so straightforward. The pleasure ground ideal was subtle, and along with hypocrisy and equivocation it encouraged controversy and the making of fine distinctions. Park proponents were advocates of enjoyment, an ideal opposed simultaneously to mere amusement and instruction. The pleasures derived from amusement operations were considered superficial, and lessons or formal instruction too much like the normal round of rational, daily structured activities. A workable definition of enjoyment emerged from the discussions about whether or not to include museums and other cultural institutions in parks. The purists among the enjoyment advocates resisted museums, exhibits, and galleries. A Chicago booster and officer of the *American Builder*, for example, insisted that parks should not have any collections of art that would invite examination and study, and in New York *Scribners* opposed an arboretum, a botanical garden, or a zoological garden for their park because they would detract from the character of the park as a place of recreation: "Science and art are excellent things, each in its way, but they are better outside the Park than in it." Nevertheless, policy-makers perceived a public need for cultural institutions that could be made sufficiently entertaining to create an enjoyable atmosphere: "if we can give people information in a playful way in the park, it will be a good thing to do."[20] This early judgment justified the museums, botanical gardens, zoological gardens, aquariums, arboretiums, meteorology observatories, and music halls we see in parks today. Even small, informally organized collections of animals or plants, like the buffalo herds in San Francisco were thought to serve the double purpose of instruction and pleasure.[21]

Overall, American parks were more austere than the beer gardens and amusement parks of American cities like New York's Coney Island, Chicago's Riverside, and San Francisco's Woodward Gardens, or even the pleasure gardens of European cities. Large stretches of the Prater in Vienna, for example, offered its visitors numerous restaurants, cafes, theaters, circuses, bowling alleys, shooting galleries, gymnasiums, and swings. The New York park commissioners did not see the difference as unfavorable to the American model, and Charles S. Sargent, editor of *Garden and Forest*, was outspoken about the secondary importance of mere amusement:

> No mere playground can serve the purpose of recreation in this truer, broader sense—the purpose of refreshment, of renewal of life and strength for body and soul alike. The truest value of public pleasure grounds for large cities is in the rest they give to eyes and mind, to heart and soul, through the soothing charm, the fresh and inspiring influence, the impersonal, unexciting pleasure which nothing but the works of Nature can offer to man.[22]

The transcendentalist cure for the excessive and one-sided stimulation of the psyche was to enjoy nature: "to love trees and shrubs, and open fields, birds and flowers, rivers, lakes, and skies . . . [to] see and appreciate the beautiful things about them."[23] The pleasure ground soothed one part of the mind while arousing the other. In the concept of the park as a pleasure ground no sport, no matter how wholesome, could appropriately be treated as the purpose of a park, but people misunderstood the function of parks. The drives, rides, and walks became more important than the scenery, and the open greens were used for athletic games, the woods for picnicking, and the waters for rowing, sailing, or skating, according to the season.[24]

As a result of differing conceptions of park purpose even walking on the grass which was being destroyed in the course of use became a controversial matter. While in New

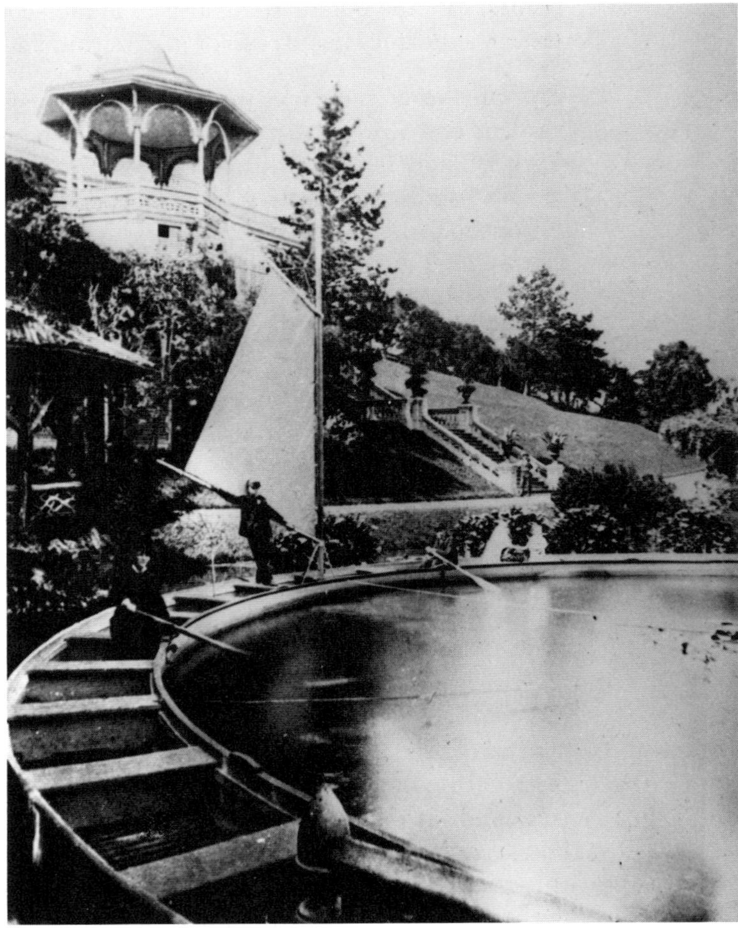

Fanciful activities included this sail- and oar-driven boating ring in Golden Gate Park. Undated. Courtesy the Bancroft Library, University of California, Berkeley.

Although stereotyped as passive, the pleasure ground hosted active sports, including lawn tennis which was popular with both men and women. After 1893, Jackson Park, Chicago. Courtesy Chicago Historical Society.

The airy structure of conservatories offered the exoticism needed to overcome the drawbacks of buildings—their rectangular bulk and association with mundane business. 1900, Lick Conservatory, Golden Gate Park. Courtesy Bancroft Library, University of California, Berkeley.

York the commission was criticized for restricting the use of turf for ball games, in Chicago playing games and even resting on the grass were prohibited. In San Francisco, however, Park Superintendent John McLaren had "Keep off the grass" signs banned. Sargent, a proponent of the pleasure ground principle, argued that the pleasure of walking on the grass was exaggerated, and to another columnist's complaint that "Keep off the grass" signs looked inhospitable in parks whose purpose is to welcome visitors tired of walking on stone pavements, he replied, "An appeal to the eye is stronger than one to the soles of the feet."[25]

Some activities were widely popular but excluded from park life; these exclusions further describe the ideal of enjoyment and reveal its class bias. Gambling stimulated the emotions and acknowledged the importance of fate rather than rational control, so it had to be driven away from the park. Folk entertainment like horseshoe pitching, tomahawk twirling, and bullet throwing were not refined enough for city parks despite their popularity, and vaudeville filled the newspapers but not park programs.[26] Other popular activities like baseball and bicycling were assimilated into park programming only after a period of resistance.

Violence and fighting constantly erupted in cities, but fistfighting, wrestling matches, duelling, and any other blood sport or unruly behavior and quarrels were strictly forbidden and were violations of park ordinances. Whenever annual reports and newspapers commented that a crowd had been unusually well-behaved, even for its large numbers, it was evidence that a park event had been successful. Workers pouring into the city from rural areas and peasant immigrants from other countries did not share, of course, standards of behavior in public places, so that rules against spitting, swearing, drinking, raising of the voice, or running underscored the need to create a civic order. The commissioners hoped that through the enforced codes the conduct of the masses would be elevated in all aspects of city life. The fact that these ordinances against improper use of the park existed indicates the heterogeneous, often unsocialized character of the peoples who visited the parks.

Restaurants too were regarded as intrusive in the setting of a park, particularly in San Francisco. A children's refreshment depot was prevented from degenerating into a mere restaurant.[27] The Victorian roadhouse in Stern Grove which had been a retreat for the rich, where they could enjoy the lily ponds, beer graden, deer park, trout farm, and outdoor dance pavilion, was converted by the parks department into a meeting and reception hall. Golden Gate's neoclassical casino was turned into a museum after some scandalous brawls and exposures that it was a haunt of loose women and obnoxious mashers: apparently five rooms on the second floor had come into popular demand for continuous orgies. When seven years later Park Commissioner F. W. Zeile resurrected the idea of the casino, he wanted to dignify its atmosphere with music, clinking goblets, dazzling lights, gay women, gallant men, Tahoe trout, terrapin pates. Yet, even so exalted, it would still be a restaurant, and as such aroused the pointed sarcasm of the media. Even while the San Francisco *Examiner* mocked the class bias of this scenario, they were just as skeptical about popular German or teetotaling alternatives, questioning the value of a restaurant as a place "where beer shall foam . . . while pretzels shall tangle the teeth with thirst, where the mettwurst, the sauerkraut and the sausage lay claim . . . or . . . [where] the milkshake, the ginger pop, the lemonade and the sandwich prevail."[28] The *Bulletin* was dubious mainly because the problem of enforcing temperance in restaurants had been difficult in the past, and because on principle the park was constructed for purposes other than eating and drinking.[29] Only the *Newsletter* favored the casino:

You ride out on a car with your wife and stroll the parks. You become thirsty or hungry or both. There is nothing for you to do but walk back to the cars and come home, or else patronize one of the questionable roadhouses that fringe the Park at the terminals of the Geary Street and Sacramento Street lines. A man who knows anything about the world and respects his wife will not patronize one of these establishments. He has the choice of going hungry, or thirsty, or home.

They rather recommended that the restaurant attract a broader clientele:

Have the milk-shake and the Queen Charlotte and the ginger-pop . . . and something else for those who want that. Don't make a Sunday-school picnicker out of everybody who goes there. Run the cafe on a businesslike, restaurant-like basis, and it will be self-supporting; run it as a WCTU headquarters and it will always be in the hole and somebody will be watering the milk to keep expenses down.[30]

To avoid violating the park taboo of including a commercial activity, restaurants had to be defined as a public service and thus became enmeshed in competing visions of the good life. Sensual music and food could have provided a clear-cut contrast to the regimentation of urban and industrial life, but they were not welcome; temperance forces were victorious, and drink has been outlawed in most parks to this day. No policy-maker would solve one problem while exacerbating what he perceived as another.

Horse racing may have been a development of airing, but clearly it violated the ideal of enjoyment. The upper classes, however, did not always find their own frivolity as damaging as that of their inferiors, and, when factions among them pushed in all three cities for race tracks in the parks, defenders of the pleasure ground ideal were unsuccessful in stopping them. This challenge to their views forced them to articulate their ideal of enjoyment with particular fullness.

The resistance to a speedway in Central Park in the 1890s was especially vehement. Naturally, Sargent objected to a speedway as unbecoming both to the form and the program of Central Park:

Just now certain wealthy gentlemen of this city have revived the project to run a broad, straight, and perfectly level road through Central Park along its western boundary line, to be used exclusively for driving horses at speed; and either they do not understand that this will mean the utter ruin of the park as a place of rural recreation, or, if they do understand this, they consider the use to which they propose to devote it a more important one than that for which it was originally intended.[31]

The speedway proponents argued, however, that provisions already existed for pedestrians, equestrians, carriage riders, and why not, then, a special place for speed trotters? Sargent answered that the roads and paths existed in the park not primarily as places for walking and driving but to enable people to enjoy the park in different ways.[32] He compared it with lawn tennis, skating, and some other sports that complemented the quiet scenery and pointed out that no portion of the park had been turned into a desert, replaced by gravel, or substantially stripped of trees to make room for them. When proponents of the speedway justified the plan on the grounds that the portion of the park in question was unused, Sargent sneered, "It seems to be a prevalent opinion that land which cannot be driven over or trampled on or covered with structures of some kind can serve no useful purpose."[33]

In March 1892 legislation was passed authorizing the construction of a speedroad. The park board voted funds for the project and ordered their engineer to begin plans. But nearly every newspaper in the city attacked the idea, and a volunteer committee of citizens circulated petitions against it. At a public hearing on the question opponents appeared in force, and the board rescinded the action. Throughout the campaign against the speedway, thousands of names and money poured in to finance and support the citizens' committee, and newspapers kept up the attack. Labor unions defended Central Park against this proposal on the grounds that it had special value for working-class families who could not get away to the mountains and seashore for the summer.

Three years after the exclusion of the speedway from Central Park, new legislation established a speedway along the Harlem River, and by 1898 the annual report of the Park Department could announce blandly that the speedway was a new acquisition to the department, a novelty in park administration, next in public interest after Central Park, and popular with the general public as well as with horse owners.[34] The busy scene in Currier and Ives's lithograph "Fast Trotters of Harlem Lane, N.Y." confirms this claim.

Discussions of politics and religion were heated and exciting, and rallies and public meetings over religious and political issues were evocative of the city proper. As a result they were almost always kept out of park programming. Applications for Sunday services were periodically submitted to the park commissioners and always rejected. Boston commissioners did not allow parks to be used for public meetings, and, in defending themselves, they reported that other cities were divided on this issue as well.[35] Philadelphia allowed only religious meetings. The South Park system in Chicago forbade public meetings that would lead to crowds and speechmaking, and the West Side Park Department allowed no large gatherings for public meetings of any sort. Brooklyn only permitted such gatherings for a parade of Sunday school children.

Politics and religion were divisive, and commissioners needed the parks to appear nonsectarian to justify public spending. Conceptually, the pleasure ground was meant to transcend, not reflect, the evils of urban life, of which division was a prominent symptom. As a line of reasoning, this was consistent with military use of the pleasure garden, both before and after 1900: politics entails debates within a society; military power was supposedly on the side of one unified nation. In any case the original program for the competition for the design of Central Park called for a military parade ground, and the arsenal was retained within the borders of the park. In San Francisco the park commissioners gave regimental and company officers freedom to use the grounds for purposes of drill.[36]

Sargent alone waged battle against the military use of Central Park:

If the Park Commissioners do not know that military displays are entirely out of character with the purpose of the park, which is to afford quiet and refreshment to the people, if they do not know that in this especial case the admission of the military would be utterly destructive of the beauty of the park, and that it would cost thousands of dollars and years of time to restore it, they are incompetent.[37]

Picturesque Theory

The beauty of the park was to evoke a sense of what art historians call "picturesque." To pleasure ground designers, the informal picturesque approach to organizing the landscape was the ideal antidote to the highly artificial American city. European palace gardens like Versailles were artificial—symmetrical, rational, geometric, and heavily architectural—and thus an unsuitable model. In fact, Olmsted, who was largely responsible for promoting the idea of the picturesque landscape park, felt that pure wilderness would provide the best and sharpest contrast with civilization. But because he recognized that the wilderness would be hard, if not impossible, to simulate within a city's boundaries, he decided that the picturesque—the pastoral middle landscape—was an appropriate compromise. Its informality was democratic, and it offered the right synthesis of the beautiful and the sublime: an overall composition of smoothness, harmony, serenity, and order, with an occasional reminder of the awesome grandeur of a mountain, a deep crevasse, long waterfall, or steep crag.

Olmsted acknowledged that a wilderness park would be impractical, but in any case the theory of the garden in both England and the continent had already established that uncultivated naturalness was undesirable. The European pleasure gardens of the seventeenth and eighteenth centuries had been designed according to three rules prescribing the relationship between nature and art: (1) the garden should orient itself to the image of nature; (2) in mirroring nature, it should be differentiated from the surrounding landscape and recognizable as something different; and (3) this difference should not be an unnatural contrast but rather a heightening of nature in the image of nature and reason.[38] Accordingly, the goal for the American

Before the municipal park movement city parks were typically small squares landscaped in a formal Beaux-Arts style. Union Square, San Francisco, ca. 1900. Courtesy the Bancroft Library, University of California, Berkeley.

pleasure ground was to heighten the idea of naturalness with forms suggested by nature but not to rely on what nature actually provided.

Despite this, Americans sometimes failed to realize that deliberate naturalistic landscaping was itself artificial. True naturalists tried to keep this artistic concept of a naturalistic setting in check, as did one San Franciscan when a proposal was made to allow a railway to use the unimproved portions of Golden Gate Park:

If the term (unimproved) is applied to the strips of undulating land covered with bent grass, lupine, and crops of wild plants which the vulgar and ignorant call weeds, it is nonsensical and misleading. To many these spots are more interesting than the beds of flowers and plats of lawn so carefully watered but so dreadfully artificial. The Presidio in its wilderness has many charms the Park has lost.[39]

Still another challenged the very policy of imitating nature:

The trouble with many public parks is that there is too much landscape gardening and so on. That is the trouble with Golden Gate Park in San Francisco. It is all too artificial. The beauties of nature have been marred by man's handiwork. You can't improve on nature.[40]

Site Selection

Site selection was compromised by political, economic, and demographic considerations. One of the first considerations was finding the land. Nineteenth-century cities had only a few parks before the large pleasure grounds were established. In San Francisco the western addition was laid out in 1855, with seven large squares set aside for recreation; the Potrero plan had included three similar squares. The New York City plan of 1811 was not even this generous, offering only a few open squares. Before 1869 Chicago made no plans at all for open space preservation; instead small bits of land—triangles between intersecting streets, unsuitable for other purposes—were donated to the city by private citizens. Before the park movement got underway, recreation took place in whatever small pockets and central areas were nearest a person's residence or work: burial grounds, plazas, market gardens, tenement courts, settlement houses, schoolyards, and streets, or in commercial establishments like beer gardens, ocean beach resorts, and amusement parks.

Some park advocates promoted the park to replace certain land uses while others saw them as complementary to existing open spaces. In Chicago, for example, a Dr. Rauch would insist that the cemeteries be removed from the city center altogether and replaced by healthful parks, whereas in New York *Scribner's Monthly* would endorse Central Park as an addition to the city's open spaces:

> . . . however beautiful a Mount Auburn or a Laurel Hill might be made with winding walks, and trees and flowers and quiet pools, it could not be a place where one would go to shake off sad throughts, or escape from the company of care. Cemeteries are good schools, . . . but a garden is no less a school, and such places of recreation are necessary in every great city for health of body and mind.[41]

In New York City a dumping ground at Rutger's Slip was cleared up for a playground, and existing plazas were prepared for a radical transformation. In San Francisco it was the criticized Portsmouth Square, "a general depository for everything, from glass bottles, to drunken women, lime, watermelons, and old rags" that was coveted by park advocates, as editorialized in the *Alta*:

> It certainly is a Public Square in every sense of the word, for an individual appears to consider himself perfectly free to occupy it for whatever purposes he pleases. It is converted into a cattle show, mule mart, vegetable and fruit market, hay market, lumber yard, auction yard, wheelwright's shop, carpenter's shop, engine house, and cart stands. . . . vehicles of all sorts cris-cross it . . . , it resembles a rag fair or a marketplace in a western city.[42]

The redeemed site would have instead

> . . . trees planted, the fence built, the walks rolled, the benches made, the fresh, bright, green grass springing up, intermixed with fragrant clover; little boys and girls endeavoring to paddle in the basin and catch the goldfish, stout old men in voluminous white waist-coats restraining very small boys from precipitating themselves into the

> water, nurses endeavoring to amuse their charges, lovers prattling soft nonsense to their mistresses . . . and in the foreground our worthy Mayor contemplating the completion of the picture he drew in his inaugural message.[43]

The first order of business in the creation of Central Park was to remove squatters whose shanties with their bone-boiling establishments, piggeries, and stagnant water emitted a most offensive odor.[44]

Sometimes park advocates tried to defeat a morally dubious venture by denying it any land whatsoever: reformers hoped to eradicate the amusement park, the tavern, and the beer garden altogether. Amusement parks, however, were too popular to supplant; they usually survived until burned down or badly deteriorated. Woodward's Gardens in San Francisco, which had its counterpart in most other cities, was visited daily by hundreds. It was considered the best resort on the Pacific slope, offering along with a museum, art gallery, zoo, picnic grounds, boating, a library, a refreshment saloon, Sunday concerts, balloon ascensions, and a popular aviary, a Mecca for outdoor amusement until the popularity of Golden Gate Park increased toward the end of the century.

Contrasts between Coney Island and municipal parks appeared frequently in popular and park writing, but not always in support of the pleasure park, as this excerpt from the *New Republic* shows:

> You come upon it, the municipal Seaside Park, at the end of our dirty white street. Within a thick hedge there is a level greensward. Huge trees shade its borders; like all respectable parks it has flowers and rubbish cans. But with us who go to Coney the park is not popular. Not enough jazz. Too quiet. You can see an old park anywhere, but Coney is the place of the hot dogs, the dance pavilions, the African dodger, the ring toss with its prizes of candy and kewpie dolls. The park department has done its bit for Puritanism with its absurd sign: 'Persons in Bathing Suits Not Allowed in This Park.' Except on the warmest day it is needless.[45]

Not only was the pleasure ground in competition with the amusement park, but also it had to contend for open land where there were already residential parks like New York's Gramercy Park. Another, in San Francisco's South Park, was a speculative housing project with building lots fronting a central oval nearly a quarter of a mile long, modeled after the ovals and crescents of London. The oval belonged in common to the lot holders, thus offering them spacious ornamental grounds instead of a dusty, sandy, or planked street. This kind of elegance was precisely what the pleasure ground advocates were trying to steer away from: the park they would plan in the nearby Mission district they described as a "people's pleasure ground in every sense of the word, not merely a square amid a lot of houses."[46]

Thus in practice the sites selected were simply those for which there was no competition at all, those unusable for other purposes. Chicago's South Park system was a swamp, considered wasteland; Louisiana's central park was a swampy jungle inhabited only by Indians; Golden Gate Park was shifting sand dunes; the Back Bay in Boston was selected in part because its gullies were too steep for construction; land for Morningside Park in New York was too rocky for farming or building; Central Park had poor, rocky soil:

> Never was a more desolate piece of land chosen for a pleasure ground. The barren ledges of gneiss were covered here and there with patches of unsightly vegetation, or, what was still worse, with clumps of squatters' shanties. . . . There were strips of marsh, covered with coarse grass, and in the hollows green, sluggish pools served as bathing places for ducks and geese. . . . Pigs and goats ranged over the rocks, and snuffled in the stubble and weeds. Indeed, the soil, spread in a thin layer over the gneiss, was too shallow to support any vigorous vegetable life.[47]

In the case of Central Park, a remote site satisfied the park's designers in a number of ways: Its remote location made possible its generous size, which could then accommodate lengthy carriage drives and other activities that required open ground. Size also allowed spectators to look on from a safe distance, while still others could seclude themselves in privacy from participants and spectators alike. In

Chicago, a booster congratulated his fellow citizens for their farsighted selection of remote, generous grounds:

> It is unquestionable that the park and boulevard system of Chicago was planned and carried out far ahead of the city's actual needs. In truth, even at the present writing (1891) they are beyond all proportion to the use made of them. . . . This being so when the city has long passed the million mark, how almost absurd they must have seemed when they were laid out encircling (though far away from) a town of only three hundred thousand souls! They fitted about as well as a wedding ring on a baby girl's finger. . . . If it had not been done when it was, it would have been impossible ever afterward.[48]

Nonetheless, when the choice of available land was actually made, considerations of landscape, cross-ventilation, view, access, circulation, and topography although not insignificant, were ultimately secondary to economic and political expediency. Often these site selection criteria were simply abandoned to accept gifts. In New York site selection for a public park involved a conflict between proponents of Jones' Woods and the future Central Park area which was weighted with economic considerations. Jones' Woods was a wooded waterfront site of 153.5 acres on the east side of Manhattan near the tenements, while the Central Park area was a treeless, rocky site miles from the city. The legislature first authorized funds to buy Jones' Woods, but the decision was hotly contested.

Jones' Woods was closer to New York's population, had a river front and trees, and would offer immediate returns. The opposition included the horticulturalist Andrew Jackson Downing, who challenged the feasibility of using this land for park purposes because it could be used for commercial docking and because a shore site was healthful and pleasurable without a planned park on it. The Central Park area was proposed as an alternative that would offer cross-ventilation, access from two sides, and easier conversion to a park than Jones' Woods, which had too many trees for open space. A tract of land as large as Central Park could better accommodate population growth. The cost considerations of purchasing the land also worked in favor of the

Central Park location. Although as a parcel Jones' Woods cost less, the per acre price of Central Park was lower. The planners could not ignore that in the long run Central Park was to have taxable property on all four sides, although some of the land around the arsenal and reservoir was already public property, while Jones' Woods could not have property owners along the riverside. Much of the public clamor over the choice of Jones' Woods was, however, that the benefits would be disproportionate. The taxing system at that time did not require the adjoining property owners to pay extra taxes even though their property values would go up.

The committee assigned to study the issue of a public park in New York concluded that both sites should be purchased, but the act authorizing the purchase of the Jones' Woods site was repealed in 1854. In retrospect the argument that Jones' Woods did not offer enough space might seem farsighted, but the charges and countercharges in the New York State Senate minority and majority reports for 1853 suggest that it was financial interests, especially commercial docking operations, that won the day.[49]

In San Francisco, the selection of the land for Golden Gate Park had highly political motivations. The ordinance establishing Golden Gate Park resolved a violent and bloody conflict between the city and squatters who had made competing claims to land that included the present park site. The squatters were given clear title on the condition that they give ten percent of their claim to the city for the park. In a certain sense the idea of a public pleasure park was compromised through a face-saving trade. Olmsted's plan for a carefully sited system of connected parks at what are now Aquatic Park, Van Ness and Divisadero Avenues and the Mission district in downtown San Francisco was no competition for such a political opportunity.

In Chicago public access was the principle that governed the location and use of parks: Lincoln Park depended on horsecars, but all the other parks were laid out near routes used by the commuter trains of the major railroads. In practice elsewhere transportation was not the primary design principle; yet Olmsted continued to advocate the use of drives and boulevards to link parks into an entire system that would also define different parts of cities like Seattle, Boston, and Minneapolis and give them structures around which to organize. For New York Olmsted and Calvert Vaux had conceived of a chain of parks from Prospect Park in Brooklyn to the ocean, back up behind Brooklyn linking a series of small parks, crossing the East River into Central Park and over the Hudson River to New Jersey's Palisades, ending in the Orange Mountains.

Whatever little success designers had with these plans, once a site was selected, its almost invariably peripheral location required that primary attention be given to street connections. In San Francisco proposals were made to link the tops of all the highest hills via boulevards and to run an avenue from city center to Golden Gate Park and from there to the Presidio, a military reservation. In Boston the parkways followed the watercourses of the community—the cheapest way to solve the problem of surface drainage while at the same time creating a pleasant view. In Chicago Horace Cleveland proposed planting the boulevards with every variety of tree and shrub that would thrive in the climate, allotting to each family a length corresponding to its importance.[50] With parkways and street-car lines supplementing carriage travel, and thus increasing popular access to the parks, public grounds need not be located in poor sections of the city. Good transportation was a compensation for a remote location. The San Francisco Report for 1890 explained, "the ever present cable car lines furnish pleasant, cheap, and expeditious transit to and from our great park, thus equalizing the facilities of the entire population for enjoying its advantages."[51]

Design

The ideals of naturalness and informality suggested meandering roads, gradual changes in grade, luxuriant, almost tropical planting, and permanence. Park designers often were pressured to solve problems piecemeal because politicians did not understand the need to treat the landscape as a whole. The general public might be fond of flower gardens or clipped shrubs, but designers insisted that they should be subservient to the larger composition, a park being superior to the mere frippery of a decorative garden. Gardens that are like miniature paintings in their attention to detail had no place where the broad, grand scale of landscape architecture was needed. As an informal adviser to the San Francisco Park commission, Olmsted aptly defended this view in a letter in which he stated that a garden was "no more an essential part of the rural park . . . than is a picture hung in a frame an essential part of the house that holds it."[52]

The program issued by the park department for the Central Park design competition required four or more east to west crossings, a parade ground of forty acres, three playfields up to ten acres each, sites for exhibition halls, a large fountain, a prospect tower, a speeding ground, and a three-acre flower garden—all for a $1.5 million dollar budget. The winning team of Olmsted and Vaux fleshed out the skeletal requirements in several ways: they devised a complete separation of the east to west crossings from the interior circulation of the park, added cricket grounds, divided the site into two basic parts—a sweeping, broad part to the north and a rocky, more picturesque, part to the south—and planned a wall of vegetation around the perimeter to insure that buildings remained visually insignificant. The Ramble was treated as the heart of the park and offered the epitome of picturesque intricacy and variety with its irregular clusters of shrubbery interspersed with patches of open ground and winding paths that opened up new views or vistas at every turn and conveyed the impression of a much more spacious area than it really was.[53] The popular press took a great delight in writing about the *Glorietas*, or rustic summer houses, that dotted about in odd corners of the park.[54]

Golden Gate Park's first superintendent, the young engineer William Hammond Hall, advocated architecture and gardenesque landscaping for Golden Gate Park, but his reason was that general aesthetic standards for the pleasure ground needed to be modified according to local circumstances. For example, ocean winds required an artificial warmth of feeling that would be supplied by graceful architectural shapes and a gay and sprightly treatment at certain localities. The pastoral landscape could be prevented from becoming monotonous—it could be made sprightly—by the use of "local passages, strongly contrasting in the picturesque and gardenesque."[55] But Golden Gate's next superintendent, John McLaren, was attacked vehemently for failing to meet the standard of unity, variety, and harmony. A fellow landscape gardener charged that he totally ignored "all the theories and principles of the art of landscape gardening. His ideas, executed at great expense, are odd, bombastic, conceited and whimsical."[56]

The consequence of naturalness was that the finished product looked unimproved, and, since the public was asked to spend its money without obvious effect, informal designs were hard to defend. In San Francisco a grading company proposed to grade the entire park, cutting "things down to a plane like a public square. Hills, valleys, undulations were to be done away with. There was a hot time in the inner circles."[57] Although the matter was killed before it reached the board, and the vision of a naturalistic park won in competition with other designs, the vision did not always win against encroachments that were to follow.[58]

Drives

The form of internal circulation paths aroused little disagreement, since most designers agreed that they should be curved. The flowing lines of an arabesque would contrast with the wearisome rectangularity of cities.[59] The winning Greensward plan for Central Park avoided long, straight drives in order to squelch trotting matches. In San Francisco a special condition reinforced the curvilinear solution; a system of turning roads and walks, planted with clumps of trees, would avoid the sweep of the wind. Psychologically, in response to the damp climate, more

Curved circulation systems, typical of pleasure grounds, countered the surrounding grid and created open meadows. Courtesy the Bancroft Library, University of California, Berkeley.

warmth would be felt in a diversified plan than in one using straight avenues.[60] In the midwest, landscape architect Cleveland dissented, arguing for straight roads if there was no reason for a curve.

The pleasure ground characteristically separated its transportation systems: landscape and planning historians have considered this one of its most distinctive features.[61] Vehicles and pedestrians had different drive- and walkways, so that a toddler, a pair of lovers, or picnickers could use the park without being harried by vehicular traffic. The designers of Central Park separated carriage from pedestrian traffic in the handling of the four transverse roads, but usually ran footpaths close to carriage roads to take advantage of the view of the equipages and their occupants.[62] The parks of Chicago and San Francisco followed this example. Driveways for vehicles, walkways for pedestrians, and tracks for cyclers required special bridges and tunnels, and sometimes roads were sunk at points of intersection so that one kind of road could be carried over another without incident, visual or physical. European carriageways were carried over promenades on causeways with high arches, but this was unacceptable in America because such forms would disrupt wide vistas and introduce unwanted construction.

Water

The artificial lakes, important features of large parks, required sophisticated drainage systems to allay fears about seepage, evaporation, lack of movement, and freshness of the water, so designers considered them worth the effort.[63] From certain vantage points broad expanses of water that would merge with the sky would create an illusion of infinity that contrasted with the finitude of the urban grid. Flat sheets of water suggested placidity, so the masterful landscape gardener of Chicago's West Park, Jens Jensen, treated the lagoons as if they were sleepy Illinois rivers, winding their way in typical S-curves through the flat prairies. A cascading stream was useful only rarely where a picturesque element might be needed to enliven a setting; for example, Jensen created a waterfall which cascaded over stones and collected in a great basin before plunging into the placid lagoon.[64]

The bodies of water artifically created to express the social content of the parks were more important than natural shorelines. In San Francisco Hall complained about the low priority given to treating the ocean beach, and in Chicago the creation of a permanent beach along Lake Michigan took place well after the creation of lagoons and lakes, even though the lakeshore was always in the public domain. New York gave up its shore site at Jones' Woods in favor of Central Park; much later waterfront recreation in New York's Riverside Park was promoted as complementary to the pleasure ground at Central Park.

Flora

The value of shrubs and trees lay primarily in their capacity to form and modulate space. The pleasure garden designer arranged masses of trees to form long vistas leading the eye into imaginary distances and to create the kinesthetic experience of moving through spatial sequences.[65] The woods opened and closed around meadows, beckoning strollers forward through narrow passages intended to pique their curiosity about what was on the other side. Banks of trees also created backdrops for the staging of dramatic natural spectacles—occasional reminders of the awesomeness of nature in the wild. Plantings screened the border of ugly urban surroundings.

According to picturesque theory the designer avoided calling attention to the individual tree, its bark, leaves, and other details. Hence native varieties rather than exotic ones were preferred. (Olmsted tried to achieve a tropical effect of luxuriant growth in his parks, but he used hearty native plants to do it.) Specimen planting, later popular in the gardenesque style, was to be avoided, which is why arboretums are not more common in parks and along parkways. In Mount Royal, Montreal, Olmsted chose different plant material for each level to enhance the illusion of height,

Chicago opened its lakeshore for swimming in 1895; photo taken ca. 1900. Courtesy Chicago Historical Society.

Picturesque flocks of sheep and herds of deer or reindeer kept meadows mowed before departments purchased mechanical mowers in the 1930s. Woodland Park, Seattle. University of Washington Library.

which he intended as an environmental illusion rather than a botanical lesson.

Trees clustered into forests were preferred aesthetically for their sylvan effects and luxuriant foliage and in particular for their imagined role in preventing malaria and the diffusion of fever germs. Pine forests in particular were valued on the theory that the turpentine they diffused into the air would purify it by destroying deleterious gasses.[66] Trees produced a clean, fragrant aroma, valued for its association with health and for its aesthetic release from the stench of the city's open sewerage system. The public, not understanding the scientific justification for pruning and thinning these prized stands, often protested. When they won, trees crowded themselves out of shape, died prematurely, or harbored insects.

Mowed grass was basic to the pleasure ground. An urban park should provide an antithesis to bustling, paved, rectangular street blocks; this requirement would best be met by a large, open, tranquil meadow-like park.[67] In San Francisco dunes and frog ponds were transformed into lawn where buffalo herds, like sheep and deer in the park systems of other cities, grazed on the grass, simultaneously practical and picturesque.[68] Lawn was protected: when a children's playground was proposed on the site of the picturesque north meadow in Central Park, the Park Commission relegated it instead to an area of less important landscape.

Playing fields for sports, such as baseball, football, and even polo, and general playgrounds for less formal ball games were usually relegated to a space near the edge of the park. This provided easy access and preserved the tranquility of the inner core. The park reports, however, gave little attention to the way these sports areas affected boundaries, surfaces, and other landscape elements; their purpose was simply to meet the demand for sport, rather than the more important one of stimulating and orchestrating a special kind of psychological experience.

Some sense of the importance of greenery to the pleasure ground ideal can be derived from considering the extent of the struggle to establish it on the dunes of Golden Gate Park. The prospects were dismal. The dunes attracted no one except men hunting frogs for San Francisco's already famous French restaurants. In 1866 four prominent newspapers denounced the idea of building the park on the dunes. Important civic leaders and landowners also resisted the project. Nevertheless, Engineer William Hammond Hall began to mount a case for the feasibility of reclaiming the dunes. Sand reclamation accounts were translated from French and other European languages, attention was called to the foresting of the Bay of Biscay in France, and the first experiments in planting the dunes were made. But even Olmsted doubted the chances of succeeding on this land.

One objection to reclaiming the tract was that, even if the effort was successful, the winds would blow sand from the adjacent dunes over the new plant material, undoing reclamation efforts. But others optimistically assumed that reclamation of these sand drifts would "stimulate the owners of adjoining property to turn the desert into a garden."[69] Indeed, once people saw with their own eyes that plants could grow on the dunes, their worries subsided.[70] By 1875 all editorial opinion had aboutfaced.

Designers relied on the haze and obscurity of irregular planting to suggest the feeling and idea of distance and tried to avoid the use of flowers or even colored foliage. Olmsted felt that flowers revealed the hand of man, which the park visitor saw all too much of in the city. Sargent decreed that the introduction of bedding plants was "altogether out of harmony with the spirit of the place."[71] He thought that, because bright-hued leaves did not grow in the United States, their jarring, exotic aspect, although fashionable in Europe, must be eschewed here in order to follow nature.[72]

Olmsted relaxed his standards only in the case of large naturalistic bands of one species of one flower or decorative gardens confined to narrow bands and formal plots around buildings. Even such a policy of restraint, however, proved to be dangerous, for once flowers of any kind were introduced discipline might slack, and this could open the way to Victorian excesses.

Park purists wanted to exclude the Victorian practice of making pictures and allegories with flowers and plants altogether. Planting should be luxurious and permanent, not seasonal: if there were flowers, then they should be wildflowers. But the local press liked to describe the elaborate, sculptural floral displays, and this reinforced their importance.

In fact, carpet bedding was the most powerful force eroding the controlled use of flowers. From the start, Chicago specialized in allegorical planting which conveyed political and religious messages. Flowerbeds were shaped like stars, baskets, cornucopias, and pyramids. San Francisco began to indulge in carpet bedding in the 1890s. Newspapers billed intricate floral works as the latest attraction and proposed floral maps of the United States or California.

Architecture

Buildings, like roads and walls, were necessary evils required to make parks usable. As in the case of flowers, even their restrained introduction into the parks posed a danger to the pleasure ground ideal. According to that ideal, architecture was supposed to subordinate itself to the overall composition of the landscape plan. Sargent and Olmsted adamantly denounced architectural features that made a park confused and fussy, like a garden or a rural cemetery. Sargent acknowledged the pleasures of throngs of men and women meeting in a holiday mood on some spacious urban plaza, but he argued that there was no excuse for a vacillating compromise between a pastoral park and an urban square.[73] During the height of the neoclassical revival of the 1890s in New York, Commissioner George Clausen stated that his administration would protect natural scenes from architectural encroachment with the same jealous care as

Top:
Victorian "bedding out" eroded the naturalistic ideal of the pleasure ground by introducing garishly colored plant material and geometric layouts. Washington Park, 1889. Courtesy Chicago Historical Society.

Bottom:
Chicago's South Park system became notorious for allegorical flora displays such as "The Flight of Time." Washington Park, 1889. Courtesy Chicago Historical Society.

The German landscape gardener Kanst earned notoriety among pleasure ground theorists for such displays as "The Globe," Washington Park, ca. 1892. Courtesy Chicago Historical Society.

In "Rowing for the Presidential Chair," the owl atop the pole asked: "Hoo" will be president in 1892. Courtesy Chicago Historical Society.

did the creators of Central Park.[74] Accordingly, he removed buildings in front of the arsenal and replaced them with grass, flowers, and shrubs. A simple wall around a cemetery in New York's Hudson Park was criticized because it treated the masonry more architecturally than was appropriate to park theory.

Park buildings were generally only one or two stories, to keep a low profile. Galleries and balconies on the second story often provided scenic viewing points. Ideally, large public buildings were to be outside the park entirely, but, if they were necessary for the park itself, they were to be erected on the edge of open grounds, curtained by trees so that never more than one was seen at a time. Commissioners in most cities felt that park buildings should be durable and permanent, and they were willing to build slowly to make the investment in substantial structures. When San Franciscans had to decide what to do with the temporary buildings left from the midwinter fair of 1893, they concluded that park buildings of any importance should be built of stone or marble, "or at least of enduring materials that will possess the elements of beauty and dignity," and removed them.[75]

Some of the rejected entries to the Central Park design competition vividly illustrate inappropriate architectural treatment. W. Benque proposed a series of four open squares with promenades and formal planting separated from each other by three blocks of buildings, including great boarding houses, schools, block-sized bazaars divided into salesrooms, libraries, opera houses, theatres, and first-class hotels.[76] One scheme, called "The Eagle," centered on an emblematic national fountain of thirteen star-shaped basins surrounded by American eagles. Water came out of the beaks, then from star to star. The "Rustic" scheme introduced an Italian campanile, seventy-five feet high, with a reservoir on the top. The "Manhattan style" scheme had an Italianate central avenue.

A park required many structures that were not buildings in

Architectural style ranged from the rustic to the neoclassical. Lewis Miller sketch, Central Park, Museum of the City of New York.

Ideally, buildings should contribute to the landscape composition but not dominate it as here in Douglas Park, Chicago. Pre-1900.

the fullest sense but, nevertheless, received architectural treatment. Any urban park was thought to deserve a wall to prevent the boundary from being overrun, regular walks neglected, and tracks beaten in the grass. Elaborate entrance gates were common in most pleasure grounds—a message that the parks should be taken seriously as an expression of a high level of cultural achievement. The terrace at the Central Park esplanade, although not a fully enclosed building, had extensive floors of ornamental tile. Similarly, the Central Park belvedere was a cross between architecture and landscape architecture.

The belvedere and terrace were points of focus in the landscape as well as observatories and gathering points. In contrast, buildings like depots, refectories, boat landings, and greenhouses were never aesthetic elements in their own right and were styled to fit modestly into the pastoral setting. Showing machinery for what it was might have been natural, but, because it appeared man-made, designers ornamented it. Thus a waterworks in Golden Gate Park was enclosed in a concrete Moorish style building, and the valley surrounding it was designed as an old-time fairy dell rather than betray an intricate twentieth-century piece of steam machinery.[77]

For about ten years, the park departments preferred a rustic anything: railings, bridges, pergolas, pavilions were made from small trees with the bark intact. For Golden Gate a special tree was imported from Japan because it branched evenly into a Y-shape at the right height for a railing. Pergolas and bandstands were light, airy structures, usually wall-less with peaked or lattice roofs in the Victorian stick gothic style. Museums and other places of exhibition that required walls compensated for the intrusion by their unusual shapes and associations with exotic places. Most conservatories were built of wood and glass and resembled the delicate Victorian pavilions erected at late nineteenth century expositions around the world. The rustic and Victorian stick styles soon gave way to Richardsonian Romanesque—sloping roofs, asymmetrical plans, staggered rusticated

Top:
The rustic style could be found nationwide from Seattle to the Bronx. Pelham Bay, 1916.

Bottom:
Rustic materials and style were naturalistic but difficult to defend as worthy expressions of public spending. Lake Washington Park lunch room and bicycle path, 1900–1907. Seattle Historical Society.

The Victorian Gothic and Richardsonian Romanesque became favored for public buildings because the solid materials and large scale seemed worthy of public expenditure, yet these styles retained informality: asymmetrical plans and elevations, sloping rooflines, turrets and garrets, irregular windows, varied materials, and arched entry. West Chicago Park Commission Offices.

Top:
Richardsonian Romanesque arches offered an easy-going formality at this boat landing in Humboldt Park, Chicago.

Top, Opposite:
Rusticated stone work, shingling, and half-timbering reinforce the informality of the irregular plan and elevation of these stables in Humboldt Park, Chicago.

Bottom, opposite:
Private donors often preferred the symmetry, colonnades, and polished stone of neoclassical monuments in exchange for their generosity. Douglas Park, Chicago.

This rustic staircase was redone in 1916 as neoclassical, reflecting the move toward more ostentatious styling. New York.

stonework, irregular window placement and shape, and round turrets—which also provided a picturesque contrast to commercial buildings. Yet the informal picturesque ideal was somewhat undermined by the neoclassical revival, which was given a great boost by Chicago's Columbian Exposition of 1893. In Golden Gate Park music was initially performed in the open air or in Victorian bandstands, but its new music concourse was designed as a "grand corso 160 feet in width and making a complete circuit of the coliseum" which would permit a double stream of carriages to move in opposite directions without interruption.[78] The new stand, a gift of Claus Spreckels, sugar magnate and civic leader, was in the Italian Renaissance style, and, hardly an inconspicuous support structure, it proclaimed clearly the impressive status of its donor.[79]

Ornament

Despite neoclassical competition, the picturesque ideal was never abandoned entirely. As late as 1893, the year of the Chicago Fair, the design of the boathouse in Strawberry Lake in Golden Gate Park was informal, rustic, and picturesque. But the statuary that was introduced into the parks by ethnic groups and wealthy donors was a blatant intrusion, as remote from the picturesque as the speedways, another intrusion of the rich, were from "airing."

Statuary reminded the viewer of man's handiwork, not nature's, and, because it was associated with European aristocratic formal gardens, it was an anathema to democrats. Some San Franciscans expressed a desire that "the passion may never come to make our park a pantheon, remembering that art is subject to criticism, but vegetation pleases all."[80] Chicagoans, ever pragmatic, said statuary, fountains, and artificial decorations of all sorts could be introduced but shrubbery and landscaping should take precedence.[81] Most designers objected to statuary in general, although laymen tended to object only to specific pieces. The American Park and Outdoor Art Association was wholly against what it called effigies in the parks:

There should be no place in them . . . for granite pantalooned remembrances of dead musicians and soldiers and statesmen. If we cannot teach people to realize that they should keep their effigies of statesmen where they belong, then let us hide them in thickets. . . . We should put nothing in our parks which suggests unrest or anything disagreeable, or that will frighten children, but we should put in objects that will suggest woods, trees, water and nature.[82]

Only in limited circumstances would theoreticians consider statuary and ornament appropriate. Formal promenades were permissible settings, and rustic vases full of plants and blossoming vines punctuated the planting beds along Chicago's parkways.

Sargent explained that pressure for statuary was formidable:

We may give our commissioners too much credit if we take it for granted that they all know how bad the "Scott" is, or the "Morse," or the "Elias Howe," or the "Tigress with her Cubs," but some of them do, and these could give reasons that might convince the rest . . . however, you have still to convince the public, and this is a harder task. For, the public is only half-educated in matters of taste, and not only admires these very bad figures, but is continually pestering the commissioners to put up more like them.[83]

They would have to be more than men, he said, if they could face the wrath that would follow their refusal. Thus a memorial arch to Golden Gate Park was donated in the memory of a widow's husband and son, and both Chicago's and San Francisco's German communities installed monuments to Schiller: "Whenever a German emmigrates, Goethe and Schiller emmigrate with him."[84] The temperance advocate, Henry Cogswell, donated an elaborate fountain inscribed with the words Vichy, Congress Water, and California Seltzer—all intended to proclaim the virtues of ordinary drinking water.

Transition

Gas lighting could not be used near trees without killing them, but in any case Olmsted did not want manufactured

Despite the dual proscription against statuary and instruments of war, these relics from the Spanish-American War found their way into Lincoln Park. Ca. 1900. Courtesy Chicago Historical Society.

For a few years planners thought they could create small versions of the pleasure ground in tenement districts. In this transitional small park the buildings are inconspicuous, berms obscure surroundings, the open meadow and lazy body of water create soft edges and serenity. Chicago Park District.

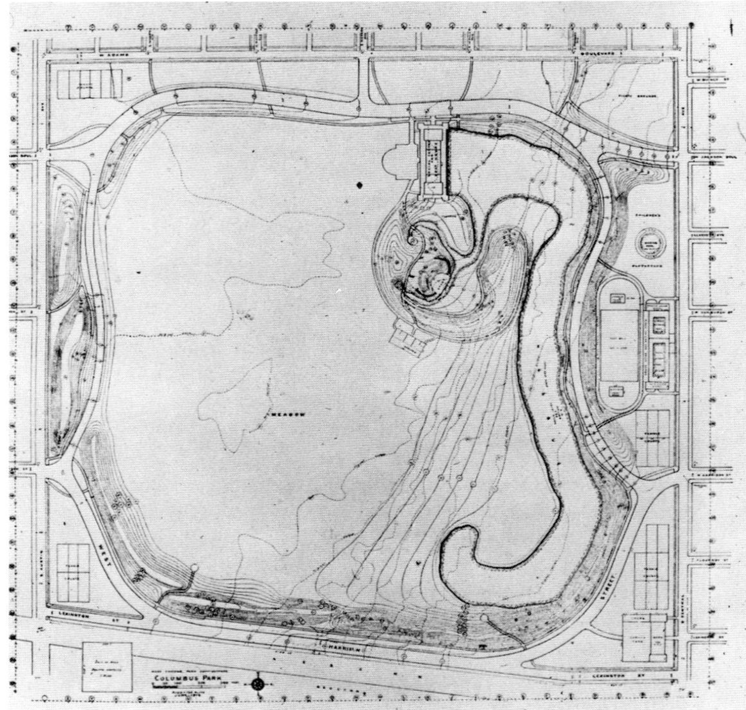

lighting fixtures marring the pastoral illusion, so he accepted the constraint happily. For most cities' parks he proposed that only a large, open meadow be lit for night use. As the importance of direct use, however, came to rival that of picturesque effect, the way was open to electric lighting. In San Francisco, for example, the owners of the pleasure resorts and restaurants near the Cliff House area organized in 1895 to promote the lighting of park drives. Liverymen, cycleries, members of bicycle clubs, and wealthy horsemen joined the owners in making private contributions to the electric lighting scheme. Yet there was truth as well in McLaren's democratic rationale that "lighting the park would make it available to many who, working in shops and factories through the day, cannot go out except in the evening."[85] By 1898 the bicycle paths in Golden Gate Park were electrically lit from 6:00 p.m. until midnight.

In fact, by the end of the pleasure garden era around 1900, administrators showed an equal interest in the use of parks and in their form.[86] Despite forces of disintegration the ideals of the picturesque which had dominated park design for fifty years persisted into the reform era and beyond. The first playgrounds tried to integrate play equipment into an overall picturesque composition. Designers organized these playgrounds around a central open field, encircled them with curved walks and clusters of shrubbery, and protected them with berms. Architecture stayed to the side, and, where possible, a lake or mere completed the pictures. Because the principles of layout were so similar, with only the size and location of the site changed, this transitional type was called the small park. But in a short time new principles of composition and a new language governed their design.

2

The Reform Park: 1900–1930

The Need for Structure

The popularized transcendentalism that lay behind the creation of the great nineteenth-century pleasure grounds was to yield to turn-of-the-century progressivism in the urban parks of the early 1900s. Parks, such as Chicago's Pulaski Park, New York's Steward Park, San Francisco's Funston Park, were created and run with a reforming zeal, and at times their advocates spoke of them as if they were municipally run settlement houses. The keynote approach of reform parks was to organize activity, since urban park planners now considered the masses incapable of undertaking their own recreation. Organized activites, of course, contrast with the unstructured pursuits of the pleasure ground. Yet the organization motive, parallels the restorative function of fresh air and landscape in pleasure ground thinking. The presiding spirits of the pleasure ground—landscape architects like Olmsted and gardners like Chicago's Jens Jensen—gave way to reform park organizers, park leaders, play directors, and efficiency-minded experts in recreation.

Using the new parks were mostly children and adult men of the urban working classes. According to reform park thinking, they were incapable of undertaking their own recreation, not so much because the city provided no space for it as because it gave them recreational needs for which mere space was insufficient. Organization was the key to getting the most out of free time. Thus for working men deliberate, organized sports would ensure their exposure to a full complement of human experience, acutely needed since office and factory work was perceived as routine and dull. Ironically, the substitute for the loss of the traditional creative satisfactions of work was to specialize recreation in the same way that work is specialized rather than to try to reunite human activities. Similarly, children's schools were molded in the image of such economic institutions, and their play was comparably routinized.[1]

In the early 1900s larger incomes, earlier retirement, shorter work weeks, and longer vacations left more people with more time on their hands. Accordingly, the phrase "leisure time" first appeared in *Recreation Magazine* in April 1907.[2] Whereas the older word "leisure" suggested a stroll or a picnic, and thus a pleasure ground, leisure time suggests planning, scheduling, and a gap to be filled. One main line of reform thinking, which persisted well beyond the 1930s, was that this gap of free time generated a demand for increasing recreational service, and during the first three decades of the century demand in itself justified the sudden creation of municipal facilities, beaches, golf courses, stadiums, tennis courts, and picnic areas.[3] Generally, for its advocates the reform park was a moral defense against the potential for chaos that they perceived in this new abundance of free time, just as the pleasure ground had been an antidote to the old lack of free space. Spare time, in short, was a threat to society. It could be as easily spent in the saloon, the dance hall, and the picture show as in the church, the YMCA, and the library, unless reform advocates competed to channel time their way.

Jane Addams observed that the failure of the modern city was "all the more serious because of the unprecedented monotony and division of urban industrial labor, and because young people were now released from the protection of the home and allowed to wander unattended through the city streets."[4] Unattended children promised particular threats. Many park reformers used the vulnerability of children as argument for their cause. Thus they pointed to children's death rates in hot weather to shock the public into supporting playgrounds.[5] Unlike the pleasure ground, which encouraged family excursions and recreation, the reform park segregated the ages and sexes. For the first time children became a distinct and important focus of park planning. The reform park movement, in fact, stemmed in part from the late nineteenth-century playground movement, and the early reform parks were often aptly called playgrounds.

Playground and Park

The playground movement came into being several years before it was institutionalized in municipal park service. There was a Boston schoolyard devoted to play by 1868, a playground in the athletic fields of Chicago's Washington Park by 1876, and in 1885 Dr. Marie Zakrzewska started a children's sand garden in Boston after seeing one in Berlin. The idea soon spread through settlement house work. It became popular enough to force city governments to begin to install play equipment in existing parks and public squares. Before 1900 New York, Chicago, Philadelphia, Pittsburgh, Baltimore, New Haven, Providence, and San Francisco had such playground facilities, although these municipalities had not yet passed legislation enabling them to purchase land specifically for this purpose. Boston's City Council pioneered in the movement and dedicated its first playground in 1890; New York's Small Parks Commission was appointed in 1898, and Chicago's legislation was passed in 1901. A further landmark of the movement was its national institutionalization, in 1906, in the Playground Association of America.

San Francisco's Playground Commission was established in the city charter in 1907, after ten years of agitation. A brief account of these years gives an idea of trends and forces. When the push for a park in the working-class Mission district began in 1897, people viewed it as fundamentally different from Golden Gate Park; they felt that they were at

Settlement kindergarten class in sandlot in Davis Square. Undated. Courtesy Chicago Historical Society.

the beginning of a new order of things, a new era.[6] A grand jury investigated the Parks Department in 1898 and opposed the acquisition of more land for park purposes unless it was east of Van Ness Avenue, that is, in the crowded districts. A women's club recognized the necessity for public playgrounds and sponsored the first public playground on school property. By 1900 the playground movement was closely allied with general urban reform in San Franciscans' eyes, so the entry of the municipal government into the field was inevitable.[7] Thus in 1901 the Board of Supervisors gave the Board of Education $12,000 to equip a playground in a working class neighborhood, in 1904 a bond issue passed for $740,000 for the purchase of two more playgrounds, and in 1907 the Playground Commission was established.

Since park advocates were arguing for the location of new parks on sites more accessible to the working classes, they were natural allies of the playground movement. In fact, the name "small park" reflects the continuity they imagined between the pleasure ground—now called the "large park"—and the new sites. In the beginning parks departments regarded these sites as parks first and playgrounds second. But the balance shifted so greatly over the course of time that the term "small park" became something of a misnomer: the parks were by no means miniature pleasure grounds and, in fact, were distinguished less by their size than by their intended function. "Playground" is more accurate, but only because it has come to be associated exclusively with children's play, suggesting outdoor activity. I am calling the parks that appeared and flourished during the first three decades of this century parks instead of reform playgrounds.

Organized Play

There was little debate about the purpose of the new type of park. Those who felt that it was primarily a place other than the street for children to go for spontaneous play or athletics, gave way to the majority opinion that such parks should be places for organized play. Rather than debate there was development, from a focus on play to a focus on organization itself.

Park leaders considered play, whether spontaneous or supervised, as a natural instinct which would find an outlet in deviant behavior if thwarted.[8] Play was the essence of the child; or rather, as an early recreationist, Joseph Lee, said, "Play is the child." Lee assured the public that play was serious—it is the "letting loose of what is in him, the active projection of the force he is, the becoming of what he is to be."[9] Hygiene alone demanded that children be given the chance to play, and games, especially those of adolescence, encouraged self-reliance and initiative.[10] Games, in fact, were regarded as an improvement on simply play, since they involved a definite program and conclusion.[11] Professionals conceded that play was instinctive, but they maintained that games had to be taught. The playground then provided not just an outlet for the instinct of play but a setting for the teaching and learning of social content through games.[12]

Eventually focus on play was broadened to include a general range of activities for young and old. In the thinking of the period, parks were for activities as well as landscape beauty—in other words, they were not mere pleasure grounds. But soon this distinction lapsed into unimportance, and a distinction between organized and unorganized activities emerged in its place. Activity in itself would no longer suffice; it had to be organized by knowledgeable leaders to mold the user's experience effectively. In the metaphor of Olmsted and Nolen, "Cake ingredients dumped into a bowl don't make a cake."[13] Chicago park officials explained, "The contrast in old and new park service is striking in that the former furnished merely a place for recreation, while the latter furnishes, first of all, a scheme of recreation."[14]

In the new scheme play was systematically channeled into activities that seem to make for good citizenship rather than being an end in itself. The care of the playground was entrusted only to play leaders who understood that the significance of the play instinct was its relation to the physical and social development of young people.[15] At first leadership was needed simply to ensure order, issue equipment, organize teams and schedule games—in short to accommodate. Within a few years, however, leadership was used to stimulate sanctioned activities, particularly community use of assembly halls and clubrooms. Chicago administrators claimed, "our recreation centers include not only custodial methods of management but also expert leadership."[16] A good play leader would want to avoid becoming a mere caretaker who only taught a few of the bigger boys some more or less dangerous tricks or stunts, while the weaker ones received no attention; otherwise, the moral effect of the playground would be completely lost or reversed.[17] Leadership was necessary to protect children from one another, which in itself was recognized as a means to foster a general sense of ethics: "Left alone, the tyrannies children practice upon one another compete in cruelty with the oppressions exercised by the brutish governments of grown men. . . . More ethics and good citizenship can be instilled into our embryo rulers by a play master in a single week than can be inculcated by Sunday school teachers and Fourth of July orators in a decade."[18] By 1923 it was simply a matter of definition that the modern playground was supervised.[19]

Because children are imitative, the character and qualifications of the instructors were paramount. Equipment and physical facilities were secondary to the appointment of the "man with sufficient education, refinement, initiative, and social training to be head, guide, and promoter."[20] Qualifications for the position were spelled out precisely: the instructor should always appear neatly dressed, cleanly shaven, with well-groomed hair; he should praise boys and girls for sacrificing themselves for the good of the team, enforce the rules of the game and insist on fair play, and play frequently, setting a pace for vigorous action.[21] Rather than trying to rely exclusively on a combination of informal recruitment and screening by examination to find such upright characters, some parks departments instituted formal training courses for all aspiring playground directors.[22]

In Chicago a three-day institute giving special instructions to summer leaders was started in 1913. As the emphasis on leadership grew, the area over which leadership was meant to hold sway expanded. The 1909 textbook for professional play leaders, *The Normal Course in Play*, was renamed *Introduction to Community Recreation* in 1925. Playgrounds, in fact, became recreative centers, combining playground features with some of the social aims of the settlement house.[23] In organizing activities like music weeks, community days, community singing, lunchtime sings in factories, street play, holiday celebrations, community drama, pageantry, and neighborhood talent programs, they sought to ensure a wholesome expression of community life and the socialization of residents to a common core of American values.

From this base Chicagoans even tried to build a political organization for the solution of neighborhood problems, although these efforts proved unfruitful. They thought of their recreation centers as community clearinghouses through which neighborhood problems could be solved cooperatively by several different agencies, and many park districts formed advisory councils and started to train leaders in community service.[24] Probably the cultural divisiveness of the twenties would have made efforts of this kind futile for any agency. In any case by the Depression park service had lost any pretensions to being an agent of social change.

Reform Programming

The pleasure ground imitated nature, and its use was curtailed by nightfall and in rough weather. In contrast, the focus of the reform park on organized activity led to its use during times when it would previously have gone unused and to the strict scheduling of its use. This new attitude toward time wedded recreation more intimately to the pace of urban life. The day was broken into parts according to temperature changes and the schedules of school children, mothers, and workers: early morning through midday, early afternoon, late afternoon, and with night lighting, evening. The modern city was on a seven-day week, and even Sunday, the day of rest, was opened for active recreation, although in some cities the playgrounds were closed until noon. Once park life was no longer a substitute for rural summers but a response to relentless urban rhythms, the rationale for exclusively summer programming was eroded. Chicago kept eleven centers open year-round beginning in 1912. One consequence of year-round recreation was an increase in the popularity of winter sports. Skiing became popular in Chicago's West Side Humboldt Park in 1917. In New York, a portion of the speedway was proposed as a "splendid toboggan and coasting slide," and in the exceptionally mild Chicago winter of 1921, ice-skating competed with out-of-season golf and tennis.[25] New York park commissioners reversed a prohibition of sleds by 1915, welcoming them by tens of thousands.[26]

Park programming commonly divided recreation into categories such as physical, social, aesthetic, and civic, or active, passive, and social.[27] These groupings indicate the widening range of activities programmed for parks in the reform era.

Athletics were a primary focus. German immigrants had set up turnvereins in the early nineteenth century, and the YMCA integrated the gymnasium into the culture at large in the decade from 1886 to 1896: park departments merely adopted the already existing form.[28] Park gymnasiums were both indoors and outdoors; the outdoor equipment dovetailed nicely with the equipment provided by the playground movement.

The pleasure grounds had accommodated tennis, but now the sport spread, as tennis courts became extensions of the gymnasiums. In 1901 the San Francisco commissioners converted an old bandstand into a locker room, with showers and cots for the convenience of tennis players. The courts were so popular that time on them had to be limited. By the early twenties "golf for everybody" had become one of the goals of recreation divisions, although finding space for it was a major inhibitor. Archery became popular in the Chicago system during the first decade of the century, looking more like a pleasure ground activity than the pools and gymnasiums shown in other photos of the reform park era.[29]

While all of these activities presented attractive spectacles, that was no longer their principal rationale. Similarly, park meadows, when used for athletics, were more like extensions of the gymnasium than pieces of landscape, and many had football fields laid out in them. In Chicago ice hockey was played in the large parks, and nearly three dozen baseball diamonds were regularly maintained, along side of which were others laid out informally on the grass. On the Washington Park meadow, as many as thirty games went on at the same time.

Swimming baths were introduced to encourage working class people, many without private baths, to be clean. Showers were part of the gymnastic equipment but also served as public bath systems. Gym instructors encouraged the use of the showers as part of training and for hygiene, the importance of which was also evident in the meticulous washing and sterilizing of bathing suits in park laundries and in the care taken to see that each bather took a thorough bath before entering the pool. The Chicago South Park commissioners discovered, "The adult population in most of the park communities seems thoroughly aroused to the opportunity and the value and luxury of bathing. Weekly and more frequent journeys are made to the baths by entire families."[30] As swimming became a sport, swimming baths became the necessary recreational and social equipment. The first baths in New York, at Seward Park, were so popular that management kept them open at night for those who worked in the daytime and for women during special periods. In exceedingly hot weather the baths were kept open all night. Playgrounds and baths together drew

Swimming originally was introduced as a public health measure in pools intentionally too shallow for swimming; it soon became popular as a form of recreation. Chicago, Eckhart Park, ca. 1915.

such enormous crowds that keeping the park clean required constant attention, and flower beds became impractical. By 1911 Chicago's pools were so popular that groups had to be admitted hourly, each group having one hour for the process of marching in, receiving suit and towel, changing clothes, showering, swimming, dressing, and making way for the next group. Chicago's first swimming meet was held in 1913.

Athletics were further organized into communitywide tournaments. New York's first interpark athletic competition was held in 1911, with medals for winners. In Chicago a general athletic rally was held in 1908, and by 1921, separate tournaments abounded in practically every sport, including horseshoe throwing, skipmobile racing, bicycle racing, kite and model airplane flying, and games such as checkers, marbles, jacks, and top spinning. To turn sports to the purpose of community integration, Chicago developed a system of points that rewarded team spirit and cooperation as much as athletic achievement. A Supremacy Banner was awarded each month to the park that scored the highest aggregate of points in all events, including crafts. San Francisco adopted a similar system in 1922; a series of prizes, letters, and pennants were awarded to teams.

By the first decade of the twentieth century, folk dancing had been assimilated into park programs as a form of athletics and was taught in gym classes. Folk dancing was the lesser of two evils, being relatively wholesome compared to the social dancing and practices of the dance halls.[31] But in time, in hopes of competing more effectively with the dance hall, park programmers offered social dancing. New York and San Francisco introduced it in 1913, and in Chicago it became the most popular of all social activities. The Director of Recreation felt that proper moral supervision was a key to success: "the open public dance (open to girls unattended and to any one without qualification or classification except age restriction) is a weak method of presenting or handling this form of social recreation. Accordingly

Park departments nationwide assumed the responsibility for offering municipally sponsored, chaperoned social dances in hopes of competing with the private dance hall. Stanford Park, Chicago, ca. 1915.

Top, opposite:
Meticulously regimented plots for children's vegetable gardens started on New York's West Side in the 1900s and spread to other cities like Chicago Eckhart Park, ca. 1915.

Bottom, opposite:
Branch library in a Chicago field house, antithetical to the pleasure ground but an ideal for those trying to turn reform parks into civic centers. Pulaski Park, Chicago, ca. 1915.

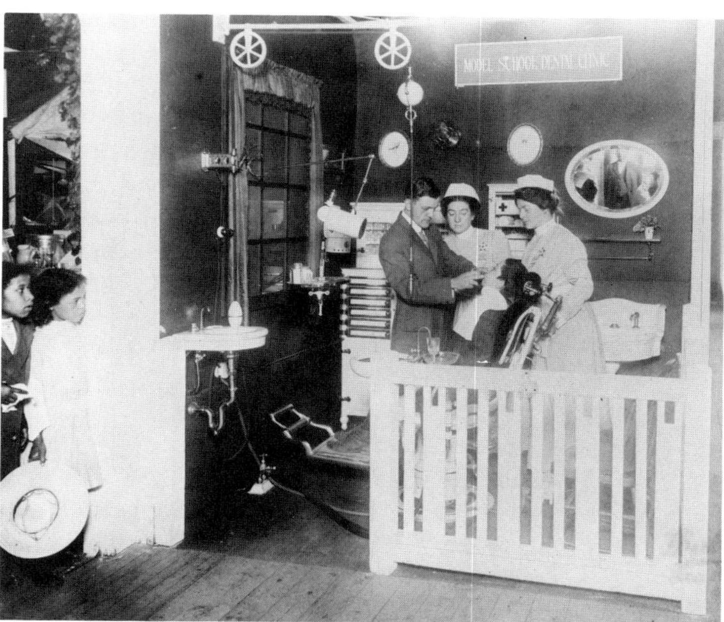

Model dental clinic in a Chicago field house educates working-class families about dentistry and a potential career for children. Two black children look on, but park services were distinctly oriented to whites, whether native or foreign born. Undated. Courtesy Chicago Historical Society.

the open public dance is not permitted in the South Park field houses. Natural groups, representing various strata in society, are given the halls in rotation for dances of the particular groups."[32] By 1920 the national literature reported that dance pavilions were very popular; it confirmed the Chicago experience that a small fee, seating for those not dancing, and male and female chaperones, converted the questionable activity into a manageable one.[33]

Just as dancing came to have a social function which overrode its athletic one, play festivals and pageants served community functions more than any aesthetic need. They were widely thought to promote real democracy by making for more inclusiveness and eliminating exclusiveness—that is, by offering to many children an outlet for the play spirit unavailable to them in athletic activities.[34] Pageantry, unlike fine art which had no place in the reform park was considered appropriate to the sensibilities of the working class. It could be stimulating and yet educational at the same time, as in New York, where a decidedly park-oriented history of New York City was staged as a musical revue in 1913 incorporating vignettes of the immigration of Irish and Germans, the first steamboat, the first coach line, the mayorality of Fernando Wood, the laying out of Central Park, the immigration of Italians and Russians, the development of Greater New York's water supply, and the evolution of playgrounds and recreation centers.[35] Chicago and San Francisco also staged festivals, circuses, and historical pageants.[36]

If painting and sculpture were not geared to the working class, crafts were, and they were welcomed into the reform park as a further expansion of its base of participation. During the pleasure ground era, crafts were considered inappropriate because of their similarity to factory work, and for the first few years of the reform era crafts such as sewing, basketry, and carpentry were occluded not only because physical and social development was more important than activities involving accessory muscles but because crafts were considered an additional evil to the unhygienic ills of factory life and schooling of children.[37] Of the three cities, New York's capitulation to ingenuity work was reported earliest, in 1911. Later, the crafts program in Chicago, which included spelling bees, kite tournaments, and whistle-making contests, was considered "as worthy of promotion as physical competition."[38] The San Francisco Park Department introduced crafts obliquely in 1912, starting with miniature yacht construction, and model airplane making became a permanent departmental offering in the 1920s, at the same time that it became a nationwide rage. By the late 1920s the San Francisco department could justify handicraft as a medium for personal expression and as a way to build up park attendance.

Vegetable gardening, somewhat similar in appeal to handicrafts, first became a recreational activity in New York's DeWitt Clinton Park in 1902, when it was divided into miniscule farms, each assigned to an individual child. Schools began to sponsor such farm programs in parks shortly thereafter, and these gardens became Victory Gardens during the First World War. As a response to wartime shortages, the Chicago Parks Department itself raised vegetable plants for distribution to the public. Demonstration gardens showed adults how to grow fresh vegetables in city-owned gardens, both before and for a few years after the First World War.

Strictly educational activity considered inappropriate to the pleasure ground was welcomed in the reform park. Thus public libraries installed branches in the small parks. Listening to addresses concerning civic issues and even noncontroversial political topics was newly appropriate, but park authorities held the line against a proposal to distribute free newspapers in the parks.[39]

A military presence was as welcome as it had been in the previous era, and park programming was organized around the entertainment of the troops. One of the inflexible rules of the pleasure ground was broken on behalf of the army in San Francisco: signs advertising for army recruits were allowed in the parks and squares.[40]

Civic meetings of all sorts were appropriate. In San Francisco the casino was proposed as the municipality's official reception place for foreign visitors, and a peace meeting was allowed in Golden Gate Park's music stand. Exhibits had a gentle alliance with education and instruction. For example, child welfare and civic-minded exhibits were organized in Chicago by the Women's City Club and other organizations. Aquariums were also advocated as educational activities, as was informal nature study. By the late 1920s even visits to municipal airports were included as a playground activity: indeed, the playground of the reform era was as much a range of activities as location.

With the abandonment of the pleasure ground ideal of the park, the park commissioners accepted and attempted to rationalize industrial culture, and they began to strive for the integration of its various elements into park programming rather than their exclusion. Thus where exclusion, as such, had been a principal strategy of the pleasure ground designers, and patterns of exclusion a clue to the nature of their ideal, during the reform park era these patterns were weaker and less revealing.

Reform parks usually retained no more than fragments inherited from pleasure ground policy, namely, their prejudices. San Francisco park reports throughout the reform era show denials of permission for political assemblies, gospel meetings, peddling, advertising, and gambling, and commercial amusements such as theatres, motion picture houses, saloons, and bowling alleys were systematically excluded. New departures were bans on assemblies in times of epidemic, and, because of the rise of injury, the occasional banning of the use of bats and hardballs.

While prohibitions were ordinarily consistent, some were contradictory. For example, the decision to allow victims of the earthquake and fire to set up refugee camps in San Francisco parks, itself contrary to ideal usage, was slowly reversed, with the refugees being squeezed out of the downtown squares, isolated in the more remote Golden

Gate Park, and eventually excluded altogether.[41] As was typical of the handling of controversial park issues, the final clearing of the park of temporary living quarters was not discussed in the annual reports or the press, but a telltale comment was made much later, namely, that the "squatters" had resisted expulsion.

Just as the number of principled exclusions declined, so too certain characteristic pleasure ground activities disappeared. These developments not only shaped the new playground parks but also eroded the original character of the old pleasure gardens themselves. For instance, boating spanned the pleasure garden and reform park eras, but just barely. Fishing from rowboats had been allowed in Chicago's Jackson Park for some time, and in 1913 it was extended to lagoons in other large parks. In New York, however, fishing tapered off, the last permits having been issued before World War I. In 1917 the Chicago South Park commissioners reported that the boating and launch service were not nearly as greatly patronized as in former years.

Concerts continued in San Francisco, Chicago, and New York past the turn of the century but dwindled in the twenties. In 1921 the Chicago commissioners let private organizations take over their support. In 1922 and 1923 band concerts, still privately sponsored, were given only at Grant Park, and none whatsoever were given at parks outside this central business district. During the same years the San Francisco park commissioners tried defending the value of a band in its death throes: "It is believed that no expenditure made by the park board is of greater educational benefit or affords more delight to visitors than is the annual sum of $15,000 for the park band."[42] But community singing was usurping the attention of park programmers, because it was thought to solidify community spirit.

The Chicago commissioners opened simple lunchrooms and an ice cream factory, and many park services offered wholesome milk, unlike the diluted or adulterated kind sold elsewhere. The demand for this pure milk and plain wholesome food increased continually. The pleasure ground attitude toward picnicking was that it should be cultivated, not only in lieu of restaurants but also because eating in the open air was desirable. Actually the number of large picnics increased over the reform years in Chicago and extended even to the beach areas, where food was roasted over little campfires as a popular evening pleasure. But the world view of the social worker, who now ruled the parks, had little room for picnics, and picnics were not mentioned in the annual reports for many years.

Auto rules had to be adopted as early as 1900 in both San Francisco and New York. Permission to drive in parks was granted only to owners of improved electrical machines, and even these were restricted to certain park roads. The number of roads made available to automobiles slowly expanded from 1900 to 1904 to 1909. In Golden Gate Park horses were important up to 1912, when the last drive reserved for the exclusive use of the horse met the fate of the others and was opened to the automobile.

Neighborhood Parks

The reform park was not so much a supplement to the pleasure ground as it was a substitute for the street. The street was attractive to children because it was so active—first a funeral, then a fire, craps on the sidewalk, a stolen ride on a freight train, a raid on a fruit stall, a fight, an accident, all kaleidoscopic confusion and excitement. Whenever reformers spoke of streets in relation to the boy, it was the way they spoke of alcohol or gambling in relation to the man: "Every year their attraction grows stronger, till their lure becomes irresistable and his life is swallowed up in theirs."[43] Teddy Roosevelt himself came out against street play: "City streets are unsatisfactory playgrounds for children, because of the danger, because most good games are against the law, because they are too hot in summer, and because in crowded sections of the city, they are apt to be schools of crime."[44] The better and safer park environment would relieve parents, truck drivers, streetcar men, and policemen from care and anxiety concerning the safety of children.

Some reformers changed their attitude toward streets and even proposed closing off some of the quieter ones for use as playgrounds in districts that did not have enough.[45] The Mission district in San Francisco and North Harlem in New York had play streets.[46] Another way of extending the effectiveness of the park system was to take advantage of the open space around buildings and schools. In San Francisco the provision of a new charter placed all the small parks, squares, and grounds around public buildings and schools under the jurisdiction of the park commissioners.[47] The mutual use of playgrounds and schoolyards by the schools and parks departments produced the school-park program, sometimes called school-playground coordination, which was instituted throughout the country. Sometimes school children were sent to playgrounds during school hours for the recreational part of the school program. After school had closed, park personnel would take responsibility for overseeing the use of schoolyards.

Beyond these improvised or ready-made park areas were new ones within densest neighborhoods. The consistent theme in justifying their location was the need to serve the largest segment of the population. Of New York's five small parks established in 1898, four were located on the Lower East Side, amid the largest concentrations of immigrants. A special park commission was set up to select sites on the south side of Chicago for easier access for the laboring classes. In San Francisco the decision to build a park in the working-class district south of Market Street at the turn of the century was justified in populist rhetoric. Residents of the district had organized to demand a high school for their section of the city, and, once successful, they began to press for a public park. After much debate, a city supervisor sponsored a new park scheme for the area, but it was criticized by the greater public for its inaccessibility:

Supervisor Curtis is on the right track in his proposal but any new park should be located near the people who need them. . . .

Before the park system south of Market should be considered completed and before any addition whatever shall be made to the park areas in other sections of the city—unless possibly on the Chinatown site—there should be small playgrounds within easy reach of every part of the densely populated district where the mass of the city's people live. These playgrounds need not be large nor need they make any pretensions to splendor or to any Paris-like effects.[48]

In 1902 the annual park report restated the need for a south of Market Street site: "we deem it the duty of those in authority to provide recreation grounds of sufficient size, within walking distance, for every child of the city."[49]

The new smaller park type was idealized because it could be tucked in almost anywhere.[50] (A more shadowy motive was that these playgrounds could be established on small bits of land that were of little use for building sites.) In time the issue of whether a city should invest in small or large parks was superseded by the general theory that a park system consisted of two kinds of parks: the local neighborhood park for frequent and regular use and the rural park for holidays. By the 1920s the more abstract inference emerged that the park system was composed of areas increasing in size as one moved away from the city center, the area of highest land value and density.

Administrators attempted to formulate standard guidelines for determining playground size. Thirty square feet per child was considered the minimum by some, although others criticized this standard for not taking into account the ages of the children, the kinds of games they would probably play, the total number of children in a district, or the amount of open space elsewhere. On Chicago's West Side a sophisticated attempt to rationalize site selection was based on the School Census of 1908, the U.S. Census figures on population density, the location of public and parochial schools, the number of existing playgrounds and parks, sanitary conditions, tuberculosis, and infant mortality rates.[51]

Some felt that population growth was going to be so enormous, or at least so unpredictable, that percentage of acreage, rather than population ratios, should be the basis for distributing parks. For example, in the borough of Queens, the population had increased 100 percent over ten years, so the park commissioners claimed that a 10 percent area should be open space and parks. Another expert concluded that one-twentieth of a city's area should be reserved for parks and squares: for every thousand acres there should be 10 acres for playgrounds and squares, 40 for large parks, 100 for streets and alleys, 5 for school grounds, 155 for public purposes, and 850 for private ownership.[52]

Ideally, a playground would be located near cheap and quick transportation systems. But topographical considerations of the location, the size, shape, boundaries, and character of the land, also were considered rational and legitimate criteria for site selection. For example, a request for a playground might be denied because the grade was too steep. A site with water was preferred, but other topographical units had to be complete, for example, no half-slopes, half-lakes, or half-hills. In the ensuing era of the recreation facility, these criteria became formal standards, in turn eroded by open space ideology that justified taking available land no matter what its size or shape.

Even during the reform era such systematic criteria for park selection were sometimes overridden or ignored when the press which could easily mount popular support and local improvement clubs put pressure on playground and park commissioners for a given playground. Often playgrounds were created because individuals offered plots of land for sale or even donated them. The editor of *Park International* commented on the

> . . . great need to secure the plotting and building of parks on a more systematic basis. . . . the location of interior parks and of playgrounds has been largely opportunist. Their opening in sections of already built up cities will probably continue to be opportunist; but new towns and the suburbs of all existing cities should provide for country

parks, neighborhood parks, formal and informal parks and playgrounds on a systematic basis.[53]

The City Beautiful

Reform parks, like pleasure grounds, were an early form of urban renewal, since they could replace less desirable land uses such as city dumps, cemeteries, slums, the empty grounds of defunct reformatories or breweries, old piers, rooftops, and vacant lots. Another opportunity for urban renewal was based on the idea of backyards for play which contributed to both the city's beautification and recreation services. Advocates of block interior parks, as these were called, had criticized the park movement for not extending its own logic far enough: if people needed to have nature nearby, it should be introduced into the city blocks where it would be closest and most appreciated.[54] They encouraged owners of unused and unattractive lots to allow the city to convert them into play spaces for children. Sometimes the communities themselves bought vacant, nearby lots to secure a play space for younger children.[55] In New York City in the 1910s the Backyard Playgrounds Association was instrumental in tearing down fences, cleaning up rubbish, and installing a common garden and interior court for the centers of large, closely built up city blocks. In the same period the New York Parks Department and the Tenement House Committee of the Charities Society tried to convince tenement house builders to use open metal rather than wooden backyard fencing to permit light and air to circulate, eliminate hiding places for thieves, and make backyards more attractive than the street for children to play in. In 1915 the New York Parks Department formally incorporated the use of vacant lots in their programming, assigning a play leader to supervise activities there.[56]

Yet, the backyard movement was never successful enough to capture the imagination of the proponents of large-scale urban beautification. Their focus was on more obvious visual features like Chicago's lakefront, which in the Burnham Plan and the Lakeshore development scheme of the twenties was considered one of the most important undertakings of park commissioners.[57] While the extensive fill created bathing beaches, its visual appeal as a continuous lakefront beach received more written attention than the services available at the site. Similarly, Grant Park was developed with great care and attention to artistic detail because it was the pivotal point of the entire system of parks and boulevards. The parks commission called it the "artistic center" of the lake front program.[58]

The City Beautiful movement influenced the selection of sites for San Francisco parks. Twin Peaks was purchased to maintain the city's skyline features. Sutro Heights and the top of Telegraph Hill were secured for their superb views; part of Bakers Beach, even though polluted in 1929, offered ocean frontage. Clearly all were locations that could not easily be used by youngsters for play. New Yorkers proposed the scenic treatment of Blackwell's Island and Randall's Island, after the design of Olmsted's Belle Isle Park in Detroit. The national park literature promoted the idea of connecting parkways and boulevards to link up all principal parks and points of interest in a city, based on the metropolitan park system planned first in Boston and discussed in New York, Chicago, San Francisco, and many other cities. Kessler's city plan for Dallas offered the high hope that connecting parkways could compensate for a lack of local parks: "since large parks in a city must be limited in number and since they are often not so located as to be of the greatest usefulness to the general public, the connecting parkways between these properties can, by careful planning, be made to serve the purposes of local parks without in any way interfering with their primary purposes."[59]

The New Park Form

In 1894 C. S. Sargent, the staunchest defender of the pleasure ground, was horrified when a Philadelphia city officer recommended that cities provide more playgrounds and fewer ornamental parks.[60] After the turn of the century park designers, who were increasingly employees of park departments rather than consultants, shifted from artistry as a design priority to utility. This changing perspective is apparent in the official reports, as the length of landscape reports diminished while the playground and gym director's reports increased.

Ideally, the playground could be both beautiful and serviceable, since most modern facilities could be decorated with trees, shrubs, and flowers without their interfering with the play space; as such, the City Beautiful and settlement house mentalities, which seemed to be at cross purposes in questions of site selection, could actually be reconciled in the design of parks themselves. The Chicago Field House was heralded nationwide as a new type of park, one combining aesthetic features with facilities for a wide range of activities. The attractiveness of greenery was even justified as being utilitarian; bare grounds required perpetual supervision, while landscaped grounds would somehow stimulate individuals and groups to work out their own activities.

As playgrounds and the reform park idea became popular, citizen groups began to request that playgrounds be inserted into existing parks, and park departments tried to integrate playground equipment and traditional park landscaping. To preserve lawn, most designers separated the areas for children's play from the rest of the park. Chicago was thought to have set one of the best examples in this respect; the strip of trees, shrubs, and paths which rimmed playgrounds made them small parks for the parents while the interior functioned as playgrounds for the young.[61]

Sometimes play equipment was installed even in the large parks, and by the end of the 1920s national opinion was that "there can be no objection to a children's area in a large municipal park, provided it is properly segregated so as not to intrude upon the rural quiet and repose of the general scheme."[62] One designer proposed dividing this transitional type of park into three zones: the meadowlike park with trees, water, and vistas, the playground with community building facilities, and a driveway with turn-around and parking areas to separate the noisy and quiet areas.[63] But some designers felt that playgrounds and the large parks should not be mixed at all. In San Francisco, a request to locate a playground in Jefferson Square was denied on the grounds that it would destroy the frontage of the bordering avenue, and the Panhandle Adornment and Improvement Club protested against the establishment of a playground in the Panhandle, presumably for similar aesthetic reasons. The New York park commissioners concluded: "The modern playground is a complete plant in itself and is most successful when segregated from a park. New playgrounds therefore cannot with safety be carved out of existing small parks."[64]

Design Elements

The designers' handling of landscape elements and details of construction shows how the tension between utility and appearance was resolved in practice. By 1922 a model reform park had at least ten acres, and at most forty. It was divided into both an indoor and outdoor plant, ringed by shrubbery. The outdoor plant was big enough for two games, running tracks, sandpits, a swimming and wading pool, an outdoor gym, a field house, and a children's playground for boys and girls under ten with swings, teeter-totters, giant strides, wading pool, sand bin, and a free game space.[65] The field house was typically located in the middle of one end of the park with the children's playgrounds flanking it symmetrically. A formal axis led to the playing fields.[66] The field house itself—the indoor plant—contained an assembly hall and stage, cloak rooms, club rooms, a refectory, a branch of the public library, indoor gynmasiums with separate locker rooms for men and women, and toilets with showers. Men's and women's gym equipment included traveling rings, climbing ladders, poles and slanting beams, pits for jumping, shot putting, and pole vaulting, a cinder running track, a ball diamond and basketball court, and quoits. The women's gym in addition contained swings.

The overall layout of the park was symmetrical and formal.

Paths and roadways were minimized to save space for games and direct use. Spatial sequence was not particularly important; no illusion of more space than existed was called for, nor were the kinesthetic experiences of moving through different volumes or meandering along serpentine paths sought after. If anything, the pedestrian was offered a feeling of order and civic importance through the formal, central, and axial array. Views were no longer carefully controlled, except inasmuch as shrubs and trees might screen out the immediate environs of the city though obviously not the skyline of industrial areas and tenements beyond. Buildings dominated the landscape, their location, size, and style making them important.

The vegetable garden for children mentioned earlier, or "school farm," although typically walled off from the rest of the park, epitomized its rigid organization. Rows upon rows of miniature small farms, four by eight feet, were plotted. The surrounding area was barren with factories and signs visible in the background. The grid and the factory environment went with an emphasis on production and discipline. Every child's plot was planted in the same way to help the children learn to recognize different crops and to facilitate the teacher's work in handling large numbers of children. A lesson given on one plot would apply to the whole school farm. Moreover, it would be "as much a mistake to allow children to plant as they please, before they have received training, as it would be to build a fine school house, open the doors, and invite the children to enter and educate themselves."[67]

The rationale of reform park design was as highly evolved and consistent as that of pleasure ground design, but virtually antithetical to it; it represented much more than an erosion of the older ideal. Thus water was not used for psychic effects but for practical ones: it filled wading and swimming pools and showered people before and after swimming. Just as the showers were usually adjacent or linked to the swimming pools, the gymnasium lockers were linked to the shower baths and to the indoor and out-

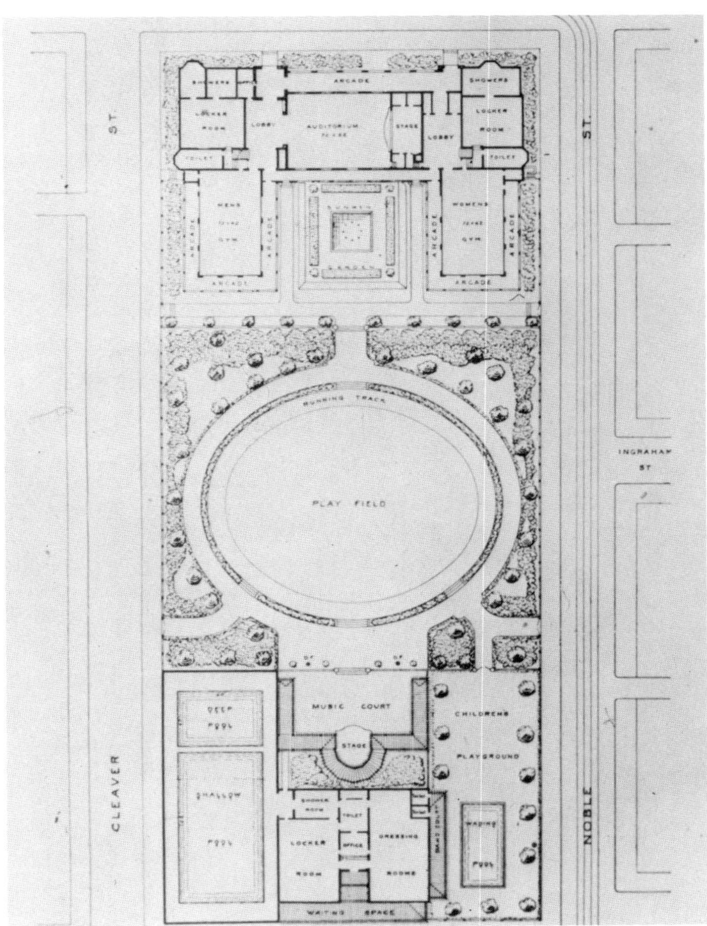

Pulaski Park has a vestigial curve and tree-dotted lawn in its plan, but otherwise reverses all pleasure ground principles of planning and is bilaterally symmetrical, rectangular. Chicago South Park District, *Report 1914*.

The design of Harrison Park, entirely relying on a grid of right angles, uses trees to accentuate lines rather than to create volume. Chicago South Park District.

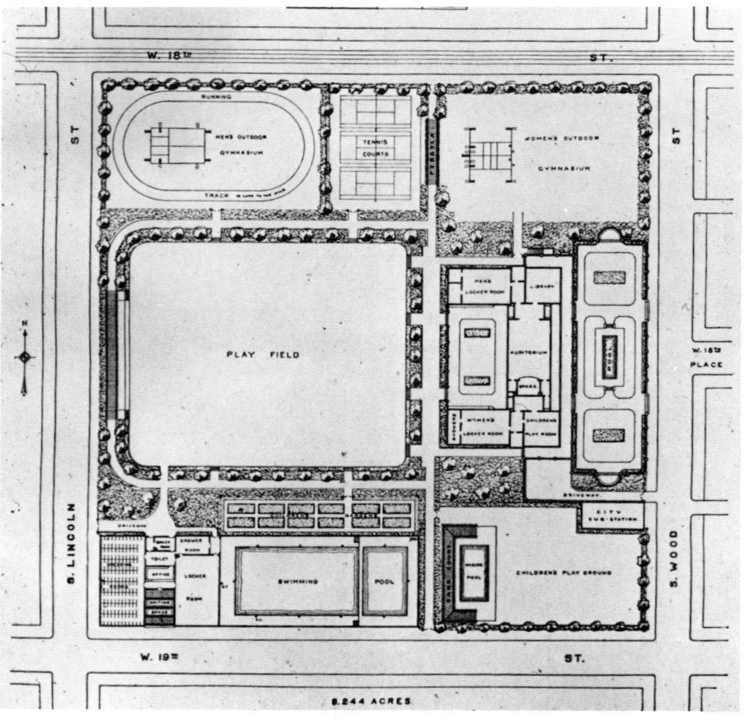

door gymnasiums.[68] Such requirements for adjacencies locked the reform park into a characteristic sequence of functions in layout.

The grounds were no longer undulating but flat to accommodate baseball diamonds, running tracks, and other equipment. Grass was abandoned in favor of hard surfaces for games; even when lawn was provided in some leftover corner of a park, it was destroyed by people cutting across it. In downtown parks maintaining grass was so difficult that paths had to be organized like spider webs of intersecting walkways.[69] Gravel was easier to maintain, so that, if a broad plane to rest the eye and mind was required, an open stretch of smooth gravel would suffice.[70]

The theoretically despised, but enormously popular, flower shows of the pleasure ground era were mentioned less and less often in the annual reports, but this was not because of any revulsion against the garishness of flowers. Park departments of the era supported the City Beautiful window box campaign, flowers edged buildings and entrances and filled sidewalk boxes, and cut flowers adorned interiors. In fact, they considered flowers a refining influence in the field houses. Their freshness and beauty, being seen by all who passed by, was said to "speak" to the patrons "as impressively as the lecturers in the assembly halls or the books in the reading rooms."[71]

Play equipment and gymnastic apparatus was distinguished by its great variety. In 1913 the New York parks department dispersed over its playgrounds the following, much of it made rather than ordered from a catalog: approach boards, baby hammocks, bagatelle boards, baseball back stops, basketball back stops, basketball courts, gymnastic bucks, building blocks, bulletin boards, chest weights, climbing ropes, croquet sets, doll houses, dumb bells, faba gaba boards, flagpoles, flying rings, giant strides, gymnasium frames, handball courts, high jumping standards, horizontal bars, Indian clubs, iron stakes, jump ropes, kindergarten benches, kindergarten tables, pursuit pins, regular size and

Utility, not beauty, was the goal of the reform park; accordingly, designers did not attempt to screen out the industrial, commercial, and residential buildings which typically surrounded the new, accessible sites. Stanford Park, Chicago South Park District, ca. 1915.

baby swings, ring toss boards, rope rings, seesaws, shelter tents, parallel bars, tether ball poles, and vaulting poles.[72]

One of the first things done to a small park or playground was to fence it in. In part an indicator of care and concern, a fence was also an instrument of social control. Thus in Corlears Hook in New York a low fence around the children's vegetable garden with a broad top rail for outsiders to lean on challenged fewer to climb over it than a high fence with dangerous spikes would have, permitted friendly conversations with adults, and prevented intrusion from dogs.[73] The proliferation of wire meshing was largely a response to the hazards of baseball. Eventually baseball was severely restricted in reform parks, but wire mesh fencing was not. It is one of today's living legacies of the 1920s.

Architecture

Since buildings had been accepted only as a necessary evil in the pleasure ground, their increasing number in the reform park had to be explained. Thus the San Francisco Playground Commission noted, "We all accept the premise of large play-fields. . . . We must also accept the premise of providing facilities for cultural recreation. . . . These arts require fine public buildings adequately equipped."[74] The editors of *Park and Recreation Magazine* wrote as if reform programming were a result of the construction of buildings: "Public recreation in 1900 consisted almost exclusively of outdoor activities, because of a lack of recreation buildings."[75]

The field house was the characteristic building type of the era. In a model field house built in Gary, Indiana, on twelve acres, seven of them were devoted to landscaping and the remainder to athletic courts, gardens, games, equipment, sand piles, swimming pools, gymnasiums, an assembly hall with stage, library, shop, and domestic science department. No major activity had to be curtailed, daytime or evening.[76]

The Chicago field house became famous for its extensive physical plant, its comprehensive social programming, and the care devoted to supervision and leadership. Other departments like Seattle's, whose field houses lacked baths, reading rooms, and branches of the public library, deferred to its superior quality: "While not as elaborate as the Chicago recreation buildings (ours) are being operated very successfully along the same general lines."[77] The editor of *Park International* preferred that this complex building form be called a community house rather than a field house, and he went so far as to say that community service should not be provided inside the parks.[78] Whether this professional liked it or not, however, the luxurious range of amenities offered meant that the field house was commonly viewed as everyman's country club.[79]

In a debate about the placement of the field house in Funston Playground in San Francisco, the criteria for siting it were unusually explicit: the location should take into account police protection, sewer and water connections, location of the streetcar line, unsightly views, exposure to wind and sun, future building additions, costs, and the preferences of local residents.[80] Such considerations were typically given more attention in park reports than the style of buildings. Thus the regular architecture column in *Park International* stated that the most important issue in design was the arrangement, the least important the appearance or the materials of construction.[81] Yet within months the magazine inaugurated a series of measured drawings giving details in design and construction, an indication that detail and style were not overlooked.

Still, a coherent field house style was not achieved. The new parks and the field houses had neoclassical elements thought to "reflect in miniature the architectural beauty of the World's Fair buildings."[82] Field houses in Chicago and New York had Palladian characteristics—tripartite windows, applied columns, arched windows with Italianate handling of brick arches. But the ends of the pitched roofs covering the sheds were never left as a simple line; the gable was turned ninety degrees to become part of the main elevation, or a perpendicular shed was attached, and an-

Top:
The neoclassical order of this Chicago field house claimed inspiration from the World's Columbian Exposition. Chicago South Park District.

Bottom:
Romantic conventions, like this sloped roof, sometimes lingered from pleasure ground days despite the neoclassical symmetry. Eckhart Park, Chicago.

other set of gables would pop out of it, creating a complex intersection of gables. Dormer windows carried the process yet one step further. This composite of rustic and classical conventions was echoed in the interior, where the trusses supporting the roofs in the larger assembly halls were left honestly exposed but the arched and classically subdivided windows aspired to elegance.[83]

The Pleasure Ground Reformed

The buildings considered inappropriate during the reform era roughly corresponded to the excluded activities of the era. Fruit stands and booths were as unattractive as the commercial activity they housed. The Chicago Bureau of Public Efficiency, a civic reform organization, criticized the construction of a new administration building in Washington Park, not just because the old building could have been remodeled but because they questioned the wisdom of locating a costly and conspicuous structure for administrative purposes in a public park.[84] Temporary buildings were still considered distasteful: the commissioners occasionally resorted to tents to house administrative functions, but they were taken down as soon as possible. This must have contributed to the decision to curtail the length of time that parks could be used as refugee sites after the San Francisco earthquake of 1906. Permanent buildings were excluded if their purpose was not considered compatible with that of a playground or small park. Accordingly, museums were permissible, but courthouses and schools were not.

The resistance to railways, roadways, and billboards also carried over from the pleasure ground era. Opposition to a railway surfaced in 1915, when the Southern Pacific Railway proposed to operate a rail line through Golden Gate Park. The board decided not to object to the operation of an auto train with a limited number of cars to each train. Citizens' groups began to protest, however, and within a year the commissioners were issuing their thanks to the citizens "for their valuable assistance in helping park commissioners prevent desecration of the most beautiful portion of

Golden Gate Park."[85] Similarly, the recreation commissioners were against letting streets traverse playgrounds and tried to resist transportation systems that simply used parks as the easiest way to cross town.[86] They also continued to oppose advertising and billboards, especially in the vicinity of parks. In New York the Parks Commission decided to get special legislation to prevent the erection of billboards within 350 feet of park areas. In one case residents around New York's Van Cortland Park who objected to a billboard nearby burned it down when the Parks Commission did not respond. Because of this incident, the editor of *Park International* recommended that a censored zone of at least 500 feet should surround all civic park areas; in fact such a zone had existed in Massachusetts since 1903 and in Indianapolis since 1920.[87]

But though billboards were beyond the pale, the strict prohibition of signs began to wane. Warning signs were installed in San Francisco offering a reward for the arrest and conviction of anyone vandalizing park property whenever damage occurred. In 1925 the army was granted permission to use portable signs in parks and squares to advertise for army recruits despite resistance to the idea of using sandwich men to enlist "vagrants and sightseers to don the uniform of military service."[88] The widespread use of the automobile forced commissioners to install danger and direction signs.[89] Finally, although it was never a widespread practice, some landscape architects suggested that the labeling of plants would enhance their educational value.[90]

The labeling of plants would have horrified Olmsted or Sargent, as would the emergency hospital built in Golden Gate at the turn of the century as a model first-aid facility. While as part of a pleasure ground it was supposed to be devoid of any association with disease, the many accidents to visitors were used to justify the hospital.[91] After a lifesaving station was constructed in Chicago's Jackson Park, the commissioners assured the public that, although the building was commodious, within a few years the plantation about it would attain some size, so that it would no longer be conspicuous.[92] Their pleasure ground conscience was pricked, but the usefulness of having a lifesaving crew nearby was justification enough.

In other ways, such as the conversion of an old music stand into a dressing room for tennis players in Golden Gate Park, mentioned earlier, the form of the pleasure ground was modified by the new park philosophy. Changes in landscaping were recommended when new vistas became available because of new structures, or when old openings became unsatisfactory because of an unsightly building on the margin of the park. Concrete was substituted for gravel, or electric lights used to decorate a Christmas tree. The twentieth-century skyline was incorporated into the vistas of the pleasure ground, and in response to City Beautiful tastes, curved sidewalks and indirect entrances were straightened out into right angles and direct access routes. Yet in Chicago modern technology enabled the commissioners to create a new picturesque element—a lily pond heated by steam from the condenser at the electric light plant.[93]

In 1903 plans were made for appropriating the Golden Gate speedtrack, adding a bit more land, making a half-mile circular track with an athletic field in the center, and creating a sports stadium. The ampitheatre, which was staked out in August of that same year with a speedtrack, polo fields, and athletic ground, was seen as an attractive addition to the "public playground of which San Franciscans are so proud."[94] Relabeling the pleasure ground as a playground, linguistically equated the two and subliminally justified the erosion of the older ideal.

Transition

The quality of experience in a reform park was markedly different from that in a pleasure ground. Rather than quiet and serene, it was noisy and organized, both visually and in terms of activity. During the early twentieth century the pressure and rigidity of industrial production were maintained or increased, and labor gains mainly took the form of compensation for them: a shorter work week, earlier retirement, longer vacations, and higher pay. Ironically, however, the reform park offered urban populations leisure experience to fill the newly available time that was nearly as rigid in its organization. Parks, like business firms and schools, followed an industrial model: age segregation, specialization of function, and a horror of waste. From the safe vantage point of the next era, Chicago park commissioners acknowledged the negative aspects of overorganization in the reform era when they claimed that their contemporary program was "not regimented . . . not a service ladled out by a dispensing agency which decrees what is good for the public according to notions of its own."[95] The industrial top-down style of leisure-time organization in the reform era did have some virtue, namely the careful programming of local playgrounds by social workers. The benefits of this control were lost in the 1930s when the desire to give everybody a playground nearby went beyond staffing abilities. Playgrounds could be built quickly using both skilled and unskilled labor, but trained leadership did not come so easily and consequently did not keep pace. Thus, despite the attempts to turn recreation into a form of community development by extensive programming and renaming the field houses and programs community centers, and community recreation programs, respectively, the social center approach of the reform era was abortive. The reasons are implicit in the ideology of the recreation facility.

3

The Recreation Facility: 1930–1965

The Age of Leisure

In the 1930s park administrators abandoned their idealistic efforts to use parks as a mechanism of social reform. In New York City the reform period clearly terminated in 1930, with the appointment of Robert Moses as park commissioner. Moses' first annual report was a sentinel: "We make no absurd claims as to the superior importance and value of the particular service we are called on to render, and we realize that budget making is a balancing of comparative needs of numerous competing agencies."[1]

Similarly, the president of the American Institute of Park Executives explicitly abandoned a reform attitude. He felt that park administrators should no longer view themselves as their brothers' keepers; if people were not already essentially wholesome, he could "hardly hope to effect their salvation."[2]

The implicit message of such statements was that "the service" needed no particular justification, that park facilities were an expected feature of urban life. Park officials around the country adopted this attitude, repeating the claim that they no longer had to justify parks and that recreation had been accepted as an essential of life, like health, education, work, and religion. "Basic," "universal," were almost as frequent as "essential" in describing the new ideologically denuded status of parks. Other terms such as "fundamental" and "important" implicitly justified the status of parks

The end of ideology in park programming was accompanied by claims that park design and equipment were "just for the fun of it." Reprinted from the 1965 issue of *Parks and Recreation* by special permission of the National Recreation and Park Association.

as a function of government. No longer luxuries or even amenities, they became necessary parts of every city.[3]

One consequence of this apparent complacency was that the underlying rationale for park activities was often forgotten. *Recreation Magazine* admitted: "Unfortunately, many of our leaders are primarily concerned with providing a 'smorgasbord of activities' without regard to quality and purpose."[4] Instead of giving careful attention to programming, park administrators now endeavored to expand the physical system. Facts, not their meaning, would speak for themselves. Recreational facilities in New York increased fivefold over the twenty years from the mid-1930s, and Moses felt that this "twenty year record of park expansion . . . speaks for itself."[5] The Chicago Park District was eager to help "build a bigger and better Chicago." Through a ten-year park development plan more parks, field houses, children's playgrounds, swimming pools, and acreage were added: "The objective has been to meet the needs of Chicagoans for more recreation facilities."[6] More and bigger were argument enough.

More facilities were undoubtedly a response to a general increase in demand for park services. The population was growing rapidly, for example, and a rising standard of living was leading people to think more of play and less of work. The exodus of families with children to the suburbs brought with it demand for park services in new areas. Nevertheless, response to demand was not the same thing as action according to purpose, and this disregard of purpose implied a lack of philosophy. As a Chicago reporter observed, "People interested in a larger modern park system charge that there is no park philosophy, only park patronage. No push for park creation, only recreation."[7]

The term "recreation," in fact, was the watchword of the era, since unlike "play" it seemed to exclude no activity or age group. In the early 1930s its use increased in the San Francisco Commission minutes: land began to be purchased for recreational purposes, not for a playground or a small park, and the Playground Commission started refer-

Top:
A demand-oriented philosophy required expanding acres of parkland and facilities for swimming pools, playgrounds, and clubhouses. Detroit. Reprinted from the 1952 issue of *Parks and Recreation* by special permission of the National Recreation and Park Association.

Bottom:
Clubhouse and pool in Los Angeles. Reprinted from the 1952 issue of *Parks and Recreation* by special permission of the National Recreation and Park Association.

ring to itself informally, and in its permanent records, as the recreation commission.[8] Correspondingly, parks became recreational facilities, the term "facility" being equally neutral and all-encompassing, and all outdoor activities in these facilities, except those of very small children, took place in outdoor sports areas.

The practical purpose of terms like these was to simplify bureaucratic procedures and streamline services, but they also reflected a park philosophy, albeit one which hardly surfaced except in their use. This philosophy, or more precisely this ideology, was rooted in another twist on the idea of leisure. In 1934 a Chicago park professional wrote an article in *Parks and Recreation* called "What Shall We Do with This New Leisure?" and the "new leisure" was a distinctive accent of the period.[9] For the first decade of the period, of course, leisure was often a consequence of unemployment. As such, it was a euphemism for enforced idleness: in San Francisco the idustrial division of the Recreation Commission was established to "confront the problem of increased leisure time due to the Depression."[10] In Chicago, more forthrightly, community groups banded together to attack "the problem of finding something to do for every person to whom idleness is an irksome and deadening problem."[11]

The solution to the problem of idleness was jobs, but jobs were part of politics, and the parks were as determined to remain above political controversy as they had been during the prior eras. Thus commissioners' reports touched on the effects of strikes on park service only obliquely, by describing parks as useful for employing large numbers of people and channeling potentially disruptive energies into constructive work. The solution to the problem of increased leisure time, which was more leisure activity, was something the parks could provide, and, in doing so, they could play their traditional role, as an urban safety valve.

Thus, from the start the emphasis on leisure characteristic of the whole period went along with arguments for the need to expand park programming, and, since the period was typified by tight park budgeting, these arguments needed to be strong ones. Moreover, since leisure time was indeed increasing, after the Depression as well as during it, the new emphasis had a basis in fact. The shorter work week, long weekends, daylight-saving time, improved automobiles and road systems, earlier retirement ages, and longer lives meant that more people had more time outside work and sleep than ever before. Though these generalizations apply equally to the previous era, and talk of leisure time was not entirely new in this one, the effects of these developments were cumulative.[12]

In addition to its factual basis, the emphasis on leisure involved an interpretation of social phenomena, calculated to weaken any impetus toward radical social economic change. Essentially, it involved the characterization of the urban mass population as a leisure class, one whose members had achieved their goals. The practical effect of these assumptions was the virtual elimination of class hierarchy—hence conflict—since any differences in income, power, or prestige were residual and did not effect basic life chances. Americans were pictured now as occupied chiefly with combating boredom or, more generally, remaining happy. A new interest in mental health—the first articles in *Recreation Magazine* by psychiatrists appeared in the late 1940s—contributed to this characterization. This interest carries over from the pleasure ground era, but the focus was no longer just on the preservation or restoration of health but on the pursuit of happiness itself. If the people were unhappy and bored, that was cause for alarm. The responsibility of the public servant, the new bureaucrat, was to fulfill their relatively mute demands. Social control of the masses no longer proceeded via improvement but rather via flattery.

System

In replacing an ideology of reform with one of leisure, park departments put themselves on a par with commercial producers of entertainment commodities. By acknowledging that their function was to meet the public demand for leisure activities, they made themselves subject to demand rather than to a norm of public service not necessarily reflected in demand. This led, on the one hand, to an increased emphasis on the efficiency with which they could deliver services on demand, and this emphasis led to systems thinking and bureaucratization. On the other, it led to a general loss of interest in the purposes of parks and of park services which was in turn entirely compatible with the bureaucratic mentality. With the loss of idealism, however, came a loss of authority and prestige, and this was reflected in park budgets, which failed to rise during the era in a way commensurate with the expansion and diversification of park programming.

The consequent economizing affected, first of all, the training and hiring of staff. The physical plant could be built quickly, using skilled and unskilled labor, and capital outlay was a one-time event. Supervision, in contrast, required skilled leaders with at least some college education or special training, and their salaries were an unending cost. Reduction in staff, however, was in keeping with the reduced concern for coherent programming.

The war exacerbated pressures to reduce staff, and economizing pressures generally. Gas rationing and restrictions on vacation times forced people to turn to their local parks, and the stress of wartime factory production demanded release in recreation. But at the same time construction activities were curtailed, and the draft and the high wages of war production combined to strip the park departments of their personnel in all ranks.[13]

Systems thinking coped with economizing pressures, rationalized them, and to some degree even fostered them. With programming expanding faster than budgets were increasing, parks began to rely increasingly on cooperative ventures with other municipal agencies. Park officials needed to look for friendly allies. The *Leisure Time Directory* issued by the Chicago Recreation Commission for 1939–1940 listed the locations of social agencies, public schools, church agencies, libraries, and Works Progress Administration education classes along with the locations of public parks and playgrounds. Parks departments had become one of many agencies in an increasingly complex web of bureaucracies, and park administrators needed the ability to navigate their way through the network. (In New York the completion of the West Side Improvement was thought to owe much to the fact that Robert Moses had this ability.[14]) Consolidation of the park bureaucracies was one way to cope with bureaucratic complexity. Moses consolidated all five of New York's boroughs when he took office in 1930; Chicago consolidated its park districts in 1935, and pushed park-city consolidation of the two police forces in the late forties; and San Francisco merged its separate Park and Recreation Commissions in 1950.

Throughout the period planning and systems integration gained in sophistication. Parks departments had been working with schools for years, but the practice only reached institutional proportions in the 1930s and 1940s, when school-park plans were developed in New York, Chicago, and San Francisco. Even junior colleges were betrothed to recreation departments. Such affairs were typically one-sided; parks spokesmen viewed recreation work as a part of education broadly defined, but few school historians even mentioned the relation of education to parks or recreation.

Liaisons with housing authorities were also common during the period. In 1941 San Francisco became one of the first cities to coordinate the Housing Authority with the Recreation Department and the Parks Department. The first assumed responsibility for programs in all public housing developments, the second paid for park construction, and the third paid for equipment and maintenance. Ideally, this housing and recreation agreement would yield community centers for entire neighborhoods which would help to break down the barriers between public housing tenants and private home owners. In keeping with this ideal, in 1948 a constitutional convention advocated the national policy that low-rent housing, rehabilitation, and slum clearance include recreational facilities.

Parks professionals had complained, since the days of Olmsted, that city planning was too often piecemeal rather than comprehensive, but now such coordination with other agencies allowed them an involvement in it. The need for city planning, comprehensive studies, and master plans was reiterated by park spokesmen during the Depression and World War II, and in 1942 the San Francisco City-Planning Commission spelled out criteria for a master plan that included guidelines for the distance between play fields and schools and between libraries, schools, and recreation places. After the war San Francisco's City-Planning Commission continued to try to combine park projects with the projects of other city departments; and the Housing Authority's interlocked slum clearance, defense housing, and cosponsored recreation programs brought the Recreation Department into the scheme of overall city planning.

The development of planning standards was a preoccupation of park administrators during the period, and this turned them into statisticians, relying on quantiative studies of the sociological structure of the populations they served. Along with pretensions to science came improved equipment, modern switchboards, and later computers, all talismans of the efforts of park organizations to adopt the professionalism, procedural sophistication, and bureaucratic complexity spreading nationally through government and business.[15] In a related development, uniform procedures for recruitment and training of staff, data analysis, and bookkeeping emulated business techniques, and for the first time park commissioners were justifying the outlay of money for publicity and park departments were hiring full-time public relations men. All of these changes, of course, meant that a smaller proportion of recreation service focused on the user and his moral welfare. Like all bureaucracies the park department took on a life of its own and came to be committed first of all to its own maintenance and enhancement.

The Demand for Services

Depression and war provided park programmers with causes, and for the duration of these emergencies this helped to conceal their growing loss of direction. For example, the Depression stimulated a relief recreation program in San Francisco, where fourteen centers containing reading rooms, games, and tools for handicrafts were opened to keep up the morale of the unemployed. In New York and elsewhere WPA workers were placed on park construction and maintenance projects as well as the later satirized "Sahara Desert Projects," leaf raking, and sidewalk polishing.[16]

If these activities served an evident purpose, and required little justification, at least to the sources that financed them the war put the parks on the defensive. Under wartime conditions, if park and recreation commissioners did not justify park activities as absolutely essential to the welfare of citizens, their budgets would be cut. In San Francisco, for example, Mayor Angelo Rossi said that he would not approve any additional employment, service, equipment, or capital expenditure in the Park Commission unless vital to the safety of San Francisco's citizens.[17] Morale was vital, though, and to boost morale many park activities, even traditional holidays and children's activities, could be oriented toward the war. Children could do Red Cross work or help entertain soldiers, and even Valentine's Day could be celebrated patriotically by using red, white, and blue.

While old activities were given a new definition, new activities such as first-aid classes and demonstrations of the proper methods for combating incendiary bombs could be introduced. In this spirit, despite earlier restrictions against selling on park property, the sale of war bonds was encouraged. Stadiums and school gymnasiums were used as casualty stations and gas decontamination units. And morale boosting turned into full scale propaganda campaigns. A manual with suggestions on "how to organize counterpro-

Top:
Parks were a vehicle for public spending during the Depression. This WPA bathhouse was so elegant that citizens did not feel certain that they had the right to use it. 1939. San Francisco Public Library.

Bottom:
Despite having to meet the test of usefulness during economic and military crises, the historic ban against living in parks was reasserted to oust these squatters' homes from Central Park during the 1930s. Museum of the City of New York.

Top:
To justify park activities during World War II administrations were quick to accommodate military activities. This WPA casino in Aquatic Park in San Francisco served as a barracks for soldiers. 1941. San Francisco Public Library.

Bottom:
The world's largest swimming pool was the obstacle course for trainees practicing keeping their guns dry while fording water. 1942, Fleischhacker Pool. San Francisco Public Library.

paganda campaigns to offset subversive and disorganizing influences" was sent to all Chicago park staff.[18] Camera clubs pledged to take pictures the subject matter of which would lend itself to patriotic purposes or "to so arrange the composition that a subtle patriotic message was involved," and recreation leaders organized drama classes, artcraft, physical education, lobby displays, news releases, and branch libraries to promote patriotism. Children's playgrounds were renamed day camps to suggest the availability, closer to home, of activities otherwise curtailed by gas rationing and also to associate children's activities with those of military camp.

The Lanham Act provided federal money for nursery schools, day care, and recreation, and day-care centers were set up in some park playgrounds and field houses to take care of children whose parents were at work in defense industries.[19] In San Francisco the Board of Education took care of preschoolers from 7:00 to 3:00 in the afternoon, and the Recreation Commission took over until 7:00 in the evening, while the Health Department looked after their medical welfare. Similarly, Victory Gardening—so named when adults began vegetable gardening in parks—was given a new rationale during the war: families would benefit the nation as well as themselves by growing their own food. Accordingly, parks departments issued permits for vegetable gardening, lectures were given in park conservatories on Victory Gardening, and private garden clubs and newspapers exhibited prime homegrown vegetables and set up educational exhibits and model gardens.

The war also made sports useful in a new way. San Francisco's Recreation and Park Departments were now offering "program services" rather than old-fashioned activities: organizations were serviced, units operated group service, and units of service were dispatched. Changes in the actual activities offered, however, were largely in terminology, as in the case of the transformation of gymnastic exercises into physical fitness programs, or the reclassification of the old stand-bys, such as boating, baseball, and skating, as physical activity services.[20] The actual range of activities was familiar: skating, fishing, tennis, children's pony rides, golf, and swimming. (Water sports were stimulated by the wartime Red Cross campaign.) What was different was that now there was a wartime urgency to the goal of conditioning youth to a harder and more disciplined way of life, and a political threat to make the unity felt by people exercising together more highly valued.[21]

Wartime Civil Defense programming in the parks furthered the tendency of park departments toward interagency cooperation. In Chicago, for instance, the program required coordination with city's traffic divisions, state medical services, the Federal Atomic Energy Commission, and private universities, and involved contacts with draft boards, local community groups, citizenship training programs for the foreign born, and programs in first aid, nutrition, and home economics.[22] This trend toward cooperation among government agencies was paralleled by an internal programming policy that favored the federation of interest groups and their integration into broad regional organizations. Contemporaries claimed that this phenomenon was the most significant aspect of the programming of the era. The basic idea was that enthusiasts in the same activity, although in widely separated communities of the city, could get together to share experiences and pool resources. But since neighborhood groups might fear losing identity or self-direction, the answer was the creation of federations of autonomous groups. Many interest groups formed such loose affiliations: baseball leagues, camera clubs, fishing clubs, archery, tennis, and dog-training associations.

The idea of communitywide events easily transformed into a new interest in large celebrations. In Chicago in the 1930s, the completion of Soldier Field facilitated mass events: football games, circuses, Fourth-of-July celebrations, music festivals, and Easter sunrise services. Outside Soldier Field there were additional parades, festivals, ceremonials, patriotic gatherings, athletic tournaments, picnics, and concerts. Nationwide, park commissioners proposed special weeks or days of nonstop celebration: Rhododendron Week in San Francisco, Chicago Week, a National Bill of Rights Week, Farm Week, Recreation Day in San Francisco, Civil Service Employees Day in Chicago, and Negro Day.[23] Fairs—like the Chicago World's Fair of 1933—were consistent with the emphasis on pageantry and particularly during the Depression valued as an economic shot in the arm.

These pageants and communitywide events had a social focus that reflected their origins in what social researcher and playground activist Clarence Rainwater, called the community development phase of the later reform era. Despite a general move to cut back on them during the retrenchment of the late 1930s, park departments throughout the recreation era encouraged activities which lent themselves to festivals and pageantry—music, dramatics, dancing, art exhibits—because of their power to stimulate community interaction and integration. But it was characteristic of the era that these activities were also advocated by park spokespeople who viewed them primarily as means of self-expression.[24] The absence of a clarion call to reform during the era allowed a carefree variety of claims and appeals to surface.

Music lent itself well to mass events. For example, open-air music concerts at Stern Grove in San Francisco became part of an annual music festival, and Christmas carols were offered by park choral groups. Symphony concerts in Chicago's Grant Park attracted large audiences—an estimated three million people came downtown to attend the series, and many more listened over the radio. By the 1960s jazz festivals were being offered at Soldier Field.

Along with music theatrical fare, ranging from dramatic productions to simpler activities like story telling, story plays, puppetry, and singing games expanded during the era. Central Park offered story telling and Shakespearean drama, and Chicago both puppetry and conventional theatre. Citywide programs were presented to the public annually, and there were smaller programs for the neighborhoods.

Social dancing which after much soul-searching had been allowed in the reform era, increased remarkably after 1930. In San Francisco weekly dances cosponsored by the Recreation Department and the Board of Education were given a trial in 1933, and public dances on Sundays were no longer against commission policy. In Chicago folk dancing underwent a very great revival which was probably far from spontaneous.[25] Folk dancing, a jollier socializing activity than ballroom dancing, was considered to "have a rollicking quality which breaks down stiffness and formality, permits people to be more naturally themselves, rids them of stiff and self-conscious restraint."[26] Nor was classical dancing entirely overlooked. In 1936 ballet was performed around Buckingham Fountain in Chicago's Grant Park: "The artistic beauty of the fountain itself made it unthinkable that a crude program should be conducted on so magnificent a site."[27]

During the Depression unemployment gave crafts additional meaning. Spare time, regarded as an idle half day or more, necessarily required more than sports, games, and physical occupations.[28] Men and boys were particularly affected, so some of the new crafts programs were developed just for them. The range of enterprises, remaining narrow in the exclusion of fine arts, was extended to include lapidary, pottery, weaving, dressmaking, knitting, costume design, millinery, crocheting and embroidery work, and leather tooling. Boondoggling, the use of material ordinarily considered unusable, was promoted: "Even the less favored neighborhoods are able to secure heavy bones from the community meat markets, and by bleaching the bone in gasoline they can make it almost ivorylike in appearance. With this inexpensive material to work on, a great deal of artistic ingenuity has been displayed by hundreds of interested workers."[29]

During the war hobbies were promoted because they could release pent-up, nervous tension.[30] After the war craft programs continued, with power-equipped shops facilitating a much higher level of expertise. Crafts, like the other social activities, were valued both for their ability to satisfy "the creative urge within us all," and to "reach people who might not be reached other ways," specifically the shy and isolated.[31] By 1961 in Chicago such benefits had to emerge through hat making, probably the most popular of all art-craft activities.

Communitywide federations and events were encouraged by those park theorists who believed the neighborhood-level group work characteristic of the reform era made children too dependent on a single play leader. Mass activities would force leaders to refer children to different leaders as they noticed their interests developing in one direction or another. Chicago experts turned to group work, and claimed thereby to have fostered a social consciousness which became communitywide in its scope.[32] But no single theory of social organization dominated park thinking during the period. Thus some social workers believed that group work should be practiced in recreation centers, that recreation leaders should work with small groups of children over extended periods of time. Others argued that this leadership function should be extended to individual counseling, with its focus clearly on psychological development rather than community cohesion.

Demand, or need, were more often put forward as rationales for programming than any particular theory. For example, teenagers—identified as such for the first time during the era—increased demand for what the young people called "Rec" centers and thereby created the necessity for more facilities. Thus teen canteens were patterned on the war-born USO canteens, and after the war the teen center evolved, a place for dances, parties, athletics, handicraft, dramatic and music activities, meetings, and games—and for "dropping in" and "hanging out." The reason that teenagers were singled out as a special group, in fact had less to do with demand than with the traditional elite practice of solving social problems of their own definition.

Legalese

Just as the reforming motives for park programming tended to hide behind the pseudoeconomic model of supply and demand, reforming motives for exclusions from programming tended to be expressed in legalese, to hide behind the law. Thus official attitudes toward commercial activity were still at least ambivalent, but decisions to exclude such activity were often—at least apparently—made by attorneys. Thus in San Francisco a controversy about a tourist information center in Union Square led to the demand for a legal definition of "recreational" and "nonrecreational" purposes. The commissioners turned to the city attorney for an opinion, and he arrived at it on the basis of an analysis of the use of the term "recreation" in other statutes around the country. He decided that "the word 'recreation' has a narrow meaning and does not mean every form of enjoyment," thereby excluding tourist information. Thus the board did not have the power to authorize such a building.[33] Commissioners relied heavily on his definition thereafter.

Similarly, when the Junior Chamber of Commerce tried to hold an aircraft show in a Chicago park, a permit was denied, citing the section of the city charter that restricted park usage to recreation. When the U.S. Department of Commerce wanted to install radio equipment to transmit signals in connection with Chicago's municipal airport, the commissioners merely claimed that they had no legal authority to lease park lands for such a purpose. Statements or principle regarding appropriateness and inappropriateness, so seriously enjoined in earlier eras, were conspicuously absent in this era.

In these cases the law was used to bolster a traditional anticommercial stand, but during the recreation era the stand was no longer uncompromising. Eventually advertising was allowed when it promoted park activities—in the 1930s Chicago city buses were allowed to carry posters advertising special park events and new facilities—or promoted commercial values generically. Thus the Chicago Automobile Trade Association received permission to decorate lamp posts on a major park avenue for a "Prosperity Demonstration."

These ambivalences in the commercial sphere had their counterpart in the timid attempts to regulate drinking and dancing. The Chicago commissioners decided they had no right to regulate—which is not to say they approved of—the sale of liquor on private property adjacent to parks or boulevards. With the end of Prohibition the park food services themselves sold beer in Golden Gate Park, though not within the same block as a playground.[34] Similarly, though the San Francisco commissioners now welcomed social and folk dancing, they still wished to keep dance halls away from playfields despite their conclusion that it was not within their province to take action—a restraint they would not have imposed on themselves in the past.[35]

The Supply of Sites

The idea of the recreation facility was powerful enough during the 1930s and 1940s to transform some older parks, but most new park construction had to wait until after the war. In fact, because long-term maintenance had been almost as slow as new construction during the Depression and war, repairs had first priority, and construction only began to boom in the 1950s.

From then on, the authors of the national literature and yearbooks took delight in describing the increase in the number of playgrounds provided. Descriptions of the number of parks, their acreage, and their distribution were endlessly repeated, with little reference to the underlying justification for their extension. Recreation and playgrounds were universal needs, and simply fulfilling the mandate to provide more of them was all that was required of park promoters.

The new parks were sited throughout the city fabric, often in the congested areas of the inner city and the public housing projects and suburbs, both newly developed after the war.[36] In order to be numerous, these new acquisitions were remarkably small—even smaller than the reform park: "It is much better, if a choice is forced on us, to acquire one block in a congested part of Manhattan than ten acres in the open areas of Richmond."[37] The establishment of parks in the projects and older areas often involved or abetted slum clearance, though the park commissioners never mentioned land values, business interests, or political-economic considerations of any kind in their reports and claimed to be responding simply to abstract demand or need.

The school-park plan, in which schools and parks were sited adjacent to one another, continued through the era, with the two agencies sharing both construction and operating costs according to circumstances. This coupling contributed to the development of the neighborhood theory, the idea that a given geographic unit and a given population cluster should have one each of a series of urban facilities (schools, housing, health, commercial, transportation), and more generally to the systematic urban planning that characterized the era. Many city-planning departments instituted master plans for recreation in anticipation of the population expansion at the end of the war, and immediately after the war Chicago came out with "More Parks for All Chicago," a ten-year postwar park development plan.[38] In 1942 the San Francisco Recreation Commission described a master plan for San Francisco's physical development, and a plan for the development of all the city's parks (variously called a comprehensive or a master plan) was introduced in 1954.[39]

Forward-looking city planning of this sort inevitably involved the planners in large questions concerning the public good and encouraged in them, or demanded of them, something of a reform or progressive mentality. Thus it fell somewhere short of the ideal neutrality of pure systems thinking. More typically questions of site selection resolved themselves in practice into questions of expediency, often involving competing land uses. Robert Moses was the harbinger of this development. Of large-scale, urban planning he said, "The city is not going to be torn up and rebuilt on a decentralized satellite or other academic theory."[40] Moses considered himself a realist who expanded and built not according to a "radical plan of decentralization," but to practical objectives.[41] He defended his catch-as-catch-can practice of siting parks accordingly: "The theorists and the perfectionists of course, say that there has been no comprehensive plan and that ours has been a spotty program. We have indeed taken what we could get in the face of enormous difficulties."[42] When addressing himself to the issue of planning standards, he disavowed any "such thing as a fixed percentage of park area to population" and, in fact, spoke out on the inapplicability of mathematical formulas to solve social needs. For Moses, "Sensible, practical people know that the answer depends upon the actual problems of the city in question and not on a slide rule."[43] In the long run this sort of realism encouraged the spread of a purely technical systems approach in park departments.

The enormous difficulties that led Moses to take "what we could get" arose largely because of intense competition for urban space. Highways, schools, shopping centers, hospitals, and public housing competed fiercely for space with the parks and, in fact, even preyed on them. In part this situation resulted from the impoverished goals of the recreation facility, which was hard pressed to take an aggressive position because of its lack of reforming zeal. In part, however, the intensity of the competition itself caused that impoverishment, in that the parks were now forced to scramble for land and could hardly afford to be consistent or principled.

Throughout the period, social program and physical form were only loosely related. This stemmed partly from the influence of a new design ideal—the multiple-use facility—which dictated what architects today call "loose fit," partly from the fact that the underlying social goals of park programs were not clear enough for park planners to recognize one style or feature as more relevant or useful than another. In practice, various features of the preceding eras were juxtaposed, and a banal eclecticism was the result. Because this model simply extended a service defined previously, and no new forms were needed, none developed. As the Chicago park commissioners put it, "The shift was not in things or properties; it was in the social meanings of those things and properties."[44]

A few people were worried about the strict facility orientation of park service, but, rather than attack facilities altogether, they took the eclectic position that a park should have old fashioned pleasure ground elements as well. In the words of one park professional:

> The city park is gradually becoming functional in its character and, if some recreationalists had their way, would all consist of baseball fields, tennis courts, shuffleboard courts, and other specialized facilities that are hot by day and ablaze with floodlights at night. We must realize that beauty and congenial surroundings are an important adjunct to such planning and, let us not forget, that some of us require a place of peace and rest even before the grave.[45]

Meanwhile, annual reports spelled out the numbers and kinds of facilities in detail: "five splendid golf courses, seven yacht harbors . . . twelve bathing beaches, over fifteen miles of equestrian bridal paths, five casting pools, one hundred eighty-four children's outdoor playgrounds, three hundred horseshoe courts and numerous running tracks, archery ranges and playfields."[46]

The real design innovation of the era was the standardization of all the old elements into a basic municipal package, one that was used repeatedly, without regard to local site conditions. Parts, materials, and procedures were reduced to a minimum—asphalt paving and curbs, standard fences and benches, and prescribed trees specified and detailed in construction drawings embalmed in blue cloth and issued to any park architect.[47] As landscape architect Garrett Eckbo said in 1962, ". . . American park design is more limited, conventional, stereotyped, repetitive, and resistant to innovation in form than any other area of design."[48]

In general this standardization served an economizing function. What has been called parkway picturesque, the lawn and spotting of trees and shrubs here and there along parkways, on college campuses, and around corporate headquarters and suburban buildings, which was a characteristic of the era, was merely a blend of minimal standards of appearance and the desire to keep maintenance and supervision costs to a minimum. Economy also led to the removal of previous planting, especially shrubbery, though here decisions to strip parks rather than fund the supervision and maintenance of planted areas could be justified as proceeding from concern for safety and ease of surveillance. Thus in San Francisco, when the Playground Commission received a complaint about "men lurking in the trees at St. Mary's Playground," the superintendent remedied the situation by making changes in the landscaping, and Buena Vista Park was stripped of its undergrowth after complaints that women and children were shunning the park because it was attracting undesirables and winos. Similarly, hard surfaces, usually blacktop, were favored during the period, partly because of the premium placed on the multiple use of facilities but also because of economy of maintenance.

Architectural Design

Buildings in the recreational facility were larger, more numerous, and more various in function than they had been in previous eras. During the war, in particular, many nonrecreational structures were built in parks: navy control stations, fire houses, air raid shelters, temporary housing (tents, quonset huts, and trailers), and stockpiling houses.

Styling was eclectic, the new constructions being Victorian, Georgian, Alpine, nautical, and, after the war, modern and even glasshouse modern. In the 1930s designers made use of some new cast and machine-made materials and relied less on hand-crafted ones: economic conditions made rustic treatment a luxury.[49] After the war some landscape architects actually began to welcome the use of industrial materials: "The mediums for expressing modern park architecture are not factory-made 'hand-split' shakes . . .

Top:
In practice the recreation facility was typically blacktopped and fenced, without even the reform park's concessions of trees in rows. Reprinted from New York City, Department of Parks, *Report for 1967*.

Bottom:
San Francisco, reprinted from the 1952 issue of *Parks and Recreation* by special permission of the National Recreation and Park Association.

sawed timbers . . . log termite havens patterned after pioneer cabins."[50] Modernists believed that park architecture should utilize the material and construction methods of other building types and not be camouflaged nor historicized. Concrete and cinder block were suddenly refreshing.[51]

Though architectural materials were typically modern, for the most part design was not. In New York park spokesmen defended this policy:

Our standards of design have been conservative. We are public officials clothed with brief authority, custodians of the common lands and not speculators risking their own, or other people's resources. Our work must be usable and durable in the esthetic as well as the physical sense. It must last a long time and survive freakish changes of style amid the modes and rages of the day. New materials and methods must, however, be recognized, and change is a law of life. Our job is to keep what has been proven good until we find something demonstrably and manifestly better.[52]

By 1973 the *New York Times* could characterize this combination of new industrial materials and drably practical design as "Robert Moses's brick-and-tile lavatory style."[53]

Recreation facility design was epitomized by the park bench and the Cyclone wire fence. Because the bench was standardized and easy to maintain, manufactured in large numbers, readily installed wherever a place needed to be defined as a park, it became the symbol of the city park.[54] Its inclusion in a park was never challenged, although on occasion there might be some brainstorming about whether or not it should be long enough to accommodate a reclining figure since more and more parks, always attempting some sort of social control, were becoming the sleeping grounds of drunken derelicts. The fence, a park tradition only since the reform era, was equally standardized as an unimaginative solution to the problem of demarcating land uses, especially the park from residential areas around it: fences also helped to prevent accidents and thus were cheaper than supervision. In San Francisco, in keeping with the more-is-better practices of the entire period, the number and height of fences at park boundaries went up over the years.

Less supervision also meant more need for signs. In the pleasure ground and reform eras they had been restricted to entrances, where rules for use of the park might be posted. Now they were used to identify park boundaries, paths, and playgrounds and in general to organize the use of the park.

Signs needed to be highly visible—strongly contrasted with their surroundings—to be useful, and this was even more true of waste containers. In 1935 a national contest for an attractive, practical design of a waste container was held.[55] This drew attention to the design potential of waste containers, and various designs for such contrivances like "garbage gobblers" dotted professional literature thereafter.[56]

Even more striking was the fact that the color of equipment now merited attention. In Chicago the formerly acceptable dingy green zoo cages were repainted a bright, "sunshiny" tan, and other colors were added to the zoo environment, with the object of getting a more lively, modern color combination than the old staid zoo green. Still administrators cautioned that a mere change of color could not always transform a dilapidated building.[57] Drinking fountains, giant strides, slides, swings, picnic tables, turning bars, and teeter-totters, along with garbage cans, were painted bright red, white, blue, orchid, rose, and lavender.[58]

A development of the period slightly more radical than bright coloration was the small children's amusement park, sometimes called Kiddieland, Storyland, or Fairyland. Storyland, developed by San Francisco to compete with Oakland's Fairyland, was a special playground with a village of fairytale houses, child-sized buildings inspired by Mother Goose rhymes such as "The Old Woman Who Lived in a Shoe," "Humpty Dumpty," and "Peter Peter Pumpkin Eater" as well as the tales of *Hansel and Gretel* and *The Three Bears*. Storyland also had a drawbridge and an en-

Stadiums and vast parking lots were two facilities of the recreation era. New York City. Reprinted from the 1965 issue of *Parks and Recreation* by special permission of the National Recreation and Park Association.

Park design has accommodated the automobile in many ways, largely without question. Seattle Auto Tourist Park, 1920s. Seattle Historical Society.

While Olmsted and Vaux had carefully sunk the transverse roads in Central Park to keep the pedestrians' experience undisturbed by vehicular traffic, planners of the recreation era paved and widened roads and expected pedestrians to wait for a safe crossing. Lincoln Park, 1921. Courtesy Chicago Historical Society.

Designers in the era of the recreation facility preoccupied themselves with details of maintenance, such as garbage disposal. Reprinted from the 1965 and 1959 issues of *Parks and Recreation* by special permission of the National Recreation and Park Association.

chanted palace, a birthday party area, a puppet theatre, and a live farm.

Until Storyland, playgrounds had become increasingly mechanized. Much more technical equipment was purchased after the 1930s than ever before, and, since supervision did not keep pace, it had to be safe, well built, and simplified. Thus the more adventurous gymnastic equipment, even the teeter-totter, was dropped, and the residue was the standard municipal playground with paved surface and fence, sandpit, swings, and jungle gym—in good municipal parlance the "pipe frame exercise unit."[59]

After the success with Storyland, park departments around the country tried to overcome the standardization of playground equipment by creating free-form play sculptures. Forms often followed a theme appropriate to the surrounding neighborhood, such as an Oriental design for a Chinese neighborhood; color and plant materials expressed the theme, and this provided both an educational and an artistic lesson. The new forms required new techniques, such as the use of glass matting and glass cloth laminated to a metal armature with synthetic resins.[60] In Chicago the designers used prefab concrete equipment in bright colors to supplement standard swings and slides.[61] Elsewhere a magic key to a talking book, actually a mechanical device for telling stories, went with the illustrated fairytales; a tiny-tot freeway helped children imagine themselves as grown-ups using freeways. Children themselves helped construct a nature study park, they used giant culverts for "spontaneous play" and a surplus jet fighter as a crawling device.[62]

The idea behind this new equipment, which anticipated the thinking of the following era, was "versatility, spontaneity, a freedom and openness of physical plan and programming, the encouragement of dramatic and imaginative play."[63] During the middle 1950s its most advanced expression was the "terrain sculpture" of Alberto Giacometti and Isamu Noguchi. But the standard argument for these innovations was merely that people had to be lured from their homes by something more than a place to picnic: "Even the

Oakland promoted one of the few design innovations of the recreation era—free-form sculptural play equipment for children. Reprinted from the 1958 and 1965 issues of *Parks and Recreation* by special permission of the National Recreation and Park Association.

RE 1 — Continuum Playground I consists of 13 abstract forms, varying in height from 1 foot to 14 feet, and occupies an area 40 by

New Playground Principle Sculpture Continuum

zoo must be glamorized and publicized. The ability to hold and attract people to our parks for any length of time is in proportion to the number of attractions offered. This competition has been met by progressive park departments with the installation of children's zoos, animals acts, birthday party areas and rides. Children's rides supplement other park attractions and have a definite place in municipal parks."[64] Even these few innovations were answerable to the characteristic logic of the recreation era: multiplication of offerings, justification by demand, defensiveness of orientation.

4

The Open-Space System: 1965 and After

Crisis in the Cities

The recreation era had provided facilities—playgrounds, parkways, stadiums, parking lots, and open beaches—but not space, much less open space. When urban parks began to be characterized as open spaces by municipal systems and federal programs in the mid 1960s, that was strong evidence that a genuine turning point in park history had been reached. A convenient date at which to fix this point is 1965, the year John Lindsay, mayor of New York City, made parks and playgrounds a political issue in his mayoral campaign.[1] The term "open space" had been used in park documents in Chicago as early as 1960, however, and in San Francisco as early as 1962.[2] Lindsay's campaign received considerable national publicity, and the shift in thinking it represented was nationwide in scope. Thus in the same year the American Institute of Park Executives changed its name to the National Recreation and Park Association to give tangible expression to the new ideal of integrating the physical park and the recreation program.[3] The National Park Service of the Department of Interior declared Central Park and Prospect Park as National Historic Landmarks, making their preservation, as opposed to remodeling, important and possible. The Chicago park commissioners wrote that they considered "1966 the start of an exciting new era in park planning, programming, and development."[4] As a final note, Henry Hope Reed, an outspoken critic of the new park ideal, designated 1963, when

Paley Park in New York is the epitome of the open-space mentality. No bigger than a building lot, this small oasis offers a visual and acoustic counterpoint to the city without escaping the adjacent street. New York Public Library.

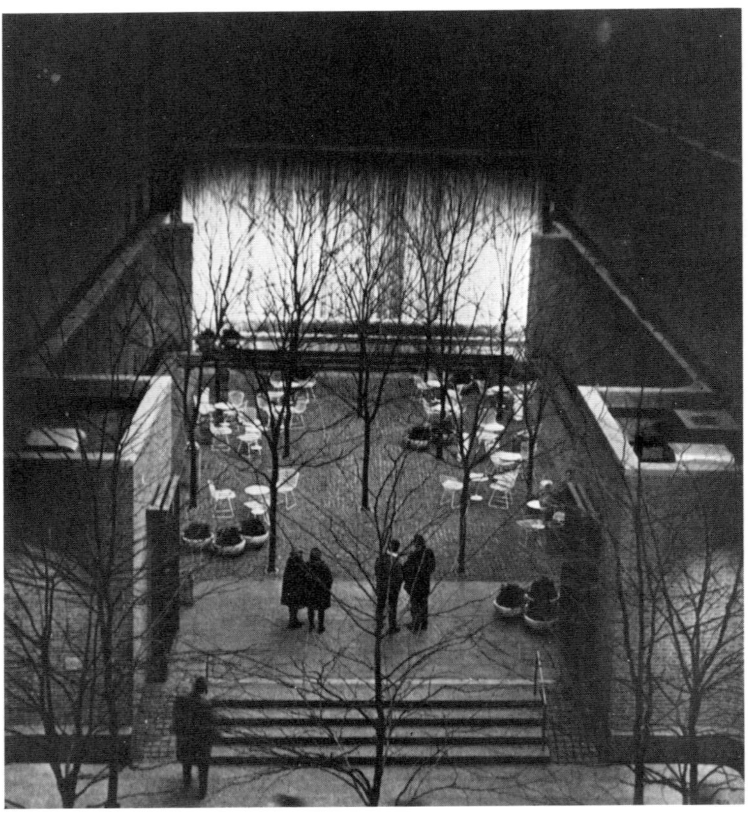

jazz and rock concerts were introduced in Central Park, as the last tolerable stage of park liberality. By 1966, he felt, permissiveness reigned and "everything was going on."[5]

The new departure in park policy was a response to the so-called urban crisis during these years. The key element in the crisis was the wholesale middle-class flight from the inner city, and the basic issue was whether community standards would be maintained in major American cities or the cities abandoned to those who had no means of escaping them.

Because of the crisis the demand for park services used during the recreation era to justify park budgets could no longer be counted on to do so. The middle class was no longer seeking park services; to the contrary, they conspicuously avoided parks, now considered so unsafe that they were part of the urban crisis rather than its cure. To use another phrase typical of the era, park practice wasn't working. This was because the city needed more from the parks than their customary safety valve function—for these were the years of riots, demonstrations, and "long hot summers." In this emergency situation for the parks to ameliorate urban conditions—to work at their traditional task—they would need to reassemble all the broken parts of the urban mass peacefully within their boundaries and thus serve as symbolls of the cosmopolitan ideal which the street—now unsafe to walk on—no longer embodied. In short, the city needed parks, but it needed them chiefly for imagery and inspiration.

The parks responded to these conditions with talk of self-examination, experiment, and innovation. Behind this talk was a philosophical vacuum: the old models did not apply and the new one, open space, was not much more than a gesture embracing the indefinite future. At its best though, the rhetorical posture could lead to an unprecedented openness to new ideas and possibilities.

If the new park pronouncements were exaggerated this was because park departments were once again openly stimulating demand for services, not just pretending to respond to it, and this stimulation, however hyperbolic, ultimately promoted the endangered cities themselves. Stimulation was the keynote in design of programming as well. The new parks were meant to be as exciting as the pleasure grounds had been programmatically unexciting, and their new image was adventurous, colorful, seductive, chic, hip, hot, and cool. If the pleasure ground had been a pious patriarch, the reform park a social worker, and the recreation facility a waitress or car mechanic, the new park was something of a performance artist.

Anything Goes

The phrase "open space" suggests a number of activities that vision and expediency began to bring into the parks after the mid-1960s. First, open spaces were wide open areas with the connotation that this was where "anything goes," and where the new permissiveness about the range of possible park activities was appropriate. Second, they were not built up but left open. They were bits and pieces of the city saved from the usual fate of urban land. As such, they were natural sites for preservation and, by extension, for not tampering with people or things at all, which was exemplified by the Be-ins and other attempts of the counterculture to promote experience as such. Third, open spaces were fluid. There was a fluidity at their perimeters, so that park flowed into city and city into park. This went with the characterization of the park as an epitome, or ideal reflection, of the city and with the use of parks for experiences of the pattern and flow of urban life—for the contemplation of the city itself as a work of art.

The "anything goes" attitude has received the most publicity, although in terms of the history of park philosophy it is the least innovative aspect of open-space programming since activities "on demand" were already the watchword of the recreation facility era. But the actual situation, by the end of that era, was that the demand for park services was apathetic because parks were viewed as irrelevant.[6] Only their potential for violence attracted the press and television. At the end of the recreation era in Chicago, a landscape architect remarked, "parks tend toward deadness in the crowded city of 1969."[7] They are deserted and unsafe, littered, with limited programming, old field houses, busy streets, and unwelcoming chain link fences.

Since nothing exciting had been done with parks for so long, they had to be shocked back into life, via newly permissive programming and the publicity to exploit it. For Lindsay's new Commissioner of Parks, Thomas Hoving, electrified programming was also the only way to attract enough people to the parks to make them safe.[8] To these ends, in New York and elsewhere, administrators brought new activities into the parks, allowed some traditional popular activities for the first time, and wove in elite cultural practices. Anything went: hot mulled wine, rock music, and bluegrass dancing on the snow for a collective New Year's Eve celebration or Check-A-Child, a low-cost child care program.[9] The Chicago Park District even considered making snowmobiles available in certain parks. Consistent with the concern for safety, dogs were no longer excluded from parks; and though this created a sanitation problem, it was remedied in San Francisco by the first canine comfort stations in the United States.

Certain activities offered during this period, such as Be-ins, Chalk-ins, and Happenings, were new to parks and to the general culture alike. (In New York, these events were dubbed "Hoving's Happenings".) Elements of popular culture, some of which had been excluded from parks before, formed the basis of celebrations: games, kite flying, band concerts, beer drinking, feasting. Some activities had been common outside parks but were new in a park context, or freshly conceived. For example, "Open the Ocean Day" in New York gathered park crowds around a sea dyed red, and in Golden Gate Park devotees of Lord Krishna organized a free feast, parade, and fair.[10] Dance and film were packaged in new ways: dancemobile, cinemobile, movie bus, and the Clairol caravan—a combination fashion show, rock-and-roll band, and entertainment.

Just as cultural events were updated, so too were athletics: surfing, trampoline, jumping, motocross, and bicycling were introduced, while horseback riding was closed in many systems. Carry-over, or lifetime, sports—badminton, bowling, golf, and tennis—were newly emphasized, giving sports a service orientation. Ghetto kids were taught the traditionally white, middle-class game of tennis. Physical fitness programs put athletics in new packages like "shape-up and fun physical fitness sessions," with instruction in tai chi, slim-and-trim exercises, karate, yoga, and belly dancing.

Elements of elite culture were welcome. New York's Creative Arts Workshop hired artists to go into the neighborhoods to work with kids. The Philharmonic concert was brought to neighborhood parks, on the assumption that most people did not attend theatre or opera only because they were intimidated by dress codes. The museum without walls concept gained parlance, and wall paintings and murals brought painting to the street. Shakespearian theatre moved to neighborhood parks and playgrounds.

Direct participation was often a central criterion in open-space programming. For example, at a banner bee held in conjunction with the Museum of Contemporary Crafts, those who had made their own banners marched in a parade with them. Because people liked to come together for New Year's, an alternative to Times Square was offered, with music, puppetry, fireworks, and dancing. The moon launch, broadcast over a giant television screen in Central Park, turned into a collective event. And at the opening of the Olmsted sesquicentennial a participatory happening centered on a giant food sculpture, a scale model of Central Park devoured by the crowd itself.[11]

Happenings were participatory—people painting things and themselves, thousands appearing in outlandish costumes on Halloween to see and be seen. Such participation, moreover, seemed to guarantee experience, the emphasis on which in open-space programming amounted to a moral imperative: "Park and recreation people must begin to take seriously their obligations to provide recreation *experiences* for people rather than recreation *facilities*."[12]

The happening, however, was also something to wonder at and reflect on. More than a simple experience, it was an aesthetic event whose subject, typically, was the urban population which participated in it. An underlying aesthetic assumption connected the happening with other phenomena of the open-space era, including the urban cultural park. In the late 1970s municipal, regional, and federal agencies cooperated to preserve segments of historic towns and landscapes such as Lowell, Massachusetts. These urban cultural parks, which were intended to preserve an important part of the nation's industrial and economic history for educational and recreational purposes, were opened on the assumption that all parts of the city—its work spaces, living quarters, and connecting streets—had equal aesthetic and recreational potential, that the city was in fact a work of art worthy of appreciation and objectification.[13]

This premium on the preservation of valued sites affected the older parks as well. With the designation of Prospect and Central Parks as historic landmarks, for instance, park service had the responsibility of preserving the historic legacy of the parks, not just responding to present demands for their services.[14] The federal agency, Heritage Conservation and Recreation Service, set high priority on reinvestment in existing urban parks through its Urban Park and Recreation Recovery Program. Moreover, ecology—the preservation of the balances of nature—paralleled the preservation of landmarks from the cultural past.

In New York walking and bicycle tours taught ecology along with architecture and overall park design. Although in San Francisco and Chicago horticultural tours and lecture series survived from earlier eras without new rationales, the National Park Service developed environmental awareness programs that influenced municipal park programming in other cities.[15]

Controversy

When the American Institute of Park Executives changed its name to the National Recreation and Park Association, they pointed out that active recreation had always been part of park programming: "Although it was not recognized as such, recreation was a key part of these early park developments—be it boating, walking, hunting,equestrian trails, skating—recreation was there."[16] But old-fashioned images such as these were a far cry from the realities of the era. The new and vigorous use of the parks, especially during the Vietnam War, was sometimes disruptive, threatening to conventional sensibilities or downright illegal. Park response was predictable.

Demonstrations against the Vietnam War (as during the 1968 Democratic National Convention in Chicago) were criticized, both as a strain on plant material and as politically inappropriate; administrators sometimes shunted demonstrators off to less conspicuous and visible parks than Grant Park in Chicago and Central Park in New York by granting them permits elsewhere, grass notwithstanding.[17] Other controversies erupted over provocative performances, such as by the San Francisco Mime Troupe. A popular cafe at Bethesda Fountain in Central Park became a haunt for marijuana users, and although the police originally thought controlling dealers and smokers would be easy if they were all in one place, the result was considered unsavory, and the cafe disbanded. Similarly, when folk concert flyers hinted that the concert would turn into a smoke-in, the New York administration revoked the permit.

These rumblings represented a deeper upheaval, indicated by a slogan of the era, Power to the people. Because park officials were committed to a permissive position based on the idea that they were obliged to respond to popular demand, they were frightened, confused, and to some degree compromised. Moreover, for understanding the new situation, they had nothing better than the traditional distinction between active and passive activities, the distinction which underlay the historic conflict between the reform park and pleasure ground and, administratively, between the recreation and park divisions. Whenever there was controversy about the use of parks during the era, the distinction was likely to show up. Thus the activities sponsored by the New York Department of Cultural Affairs were particularly controversial, but the cultural affairs director could argue that people wanted active use even though most park promoters were for passive use. In the same vein Commissioner Hoving justified activity as necessary for "certain economic levels" which "won't buy passive activity" and "have to have a pool because they don't have a racquet and river club." The upshot was that the curator of Central Park was aghast at what he considered excessive use of the park.[18]

Activists and passivists alike agreed that active and passive activities could go together, that a balance was necessary, and that both should be offered, but they disagreed sharply about what the proper proportion should be. By the mid-1970s, however, the balance had shifted to the side of those worried about overuse and overdevelopment of parks, and programming reverted to appreciation of park landscape itself.[19] A pragamatic argument against intense usage was that crowds destroyed landscaping; for this reason the Shaefer Music Festival, for example, was discontinued in 1976.

Get It Where You Can

Competition for land, particularly with freeways and housing, was greater than ever before, so open-space ideology rationalized the minipark, the playlot, and the vest-pocket park, small parks that could be tucked into irregular, unusual, inexpensive sites that had been rejected in prior eras. As Mayor Lindsay wrote, "the adventure playground is built upon almost any available site, anywhere in size from a quarter-acre to an acre and a half. If the terrain has slope, so much the better."[20] The small size of these parks was both a cause and effect of their proliferation. Ideally, they would be cast in a net over the whole city, both in the inner city and in the expanding suburban fringes, and integrated into an interconnected system of open spaces; park sites, in other words, would extend beyond their literal boundaries into the city as a whole.[21] By contrast, the classic park was inadequate because it did not cohere with the city, residential developments, and schools.

Landscape architects wanted to reveal the potential recreational use of the entire environment. (They lamented the counterproductive separation of open-space agencies which overlapped and duplicated functions and competed with one another.) Open spaces could include conceptual, temporary, and accidental openings, plazas, pedestrian walks, urban waterfronts, and bicycle paths such as those created in New York, Chicago, and San Francisco which make use of existing roadways.

The street was viewed as the "most exciting space in the city."[22] The new attitude toward streets, sidewalks, backyards, vacant lots, waterfronts, and rooftops involved them in park planning and ideology whether or not they were actually under the administrative control of park departments. Along with this attitude came a new way of looking at the undersides of freeways and bridges, interstices and hidden indoor spaces such as auditoriums and warehouses, commercial areas such as shipping centers, and abandoned industrial plants—all potential sites for the new type of park.[23]

A logical extension of distributing parks everywhere throughout a city was to make them mobile. Through the use of portable equipment, distinctive to this era, transient parks could be established anywhere—streets, empty lots, and rooftops.[24] Some viewed this possibility as a revolutionary virtue: "Future parks will have *minimum development.* The park of the future will be *flexible,* beyond any kind of token flexibility now envisioned, *convertible* to

Closing Central Park to auto traffic on Sundays brought thousands into it and helped link it with bicycle paths throughout the city. New York City, Department of Parks, *Report 1967*.

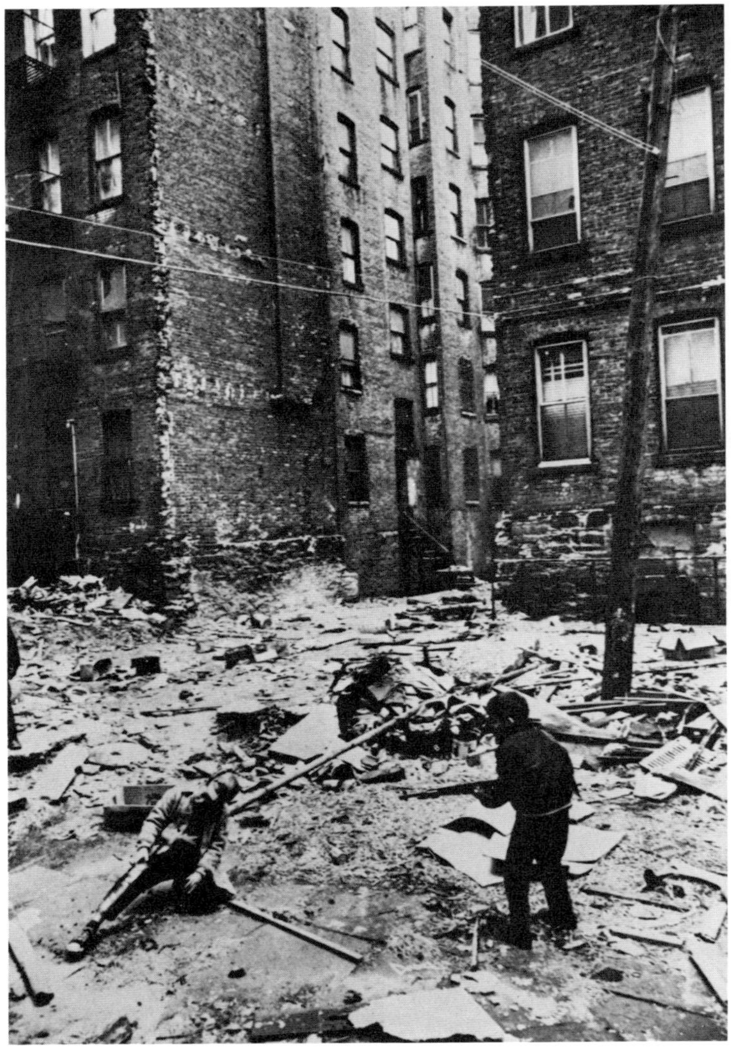

Vacant lots were the target of the federally sponsored Neighborhood Improvement and Beautification Program of the late 1960s. New York City, Department of Parks, *Report 1967.*

possibly what are now considered nonpark or even anti-parks uses, and even *disposable*."[25] In this development both ideal and pragmatic logics were at work; recreational space could be created everywhere without having to spend the money to purchase land and construct permanent buildings.

The Design Revolution

Mayor Lindsay recognized that parks do not need to be conservative, stereotyped, or dull, and asked for an attitude of creativity and experimentation in the design section of New York City's Park Department.[26] The first commissioner of parks under his mayoralty was credited with a design revolution.[27] And up to a point, these claims were in proportion. For example, Lindsay's campaign initiated the first municipal promotion of the European adventure playground idea. The adventure playground was the place where fire, water, and construction materials—lumber, nails, ropes, and bricks—could be used to create and destroy structures over and over again at the discretion of the children.

But municipal parks never accepted the idea that the children themselves should build play equipment; instead, designers transformed the children's home-made, free-form, equipment into new kinds of standardized manufactured items, with stabilized gravel and sand instead of asphalt, recirculating spray pools, vinyl spiderwebs for climbing, and interconnecting equipment. Moreover, popular understanding and use of the new model quickly became conventional. The physical forms of adventure playgrounds became similar, with no unusual requests. Designers reported that most community groups wanted those brand names of free form playstructures known for being hard to vandalize, an area for benches, and a tot lot of sand devoid of equipment so as not to attract teenagers. Despite the exuberance which welcomed this new playground type initially, it was eviscerated in no time.

In general the more revolutionary claims of open-space de-

Two vacant lots, turned into playgrounds. Chicago, 1969.

sign rhetoric—typified by those of Lindsay and his administration—were not realized in actual practice.[28] The more sedate vest-pocket parks, such as Paley Park in New York, have been more successful and probably epitomize American open-space design better than the adventure playground. Paley Park meets researchers' criteria for the design of public yard-type parks: it is sited in the heart of midtown Manhattan, people come there for a variety of reasons, its dramatic center is the sheet of falling water at the end of the lot, it has both sun and shade, and buildings enclose it on three sides.[29] Its seating is designed to provide for different views of the falling water, to accommodate people in different moods and in different social groupings.

The recurrent conflict between active and passive ideals reverberated all the way down to the use of materials and objects. Surfacing is a case in point. The intense use of open spaces required tough surfacing, but the new attitude toward freedom and flexibility required soft and changeable materials. Thus the curator of Central Park convinced the administration to take out asphalt paths. Some people felt that the new materials should be urban in order to suggest continuity with the surrounding nonpark environment, while others felt that they should give "relief from the urban hardness of concrete, steel, and glass!"[30] Landscape architect Lawrence Halprin, whose firm has designed several complex fountains in city plazas, favored hard materials intrinsic to the city but arranged to break up the city's rhythms. Landscape designers who worked for a Chicago park district were typically against the use of natural materials because they were "not safe and vandalizable," whereas citizen groups composed of designers and laymen tended to advocate natural materials.[31] Sometimes a backwoods effect was not intentional, but rather the outcome of the use of recycled materials—used bricks, railroad ties, tires, and telephone piles. The vest-pocket parks for adults were used too heavily for grassy lawns so the same sensibilities that favored texture and the feeling of looseness brought cobblestone and herringbone-patterned brick back into the designer's repertoire.

A COMMUNITY SPONSORED
VEST POCKET PARK
Made possible by the
NEW YORK CITY ADMINISTRATION
of PARKS, RECREATION and CULTURAL
AFFAIRS, and the FEDERAL DEPT. of
HOUSING and URBAN DEVELOPMENT.

The adventure playground retains little of real world adventure and places a premium on low maintenance, free-form, but standardized, elements. New York City, Department of Parks, *Report 1967*.

Water was exploited in a more innovative way in this era than in the preceding one. In the recreation era water had been used primarily for swimming, but now in addition to swimming pools came more novel treatments of water. The Paley Park waterfall, used to dampen sound, cool the air, and attract people, exemplified the new approach.[32] Seating was also addressed with new design considerations. To make plazas work as gathering points for a heterogeneous collection of people, researchers recommended that designers arrange vantage points and seating so that people would have choice about whether or not they would sit together or have space to be alone.[33] Something as unparklike as the pedestrian bridge that connects Portsmouth Square with a new high rise in San Francisco was described as having a parklike atmosphere by virtue of its benches and sculpture and broad walkway.[34]

Adventure playground designers did not even discuss trees and plants; the new urban parks required tree substitutes such as tensile structures, and the national literature explained that landscaping should be confined to low shrubbery to minimize nuisances and vandalism.[35] Urban parks continued to be stripped of vegetation for easier maintenance and police surveillance, but substitutions were met with fervent resistence.[36] Satires on fiberglass flowers, polystyrene turf, plastic grass, recycled water, styrofoam rocks, and asbestos trees and shrubs began to appear, and empirical research was produced that demonstrated the value of trees in heightening user satisfaction and increasing property values.[37]

Fencing was disappearing along with vegetation. The ever-higher chain link fences around parks of the recreation era went out of fashion in the open-space era. Open-space advocates tore them down or replaced them with more picturesque rustic fencing. Antibillboard sentiment emerged again. Buildings were out of fashion, so no new building type emerged in the era. The general mood against much building construction was for both ideological and economic reasons.[38] Campaigns were mounted to keep

Modern architecture finally surfaced in parks of the open-space era, even though dominant interest lay in restoration. Each function within the building created its own shape on the exterior; vernacular sheds, clerestories, and plain stucco surfaces completed the symbolism of modernism. Brooklyn. New York City, Department of Parks, *Report 1967.*

school buildings out of parks, reversing the previous era's idea of school-park integration, but the extensions of the Metropolitan Museum in Central Park and Chicago's Conference Center on the lakefront were unsuccessfully opposed.[39] Underground garages, once thought unobtrusive, became objectionable because of their big exhaust vents. Even park stables for horses were controversial in New York, San Francisco, and Chicago.[40]

Not surprisingly, then, interest in architectural style focused on the renovation of landmark buildings. In San Francisco the renovation of the romanesque Sharon Building at the children's playground, the restoration of the windmills, and the reuse of the Palace of Fine Arts as a Museum of Perception, Science, and Technology paralleled activities in New York.[41] There a copy of a ladies pavilion was made after the original was allowed to decay, a conservatory was restored, and the old fire department building was offered to the park system for a museum.[42]

Finally, during this period some city observers reevaluated the significance of monuments and statues. As one opinion put it, they "celebrate a city's heroes and recapitulate its past . . . "[43] But critics from every quarter attacked monumentality. The monument—whether a statue or a grandiose structure—was shunned in an era that favored keeping in touch with the human scale of things. Accordingly, the characteristic sculpture of the era was play equipment, and the sculpture actually commissioned was playful in its appreciation of movement, irregular form, and irreverent attitude. It was criticized for all these reasons. The Vallaincourts Fountain at the Embarcadero in San Francisco was called a scrap heap by a city supervisor, and adventure playgrounds and play sculpture were described as a Walt Disney-ish pastiche.[44] Yellow-painted steel panels hanging on trees in Central Park were viewed as "a desecration of our trees—like hanging a rock around a man's neck"—ignominous because their artificiality was incongruous with nature.[45]

II

The Politics of Park Design

5

The Powers That Be

American urban park policy has always been a top-down matter, but the group on top—the powers that be—have changed from era to era. The great pleasure grounds sharpened and concentrated the diffuse, irregular, and occasional character of recreational activity typical of the preinstitutionalized municipal park movement. In this sense they were vast accumulations of recreational capital, and the men responsible for amassing them were entrepreneurs who can be compared with the great capitalists of their era. They were a social and economic elite, men with considerable power and influence, acting out of more or less idealistic motives—moral entrepreneurs. They were succeeded, once the great accumulations had taken place, first by a variety of paid professionals—social workers, recreationists, planners, designers—and then by the park bureaucrats. These latter two groups can be distinguished from one another in terms of allegiance. The private interests of both groups tended to coincide with the interests of the parks themselves, as they conceived of them; but, while the professionals identified the interests of the parks with the ideals of their professions, the bureaucrats tended to identify them with the mere maintenance and enhancement of their bureaucratic structure. Thus there has been a decline, at the top, in what can be called vision or moral energy, corresponding to the decline in the position in society of the people placed there. These declines mirror a third one, more concrete: parks have gradually received a smaller and

This cartoon mocks the paternalistic anxiety of New York Park Commissioner Jesse Powers about conceding to popular taste in music.

smaller share of urban revenues and have had to turn more and more to federal assistance and internally generated revenue to survive even in a diminished role.

Those in power have had no common name throughout the urban park era. To some degree they have always been a group, but not an organized one. Some supporters became park officials, while others worked on behalf of parks as passionately involved journalists, philanthropists, politicians; and finally, bureaucrats, more employees than supporters, sustained the movement. Roughly speaking, these social groups have led the park movement in its various stages, but leader and movement suggest struggle with an organized opposition, whereas, in fact, the real enemies of the parks have been inertia and lack of interest.[1] The group to which this chapter is devoted is made up simply of those who have been interested in parks, whatever the nature of their interest, and have had the power to translate that interest into park policy. As a group, they can be distinguished from park users and from the indirect beneficiaries of park policies, such as speculators on land adjacent to new parks sites. The overlap between the group interested in parks and the group of indirect beneficiaries is a recurring theme.

Idealists, Philanthropists, Commissioners

The early park movement was manned by the same gentlemen-idealists as other reform movements. They advocated parks as a way of realizing a vision of the good life, not, at least openly, as a means of serving their individual interests. Although they saw themselves as reformers working on behalf of the people, they never doubted that leadership should stay with them. They thought of themselves as guardians of the highest cultural ideals, not necessarily as guardians of the people; because they were protecting the best of the culture, they took it for granted that they ultimately had the interest of the common man at heart.

In the early stages gentlemen interested in the public welfare met informally; eventually they created formal organizations to promote the idea of the grand parks.[2] In Chicago, as elsewhere, park promoters were social elites found among the Union Defense Committee, which was composed of so-called enlightened leaders—judges, bankers, doctors, merchants, attorneys who were also art collectors, trustees of The University of Chicago, members of elite social clubs.[3] A national group, the Park and Outdoor Art Association, fulfilled their own criteria for leadership, being public-spirited men who had travelled, and had a pretty fair idea of what a large public park should be.[4] In San Francisco the early park promoters were permanent, public-spirited citizens.[5] The idealism of these men worked in several different modes: there were groups allied by philosophic conviction or a personal passion to protect parks, civic welfare groups and charities, small-scale donors and volunteers, and clergymen and temperance advocates.

Idealism animated philanthropists as well. Even the bureaucratic recreationists acknowledged that "throughout our history, philanthropy has pioneered and government has followed."[6] Andrew Jackson Downing, an early proponent of landscape gardening in the United States, felt that the people of the United States should appeal to public liberality:

> . . . make it praiseworthy and laudable for wealthy men to make bequests of land . . . for this public enjoyment, and commemorate the public spirit of such men by a statue or a beautiful marble vase, with an inscription, telling all succeeding generations to whom they are indebted for the beauty and enjoyment that constitutes the chief attraction of the town.[7]

This happy acceptance of private support continued through the pleasure ground era, even when municipal support had been established a long time. For example, San Francisco park commissioners unabashedly hoped to extend Golden Gate Park to the Presidio on the northern shore of the peninsula by acquiring land through private donation. Regarding a proposal to extend the Great Highway to the Cliff House for three miles, the commissioners said that building it "calls for the generosity of some wealthy gentleman ready to distinguish himself by doing a proper service to his less fortunate fellow citizens."[8]

The desire to attract big philanthropists was more than wishful thinking. A list of early park contributions is a recapitulation of the big names in any city's history. In the San Francisco Bay Area, for example, most of today's major place names, both in and outside the parks were the names of prominent families: Ghirardelli, Lick, Alvord, Hotaling, Crocker, Spreckels, Stanford, Kezar, Fleishhacker, Stern, Sharon, de Young, Phelan, Hearst, Sweeney, Sutro, Haas. Parks were a major vehicle for this kind of spending, just as they were a medium for public works spending during the Depression.

If idealism, philanthropy, and public spiritedness were at one extreme in early park promotion, the simple self-interest of businessmen was at the other. Initially, New York City's business community was against municipal spending for parks. They did not want to have land taken off the market, especially not the valuable commercial dock space which would have been usurped if Jones Woods had become a park. Central Park was favored, among other reasons, because its land was not as valuable as Jones Woods. After this initial heel dragging, land speculators often became ardent park advocates. They bought land in advance of park site selection in hopes of being able to charge exorbitant prices or reap great profits on the unearned increment on adjacent lands. In some cities, like Seattle, realtors built railway lines and the parks at their ends to attract potential buyers for the land along the line. Local and municipal governments soon found that they had to protect themselves from land-grabbers, real estate sharks who might try to gouge the city.[9]

Businessmen, businesses, and businessmen's associations individually ran the gamut from direct self-interest to a disinterested concern for civic welfare. The Chamber of Commerce has been a way for citizens to promote their

A real estate speculator built both this park and the railroad line to it, to attract families, and potential buyers, on Sunday outings. Ca. 1890, Woodward Park, Seattle. University of Washington Library.

collective welfare since the middle of the nineteenth century, and, as Robert Wiebe had demonstrated, businessmen were part of the progressive reform movement, sometimes at its forefront.[10] Reformers and businessmen offered mutual support: the economic advantage of boosterism was a recurrent appeal in park literature, and when businessmen's associations promoted the economic, political, and moral welfare of the city as a whole, their actions had a philanthropic cast. The City Beautiful movement embraced economic rationales in order to legitimate many of its goals.

These strains of self-interest and philanthropy, combined with assured social position and the high-handedness that goes with it, came together in the early park commissioners. This group declined in status over time, but during the pleasure ground era, according to William Hammond Hall, Golden Gate Park's first designer, they were considered "amongst the very foremost citizens of San Francisco of their day."[11] They were lawyers, judges, manufacturers, merchants, real estate men, and bankers. They were active, politically or in civic culture at large. Of the political commissioners, some were elected to public office, others were delegates to political conventions, and still others were political lobbyists. Even during the reform era, when no full-time politicians, such as state representatives or senators, served on the boards, about half of the commissioners were active as delegates or lobbyists. The other side of such public service was the political advantage of being able to dispense park jobs to the party faithful.

Of the rest, most were active in civic culture at large. Nearly a third of the commissioners served as trustees or members of the board of directors on at least one public service or charity other than the park commission itself, such as the art institute, the public library, the local historical society, the local relief and aid society, the exposition and World Fair committees, regional park commissions, the board of education, the sanitary district, the Young Men's Christian Association, the board of inspectors for jails, or orphanages. Others were generally known as patrons of the arts, science, and literature, or as defenders of civil rights.[12] The early park commissioners, in other words, were part of an interlocking directorate, laced together by bonds of familiarity and friendship, which effectively ruled the cities.[13]

Other generalizations about the early commissioners fall in line with this picture. They were better educated than the general populace, predominantly native born, white, Protestant, male, married, and middle aged or older. The pattern of their recruitment implies that they were selected because of these characteristics and the attitudes toward society that would go with them. Yet even their high status did not dissolve issues about the proper balance between individual and collective interests. Thus their attitudes regarding the relationship between public service and private gain, between municipal and private spending, between self-interest and collective welfare were unformed and problematic. As I see it, the early commissioners, along with the general public, were in the process of delimiting the relationships between public and private, between political and civic, and between legitimate and illegitimate profit, which the culture at large had not yet worked out.

Laissez-faire economic theory assumed that if individuals pursued their self-interest, in the aggregate, the well-being of the system as a whole would be assured. The move to municipal spending from 1850 to 1900 entailed a new idea, namely, that certain functions had to be paid for and organized by a corporate body deliberately and self-consciously. But this new idea had not entirely driven out the old one, and no one doubted that individuals should always get something out of their actions, even when serving on a municipal board. In modern parlance, no one assumed that individuals were without motives.

For example, Paul Cornell, one of the first members of the Chicago South Park system, owned real estate in the general vicinity of the South Park. He initially wanted the park sited on his own lands only three miles from the center of town, but, by the time the voters approved a park district, the land had to be twice as far out to reduce costs. Nevertheless, Cornell still was able to benefit from the increased value accrued to his lands. No one found this kind of self-interest illegitimate.

In San Francisco park commissioners sometimes had clear outside interests that they felt legitimate to try to impose on Golden Gate Park. For example, Leland Stanford of the Southern Pacific Railway apparently felt no embarrassment about trying to get a railway line through the park, even though he was defeated, and M. H. de Young was indignant that the board rejected his offer as chairman of the Midwinter Fair and a member of the park board to donate buildings to the park rather than to incur the expense of having them demolished. Cable car companies benefited by being able to carry citizens out to Golden Gate Park, and eventually one commissioner became a joint trustee of the railway and the commission.[14] Public and private support of activities such as the music concerts sponsored by the railway companies and the night lighting of park driveways sponsored by an alliance of restaurant and resort owners near the ocean cliff, liverymen, members of bicycle clubs, and wealthy horsemen was not uncommon. Rather than being viewed as an illegitimate influence of money on park programming, it was viewed as another form of philanthropy, as a way to add amenities when the municipal park budget could only cover basic construction and maintenance. Some of the commissioners themselves represented the companies who were making donations in exchange for an assumed benefit, but few people saw a conflict of interest in this, probably because of the tradition of support coming from private sources. The mix of public and private support was still so close that conflicts and ambiguities were unwitting.

One of the first park theorists to object to this collision of public and private interest was C. S. Sargent. In 1895 he concluded that neither real estate dealers nor politicians should be allowed to become park commissioners. In addition he specified that the commission should be composed of a few men of taste, "public-spirited enough to serve without pay," like the boards of trustees that govern public libraries and art museums.[15] In fact, Sargent was reacting to excesses, and public criticism was reaching the high point that would culminate in reform of municipal governments throughout the United States. The Chicago *Globe* had already made a scathing summary of the political and economic interests of Chicago's South Park commissioners in 1888.[16] For example, J. R. Walsh, South Park commissioner from 1877 to 1888, used his dual position on the park commission and as the head of a local bank to capture commission accounts and then use them for his personal purposes. He bought several railraods with money borrowed from his own banks by illegal overextension and falsified records to hide this. Four commissioners, William Best, Lyman Walton, Fred Blount, and Andrew Graham, held stock in Walsh's banks and helped sway park funds to them. The grand jury indicted him on 182 counts, and he spent most of the rest of his life, after his conviction in 1905, in Leavenworth Prison.

Walsh's case was clearly beyond the pale, but defining boundaries precisely was another thing. The search for definition was reflected in the changing legal structure of the park commissions. Initially, all three park commissions were established by appointment rather than election. This was in order to free the office from political influence, since it was supposed to be above special interests, acting only on behalf of the municipality as a whole. In New York the appointments were initially made by the mayor and the Common Council, but within five years the procedure was changed so that the governor and senate made the appointments, thinking that the state officials would choose men of more mark, taste, and acquisition and who would not be subject to the selfish interests of local authorities. The compromise act that finally passed the legislature in 1857 took control away from the mayor and the city government and invested it, not in state officials, but in a new commission of high-minded local men.[17]

The governor of Illinois authorized the Chicago Park Commission and appointed its first five members; but subsequent appointments were made by judges on the assumption that their superior qualities would assure the selection of good men, and keep the administration out of politics.[18] In practice the commissioners were not free from political influence. Many commissioners did not serve their full terms, either being replaced by a new political favorite or resigning in frustration over not being able to make decisions free from political influence just when they were getting more efficient.[19]

Commissioners ideally had to be worthy citizens free from political influence. In addition they should have positive personal qualities, and these included good taste. They were criticized if they lacked it:

> . . . Mr. McLaren is no landscape gardener as his works prove by the absence therin of unity, variety, and harmony of design. . . . The only attractions . . . consist of a large band and good roads. The policemen to regulate the speed on those roads would be unnecessary had the park commissioners employed an artist as superintendent. Such a person . . . would have rendered the grounds too attractive for fast driving . . . the park commissioners are as destitute of any artistic sense as their superintendent, their conception of park management being limited to growing of plantations to stop sand drifts.[20]

High character and aesthetic sensibilities were part of a higher universalistic ideal of serving the city as a whole which was contrasted with immediate personal and political interests. L. B. Sidway was evoking the ideal when he said that Chicago's original five commissioners were very much unlike, each with opinions of his own, but that they had respect for and confidence in each other's loyalty to the work at hand and so were able to work together courteously and kindly. Sargent insisted, "It is not enough to appoint a commission of worthy citizens who . . . set themselves to adjusting the claims of rival east-side and west-side associations or up-town or down-town interests. An individual park ought to be an organized work of art."[21]

Nevertheless, for most commissioners the position was a combination of personal and political advantage with the opportunity to embody this ideal. In 1888 the Chicago *Globe* described the mixed motives of park commissioners: "All work for pure patriotism, the local love of glory; the right to spend $200,000 a year and the fun of employing retainers and dependents. . . ."[22]

Professionals

Park commissioners during the reform era were drawn primarily from the same elite as during the previous era. Yet even during these years, professional welfare agencies began to supplant private charity and philanthropy, and professionalism undermined philanthropic zeal. Once the process of hiring paid agents had begun, it was self-sustaining. Both the amateur and the volunteer became anachronisms, so that, finally, by the recreation era park commissioners no longer represented the establishment as totally as before.

Park professionalism actually started informally, during the pleasure ground era, amid the close national network of expert designers and landscape architects who designed the parks. Olmsted and his many associates and followers worked outside the ordinary structure of park employees as consultants and considered themselves, and were considered, peers of the commissioners and backers. Olmsted himself designed sixteen or seventeen major park systems in different parts of the United States; and the other designers of the era were aligned with him or under his influence. Thus, city fathers looking to hire a designer for a new city park turned perforce to a body of men as well organized, homogeneous in opinion, and powerful within their sphere as any formal professional organization. Some people might think, as did one city official, that "the woods are full of landscape-architects."[23] But Sargent could correct this misconception by explaining that no more than a half dozen men in the country were capable of overseeing the work of Central Park. Only a man of refined and educated taste could make these decisions:

> Because a worthy and prosperous dry-goods merchant can bid a cash-boy run on an errand, it by no means logically follows that he can order a statue carved or a picture painted or a park designed in the same way. This inability to appreciate the value of taste and training is the very essence of vulgarity, and men of coarse fiber can never be made to understand by argument what everyone with any refinement of mind knows by intuition.[24]

Sargent claimed that Central Park had been saved by landscape architects' being willing to stand up to the commissioners and refusing to accede to their short-term practicalities.[25] Charles W. Eliot, president emeritus of Harvard University, elevated the significance of the professional even further: "The profession of landscape architecture is going to be—indeed, it already is—the most direct professional contributor to the improvement of the human environment in the twentieth century. . . ."[26]

The reform era saw the first professional incursions into the area of public welfare—as opposed to city beautification. Social workers were the first professionals regularly employed by parks departments, and the development of the paid social worker parallels the shift from philanthropy to professionalism in park work as a whole. The profession of social work incubated in settlement houses and park field houses and then developed independently of the park system. Later the professionals came back to field houses and reform park recreation programs as employees and advocates.

Within the general category of social worker a new specialist, the recreationist, emerged, carved out as a separate profession by Joseph Lee.[27] Some social caseworkers moved into the area of recreation because they wanted to reach people who needed help but had not yet developed severe social problems: "Why stand on shore and salvage when one could be directing to safe channels from a light ship, out where things were happening?"[28]

In the main the recreationists were play leaders, trained to supervise children directly since it was no longer assumed that they would come to the parks in the company of their parents. They often quoted Lee:

> As a matter of practical experience, the opinion of those who have done actual playground work is unanimous to the effect that leadership on a playground for children between six and eleven years old is a necessity. A play leader costs something, it is true, but there is danger of being penny-wise in the matter. In a big city, especially, where a playground costs many thousands of dollars, it is poor economy to save the salary of a man or woman who could more than treble its effectiveness.[29]

Recreation specialists were drawn from diverse welfare agencies, and, once the reform parks were established, the range of support from other social and government agencies broadened. The recreation movement eventually spawned its own professional organizations, the American Institute of Park Executives and the Playground Association of America. The latter, founded in 1906, reorganized in 1910, and eventually reorganized again as the National Recreation Association, sent out missionaries throughout the country to promote and organize the idea of public responsibility for play and recreation.[30] One consequence of the establishment of this new profession was that park departments began to require playground supervisors to take specialized training through in-house service courses, special institutes and conferences, and college courses. To this end the National Recreation Association set up its own school, and the higher-ranking members of recreational organizations began to obtain advanced degrees in recreation or physical education. Recreationists were considered more adventurous, less bound by tradition than administrators.

The Russell Sage Foundation became interested in the new Playground Association of America in 1907 and gave it support, both intellectually and financially. One of the first jobs the association set for itself was to educate the American public to understand the need for professional play leaders, as distinct from teachers, park administrators, or

Playleaders, the new recreation professionals in the 1900s, were recruited equally from both sexes until the 1950s, when men "upgraded" the profession by replacing women. Ca. 1908. *American Playgrounds.*

social workers.[31] The original purpose of the association was to help "communities develop and effectively administer broad neighborhood and community recreation programs in the localities where the people lived and where their day-to-day recreation needs had to be met."[32] In little time, however, the association came to dominate these earlier traditions of local control, and once national definitions were established and standards set, the local park and recreation systems seldom deviated from the pattern set up for them.

Bureaucrats

Recreationists were typically part of the park bureaucracy, often line rather than staff workers, and among the establishment powers they had considerably less sway than the commissioner, designers, or city leaders. They owed allegiance to the ideals of their profession, as articulated in its national magazines, *Playground*, *Recreation*, and *Parks and Recreation*, but neither their profession nor their ideals had much prestige or leverage in city politics. Thus, when the reforming zeal which marked the beginnings of their profession failed, the national profession itself occupied relatively less of their attention, and the local bureaucratic structures they found themselves in relatively more. Accordingly, during the era of the recreation facility the bureaucrat emerged as the new park power, and the maintenance and enhancement of the park bureaucracy came to be as much an end as a means of park policy.

For this reason the park organization became its own promoter, and promotion came to be a regular part of park programming. In the pleasure ground era, park departments shared information about their work informally through correspondence and visits, and in the reform era administrators relied increasingly on publications such as annual reports. But in the recreation era they began to hire public relations experts to spread knowledge about and generate support for their work. The commitment to publicity became paramount: in San Francisco, "It was decided that the

Playground Commission try to secure as much publicity as possible for its yearly program."[33] Park departments thought more publicity might increase the number of users, create interest in departmental activities, and assist in securing additional funds. Park men helped each other legitimize promotional activities by drawing on patriotism and utilitarianism as rationales: during the Depression, "it was right and proper to inform the people of San Francisco of the free recreational activities offered them throughout the park system."[34] Campaigns to disseminate recreational information were thought not only desirable but also necessary. Other arguments appealed to a sense of realpolitik: "Whether you like it or not, you're in a public relations struggle too—a struggle to win public understanding and support."[35]

Another way to expand the importance of park departments was to expand their tasks beyond the normal scope of their activities. For example, in New York park advocates wanted the department to take over the responsibility for promoting the City Beautiful movement.[36] At the same time, the New York Park Department vied for authority over commercial amusements: "it is manifestly evident that the Park Department, charged as it is with the management and securing of adequate recreation for the community, is the proper authority to control and supervise commercial amusements. It is clear that such authority would make possible a very much better coordination of public and private recreation."[37]

Still another way an organization maintains and enhances itself is by rationalizing procedures. Specialization and differentiation of role within the park bureaucracy was part of the ever-growing drive toward efficiency, beginning at the turn of the century and extending past World War II. Park commissions hired efficiency experts, industrial relations experts, statisticians, publicists, and leisure experts. Extended classification systems coordinated all the different types of employees; administrators scheduled vacations, inaugurated standardized cleaning equipment and proce-

The process of transforming acreage into parkland was a major public works project which made park construction an economic stimulant and vehicle for political patronage. Courtesy Chicago Historical Society.

dures, and instituted a system of foremen's daily cost reports. Quality became equated with the sheer numbers of people served. Machinery came into vogue, and equipment carried the day: switchboards and machine-posted ledgers, and eventually computerized administration, were each said to be more efficient than manual systems. The recreation movement embraced the industrialism the pleasure ground advocates had sought to hold at bay: "We must scrutinize the technology of our process; we must introduce somehow the automatic machine and eliminate the cost and laboriousness of the handmade, personally taught, individually led, clientele."[38]

Public Spending

Whether or not the historical sequence of park leadership—moral entrepreneur, professional, bureaucrat—represents a decline, the history of public financial support for the urban parks that parallels it indubitably does so. Olmsted was particularly proud of the fact that American parks were a product of public spending rather than a gift from a beneficent aristocracy.[39] Professional and official reports and the newspapers of his era were dotted with references to the appropriateness of municipal spending on parks. By the reform park era, when the elaborate new field houses provoked visitors to ask, "'How can you afford to do this thing on such a magnificent scale?' Our reply at the end of nearly ten years experience is this: 'The City of Chicago cannot afford not to do it.'"[40]

The decline that followed can be attributed, in part, to the structure of park financial arrangements. Because park taxes and bonds have been discretionary—the taxes could vary from year to year—parks have legally been an option, or amenity, not a legal necessity.[41] Further, a recurrent issue in taxation policy has been whether land would be more beneficial to the city by remaining on the tax rolls or, if put to park purposes, by increasing the value of adjacent land. At first no one argued that municipal governments should get into the business of creating parks in order to speculate on land value, but, when New York's Central Park was so successful in precisely these terms, park advocates around the country did not fail to point out this side benefit.[42] Obversely, after the positive effect of parks on property value had stabilized, and parks had failed to stop blight and decline in property value, citizens were no longer so keen on taking potential park land off the tax rolls.

The decline is also to some degree a statistical artifact. Early municipal governments did not spend money except on sewers, roads, and schools, so early park expenditures were a high percentage of municipal monies. As local governments assumed responsibilities for an ever-widening array of social welfare functions, the park proportion declined automatically. Further, parks were once loaded with social tasks now performed by other reform institutions: juvenile courts, public housing, urban planning, pollution control, police.

In any case, after the first flurry of building in the reform era, complaints about the relative decline of park budgets began to appear in the annual reports and in newspapers. During the Depression, despite talk that parks were necessary to sustain morale, park expenditures and income evaporated. Minutes show request after request being denied for lack of funds. Even during the war, when park departments were needed to promote a spirit of calm and combat hysteria, and it was inappropriate that park appropriations should dwindle, they did. In the inflated postwar economy the parks still had to operate with a constant budget. In 1949 a planner for the National Recreation Association discovered that expenditures for parks and recreation by large cities, instead of having increased after the war to reflect increased costs in materials and services, had actually dropped. The per capita expenditure was only "a little more than half the prewar standard."[43] A HUD report on urban recreation in 1972 confirmed what the park departments had said individually and through their own professional literature: while the level of park and recreation expenditures increased continuously from 1955 to 1970, as a percentage of general municipal expenditures park expenditures showed a slow decline, moving from 5 to 4.6 percent.[44]

In the face of declining support from the municipalities, park departments had several routes available to them. One was to go back to relying on private support, especially land transfers. Land unsuitable for other purposes, such as marshes or steep and hilly property, could be donated to the city and taken as a tax deduction. Also, the editor of *Park International* recommended that private lands in congested areas used for park or playground purposes be exempt from taxation or taxed at a low rate.[45] In the 1970s, when some parks departments did not want to add to their overall acreage because of maintenance and money problems, they bought inner city vacant lots, improved them, and then sold them back to the private realm. Land could also be transferred from one city agency to another. For example, in the early days a water reservoir might become obsolete, and, rather than being sold, it would be transferred to the park department. Transfers of land from other uses or jurisdictions might come from dam authorities, drainage channels, freeway rights, unused school property, public housing, or playgrounds.[46]

Sometimes the departments paid for land but at reduced costs, especially during the Depression when property values were at low ebb and in slums where low prices made limited funds go further. Slum clearance eliminated both the problem of clearing the site of buildings and the cost of purchasing them. Joint projects saved money by making schools and community buildings available as field houses at no cost.

By 1935 the federal government had adopted the policy of granting money to states and municipalities for local projects through the Progress Works Administration (PWA) and the Works Progress Administration (WPA). The funds made possible a large amount of new construction and rehabilitation work in many cities.[47] During the war the federal government reduced its financial support, but it never stopped it. (For example, the Lanham Act provided money so that park departments could take care of children after school hours.) The War on Poverty brought money into the park districts for work training in the late 1960s, a practice continued under revenue sharing in the 1970s.

In addition park departments could raise money by generating income internally. This tactic became more popular with park departments after the budget declines of the 1930s, but even before then some revenue was generated internally through small user fees. During the Depression many systems decided to cover the operating costs of swimming pools, beaches, golf courses, and tennis courts through "small reasonable charges."[48] Renting large stadiums like Chicago's Soldier Field or San Francisco's Kezar Stadium also brought monies into the park districts. The great money-maker of the recreation era was the underground parking garage. Most cities had formal parks in their downtown centers conveniently located for parking, and garages placed under Grant Park in Chicago and under Union Square in San Francisco netted their park departments welcomed profits.

In the open-space era gestures have been made toward a new style of park leadership. Advocacy planning and grass roots organization suggest a move toward the convergence of park suppliers and users, on the one hand. On the other, the recent accomplishment of experts in working out complex and original fiscal and legal arrangements for acquiring land and funds for operations suggest a continuation and intensification of top-down planning, possible only for insiders with expertise in law, politics, and finance.[49] Parks have widespread support from many social groups; everyone is for them. This means debate is weak, the precise mechanism by which parks could help solve urban problems is often vague, and policy is often misguided; but it also means that there has been and continues to be room for enterprise. For even in bureaucratic settings the same kind of entrepreneurial talents that created the parks in the first place are needed to make things move now. Inspired change agents capable of realizing a vision, even if it takes

American parks were free to the public, whereas European parks often charged an entry fee. Americans, like this naive artist, were proud of this democratic invitation. To this day the association of free admission with democracy hampers park management. 1864. Lewis Miller Collection, Museum of the City of New York.

The need to pay for parks via internal revenues made underground garages attractive to administrators in the 1940s. During World War II women served as garage attendants. Rededication Day, 1942, Union Square. San Francisco Public Library.

shepherding an innovative piece of legislation about unorthodox fiscal packaging through a maze of municipal, state, and federal agencies, are crucial to the future of urban parks in America.

6

Users: Class and Classification

Cities are the epitome of human variety, and the users of urban parks reflect that variety in the range of types, groups, and classes they represent. But from the first, park spokespeople studiously avoided the controversial subject of social or economic class, or handled it by pronouncements of its meaninglessness or neutralization within park boundaries.

This neutralization, in fact, was an important element in early park ideology. Urbanists saw the pleasure ground as an important arena for the preservation of democracy, since in it people from different walks of life could rub shoulders and dissipate class hostilities and rivalries. The miniature yacht club of Spreckels Lake in Golden Gate Park would help integrate age and class groups: "In the common week-a-day life the commodore is the capitalist and the sailor is a 'gas man.' . . . But when these two men . . . meet on Sunday on the shore of Spreckels Lake with their boats tucked under their arms ready for action, they come together as two swaggering boys. There is no pride of ancestry or joy in being a millionaire nor misery in having to serve."[1]

Of course, this mingling of the classes was not supposed to yield an average, but rather elevate the lower classes to the level of taste and standard of the middle and upper-middle classes. Parks would equalize up, not down.[2] For this reason the park leadership closed their eyes to lower-class tastes, or at least assumed that they were born of necessity, not true preferences. Because of this blindness critics could charge that parks were designed to attract those who did not need them, and machine politicians, voicing the preferences of the working-class immigrant for entertainment, could sneer at the Greensward Ring for bamboozling the citizens with "babble . . . about esthetics and architecture, vistas and landscapes, the quiver of a leaf and the proper blending of light and shade."[3]

But even in discussions of this policy of mixing and uplifting, park commissioners tended to minimize the importance of social classes, and, whenever they could, they denied their effective existence altogether: "It should be noted that the parks are not for any particular 'class'—so called. The objectionable term 'poorer classes' has been used without a proper regard to the meaning of the words, or the odious distinction which they imply. In this land, thank Heaven! the people are not divided into classes."[4]

Despite this, however, the amount of attention paid to the laboring class, the toiling population, the working folk, those who must come on foot, those from least favored quarters, boys in the small salary brackets was disproportionate to the amount devoted to other classes: "The park is a priceless boon to the weak and invalid of all classes, but particularly to the poor."[5] This was especially the case, of course, during the reform era, when the chief rationale for the extension of park services to new sites was to locate them closer to the poor and manufacturing classes.[6] In general the poor have been major users of park services, and their welfare the chief overt concern of park officials. And at times their control has been the chief unadmitted purpose of park policy. Their existence is silently acknowledged at the very gates of parks: park advocates justified free admission as a way to demonstrate their democratic character, and those of limited means benefited in particular:

The man with a small purse and a large family should be made to feel that he has an equal interest with his richer neighbor in this one spot of the earth's surface. This equal-

The Hydrant water pluck. Pump and pipe, drinking
the good water, out of the cup.

Top:
Thanks to the temperance movement, American parks have drinking fountains to offer the working man an alternative to eating his lunch in a saloon. Lewis Miller Collection, Museum of the City of New York.

Bottom:
Dramatizations of national and local history and other types of pageantry like maypole dances were appropriate to the sensibilities of the working class, whereas fine arts and museums were not. Eckhart Park, Chicago, ca. 1915.

ity can only be assured by demonetizing money at the entrance to the park. The procession of fine turnouts and of fashionably dressed pedestrians does not inspire a sense of inequality so long as appeals are not made for expenditures which the poor man cannot afford.[7]

In the pleasure ground the rich had their place in the park, at least as models of decorum and taste. In fact, this role was substantially more. The pleasure grounds so appealed as a place of promenade to the middle class, that the reform minded worried about the working class feeling uncomfortable there. Idealizing the expenditure of public money for the less favored was easier than explaining the trickle-down economic benefits of keeping the middle class in the city. As a result in the twentieth century park policy evolved to the point that the rich were almost unwelcome:

In fact, if there is any part of the whole public to which the parks are less importantly related than any other part, it is to the group of well-to-do citizens for whom almost exclusively the earlier parks were made. . . . I do not in the least object to the use of the parks by the men, women, boys, and girls who have homes with park-like surroundings and facilities, but I consider that a mere adjunct to the use of the parks by the vastly greater percentage of the population which cannot so provide itself with recreational facilities.[8]

Starting in the 1920s, and intensifying after World War II, the middle class took care of itself by moving to the suburbs, and the city park became the almost exclusive domain of the poor.

Commissioners reluctant to acknowledge the existence of the class system readily bracketed the poor with the other social groups in the broader, less problematic category of the weak. In this way they would deflect attention away from social class toward groups who are generally defined biologically—children, the elderly, the handicapped. This biological array, moreover, can be expanded: adults, adolescents, and elderly offer a continuum of age; the elderly and the handicapped add the dimension of physical disability; and racial and ethnic categories and gender continue the biological bias. Lumped with these groups, the poor seems almost a biological classification; biological reductionism

This lithograph of the mineral water concession in Central Park shows the ideal of use by all ages and both sexes together.

lends an apparent rationality to, and hence legitimizes, social stereotyping. This is by no means the only instance of American culture turning to biology to justify its social arrangements.

Families, Children, and Adolescents

The family, at once a social and a biological entity, was the focus of pleasure ground programming. It also fell within the domain of the weak, since many observers noted that prostitution, alcoholism, the popularity of the saloon, and boarding-house living were eroding its stability. The park was accordingly a place for families to do more together, and for family life to be strengthened. Without a park a working man would take his pleasures on his own, in saloons or worse; with it he could take his family along. The same people who promoted use of the pleasure grounds by family groups approved of larger urban groups—church, school, and club—having picnics. Like the family such groups, whether related by kinship or not, were based on organic social relations rather than strictly instrumental business relations.

But during the next era, although three generations of one family might participate in park activities, they probably would not come face to face. In one reform park a boy would be on a basketball team, his father on the businessmen's volleyball team, and his grandfather a horseshoe pitcher, but they were all "working together, each in his own sport and capacity, to gain points for their park in the supremacy battle."[9] The age and sex segregation of the reform park era was not relaxed, until the next era when recreationists placed a renewed emphasis on the family: "recreation in family groups or small parties as opposed to that of the intensive, mass type."[10] Newspapers assisted by referring to the existing field houses as family centers.

Pleasure ground theorists usually assumed that children would use the parks as members of family groups—for Hor-

Planners approved of natural groups like this Sunday school class using the pleasure grounds. Ravenna Park, Seattle, ca. 1894. University of Washington Library.

Top:
The reform park accepted and rationalized industrial order via age and sex segregation, organization of activity, and utilitarian architecture. Field house, Seward Park, Chicago, ca. 1915.

Bottom:
Males and females were assigned separate days and hours for pool use. Girls' play area, ca. 1908, from *American Playgrounds*, p. 35.

ace Bushnell and other nineteenth-century thinkers, the way to reach a child was through the family. When children's activities were singled out, they tended to be unstructured, indulgent, or fantastic—treats of the kind adults have often used to pacify children in tow. An outing to a park would provide novelty and entertainment, where goat carriages and the carousel were popular rides. Menageries were popular, as were elephant and camel rides. A play environment for children within the borders of Golden Gate Park was oriented toward children's entertainment, unlike the reform style playgrounds that followed. The *Call* characterized it as "a Coney Island in miniature; with every out-of-door device for a child's amusement that has ever been thought."[11] Superintendent William Hammond Hall had proposed a children's quarter and dairy, and, when Senator William Sharon died and left a large bequest to the park, the commissioners convinced his heirs to build a modified version of Hall's plan for a children's building and playground,

> . . . quite a boon for some little ones whose parents do not like to have them on the street, and whose chance of a good frolic in the open air is therefore rare. Lots of little girls never have an opportunity of running races with each other or playing with a skipping rope, or giving their muscles exercise or their lungs a chance to expand, just for want of such a place as this.[12]

Meanwhile, settlement house workers and other reformers had been agitating for playgrounds just for children as early as the 1880s. Reformers added a developmental rationale by the turn of the century, and park documents began to be filled with claims that play was a child's work, a natural instinct which, if thwarted, would lead to delinquency and crime. Through properly supervised play, children would gain respect for property, help maintain public safety, and enforce law and order. The nation would be the ultimate beneficiary, and, as such, it properly took responsibility for developing children's abilities just as it protected and developed national resources like lumber and water. Park literature of the reform period described the rotation of children through the playground and field house as if they were crops with a concern for conserving this resource and maximizing the yield.

The developmental theory of the reform era promoted age and sex segregation and dictated many special activities just for children: special gymnasium classes, children's choruses, special juvenile sections of the field house branch libraries, vegetable gardening.[13] The recreation facility of the succeeding era was less child-oriented and more for adults. Park literature of the era was dotted with the phrase "recreation for all ages." Yet, while the recreation era did not particularly promote social reform, the child was still considered an effective vehicle for socialization: "through the play interests of the child, it is possible to instill and nurture habits of thought and action which are difficult to cultivate by precept alone."[14] During this period federal agencies expanded their involvement in children's affairs through the Children's Bureau within the Department of Health, Education and Welfare.[15] And in the ensuing era of the open-space ideology even the adventure playground, which seemed antithetical to the spirit of such engineering, had its instrumental side: it was supposed to help children discover their own physical resources, provide separate areas for different age children to facilitate their different interests, and give children a sense of independence from their parents without making parental supervision any more difficult.[16] These characteristics actually are not much different from those of the nineteenth-century Sharon Building in Golden Gate Park.

The vest-pocket park of open-space philosophy, like Paley Park in midtown Manhattan, is an oasis for the urban adult. But adults, as park users, have seldom been singled out for special attention, perhaps because they are not one of the armies of the weak. Their use of parks has been planned, scheduled, accommodated, and taken for granted; it has never been problematic.

The same cannot be said for adolescents. As the proportion of boarders and servants dropped throughout the nineteenth century, the proportion of teenagers living at home and going to school increased. This trend eventually provided the social basis for the concept of adolescence, but in the meantime youth were in an ambivalent position, and their semi-autonomy was a source of common concern. Park reports were ambivalent about where to draw the line between children and adults, the new category repeatedly going in and out of focus and changing its boundaries. Up through the 1920s eighteen- and even twenty-year-olds by and large were considered working persons, or children of larger growth, young people, older boys and girls already in business.

The terms adolescent and teenager only gained currency in the 1940s, when the category finally congealed. In 1941 the American Youth Commission prepared a report, *Time on Their Hands*, concerning the leisure and recreation of young people. The report legitimized and defined the area of adolescent recreation and chastized the adult portion of society for letting youth find their own solitary recreation and depend too largely on spectator sports, reading, movies, and the radio.[17] The report singled out disadvantaged youth for special attention: rural immigrants, the poor, girls, blacks, and other minorities.

Following this report, delinquency came to be generally perceived with greater seriousness, and local park reports began to list it as a major social problem.[18] One solution of the 1940s was a special environment for teenagers, "a rendezvous to call their own" with lounge chairs, reading tables, a jukebox, a piano, game tables, and a soft drink corner.[19] These teen centers were purposely organized as junior nightclubs—a rare park concession to popular culture—where teenagers could "cut a rug, swing it solid, and enjoy a coke."[20] Because their association with delinquents and the underprivileged undermined them, they have been replaced by special programs for teens organized around particular activities—tennis, music lessons, judo.

The Elderly and the Handicapped

As a special group, old people received minimal attention in park planning until the 1950s. In the nineteenth century parks were thought to be especially helpful for all weak and invalid people, from women and children to the elderly. Benches at view spots and as rests along long paths met the needs of this entire undifferentiated group. In the reform era designers had to remind one another not to overlook quiet places for the weak in the furor of accommodating active, outdoor recreation. But the anticipated increase in the proportion of the elderly in the population began to compete with the teenage delinquency problem as a focus of park programming after 1945.[21] In 1950 a National Conference on Aging exhorted recreation leaders to take stock of their responsibilities toward the elderly, and in 1961, the White House Conference on Aging generated a series of official recommendations which park districts hoped to be able to follow to meet the needs of older persons.

Just as recognition of adolescents as a distinct category generated its unique building type, so the new recognition of the elderly produced the senior center. Often existing buildings, such as the white elephant bathhouse at Aquatic Park in San Francisco, were converted into senior recreation centers; the old police academy in Golden Gate Park was renovated for use as a senior center in 1965. The elderly merited their own special equipment: tables for checkers, shuffle boards, paddle tennis courts, handball, horseshoes, tennis, bocce, croquet, badminton, and volleyball. They were expected to participate in crafts, games, group sessions, movies, community singing, folk dancing, ballroom dancing, and senior citizen picnics.

The new recreationists wanted to take recreation for the aged out of the realm of the rocking chair, the newspaper, and knitting needles and yarn and to avoid the association of parks with an image of despondency—of neglected senior citizens with nothing to do but sit in the park.[22] But the idea of the weak has so thoroughly permeated park planners' thinking that, despite all the talk about how old people could be as sprightly and as vigorous as other age groups, they have often been mentioned in the same breath with the mentally retarded and the physically handicapped.

Park records acknowledged the existence of cripples, unfortunates, and handicaps as early as the reform era. The crippled were allowed to run small concessions with an income of under $1,000 in New York's parks in 1915 to make them self-supporting and keep them from becoming public charges. But earning an income was benefit enough: no special programming was offered them. Special programs for handicapped children emerged in the 1920s. Crafts allowed children who might not be able to play physical sports to take part; and some special physical features were designed for crippled children, especially swimming pools and school gardens with special railings. As with the elderly it was not until the recreation era that the handicapped were mentioned repeatedly in park literature and that special programs were devised just for them. This increased attention led to differentiation: the blind were distinguished from the deaf, and both were distinguished from the crippled and those with cerebral palsy. Differentiation led to still further programming. For example, in 1946 a special day camp program was devised to join disabled and able-bodied Chicago children in activities together. Day camps for crippled chilren were successful enough so that the Chicago department initiated others for blind boy scouts, polio victims, and the aged. Fragrant gardens were proposed in the mid-1950s and elaborated in the mid-1960s: stakes labeled in Braille taught the blind about the plants, where before the fragrance was assumed to be enough. In 1977 New York City sponsored a competition for the design of innovative environments that could be used by both handicapped and normal children.

Those handicapped mentally have been probably the most discriminated against and feared of all the handicapped, and attention to them by park programmers has come last. The first sports event exclusively for mentally retarded children was held in 1968 in Soldier Field, and the New York parks had a celebration for the retarded in the 1970s. The first special olympics for the handicapped were held in San Francisco's Kezar Stadium and Balboa Pool in 1976.

Ethnic and Racial Groups

Serving the groups defined by stages in the life cycle contributed indirectly to collective welfare, but mainly it benefited them directly, as users. Women and minorities, in contrast, have been served in park districts mostly to achieve other ends, in particular societal stability.

Park response to racial and ethnic issues has been checkered; only sporadically have park officials showed regard for these populations as users in their own right. Nineteenth-century park documents did not mention race and ethnicity, but we know from other sources that the practice of segregation, "an elaborate system of public etiquette to maintain racial deference," was common.[23] In theory the pleasure ground brought all different sectors of society, presumably including its racial and ethnic components, together, but the practice of racial segregation was so unquestioned that officials did not need to call attention to it in any way.

The reform park assumed racial segregation but was explicitly opposed to ethnic segregation. The tenement-based park was touted adamantly as an agent of social and cultural integration, and its first emphasis was on the assimilation of immigrants into American culture: "Late arrivals to our shores, and the first generation of foreigners of almost every country, are meeting on common ground in the new parks and are having America interpreted to them in a helpful manner, either directly or through their children's relations to the organized work in which they are involved."[24] When the administrators began collecting statistics on the population they were serving, the distribution of nationalities was one of their primary variables. The rec-

Ethnic discrimination has pervaded park programming and was especially explicit during World War II, when the popular Japanese Tea Garden from the Midwinter Fair of 1894 in San Francisco was taken away from its Japanese owners and renamed the "Oriental Tea Garden." 1941. San Francisco Public Library.

The German community is out, despite the rain, to witness the unveiling of the Schiller Monument. Each ethnic group wanted statues of its cultural heroes installed in city parks, much to the dismay of pleasure ground purists. 1886, Lincoln Park. Courtesy Chicago Historical Society.

reation workers of the period, like settlement house workers, singled out the foreign-born for home visits. Use of the early field houses by Jews, Italians, and blacks made them cosmopolitan.[25] Park commissioners themselves described the reform park as a melting pot.[26]

Reform park leaders intended to bring all ethnic groups into the inner-city park to aid in the process of cultural assimilation, but certain parks became known as the province of one ethnic group or another. These unwritten codes contradicted official theory and policy, and in practice, rather than emphasizing Americanism and the bridge between ethnic groups, parks raised and heightened the issue of ethnicity for average citizens.

Reform parks located within working-class districts were often the setting for racial conflicts. Minorities had to interact with one another in the public parks, and during a period of neighborhood change the park became a tension zone in which the resistance of the older population toward the newcomers was expressed. Older residents of Seward Park in Chicago reported stories of pitched battles between such groups, centering around the use of the playground, gymnasium, and showers.

Pressure from the black community for unrestricted uses of beaches, pools, and parks became an area of continuous friction. The generally understood divisions between white and black swimming places at beaches, for example, were a source of tension from World War I through World War II. Race riots often began on Sundays and holidays at beaches and recreational resorts. Even after World War II, when the new consciousness tried to make sure that park services were nonprejudiced, certain parks were still considered black parks. The proposal to put the vocational high school in Washington Park, for example, was criticized because "Negroes need their recreational space."[27] By the 1950s authorities preferred euphemisms: "Work started on construction of [a] new field house in Washington Park which will serve one of the most congested areas in the city."[28]

The historian has to keep a sharp eye out for official attitudes regarding black users. Nineteenth-century documents do not refer to race, though documents from the reform era begin to do so. Annual reports rarely included photographs of black children, and the few examples are racist. One bears the caption "Historic Pageant, Central Park, 'O! That Watermelon.' under the direction of the Bureau of Recreation."[29] The children's props include straw hats, banjos, and huge slices, of course, of watermelon. Four black girls tending plots in the children's garden at DeWitt-Clinton Park deserved special mention because, this neighborhood like others in New York, Chicago and San Francisco, had never before allowed "colored children to come through the streets . . . without molestation."[30]

The black community itself had not been indifferent to years of neglect. In the 1910s Harlem residents petitioned repeatedly for a playground to replace the play streets developed by welfare organizations.[31] But only in this decade did recreationists begin to attend conferences on race betterment, and not until 1920 did the professional park literature devote a lengthy article to recreation for the black man, only "lately" having heard "of his need for recreation," having long assumed "that the 'colored man' has not time for play either in youth or thereafter."[32] Nearly all attention to the recreational needs of black people was through segregated facilities, and there were few even of them. Taken together, the 108 segregated facilities for colored children and the integrated playgrounds of fourteen cities amounted to only 3 percent of all playgrounds in the United States.[33] The 1932 yearbook of the National Recreation Association reported that of 606 recreation buildings in 203 cities, 33 were set aside especially for colored people—at best a 5 percent figure.[34]

The NRA established a Bureau of Colored Work shortly after the First World War to awaken many communities to the fact that, "for the colored soldier, the facilities were, at first, zero."[35] During World War II black people were gingerly acknowledged: a special study of their social conditions, mention of a black community representative at a board meeting, appointment of a black director, citywide celebration of a black culture event. But despite these wartime liberalities, the national literature treated the issue of black recreation obliquely. One article was devoted entirely to the account of a black police officer helping black children, but without one explicit reference to their race: only the photograph revealed whom the policeman had been helping.[36] General park policy at this time turned away from ethnicity and race toward interest groups: "we found people responding to subjects which appealed to them as individuals but made them part of a community group, club, or team."[37]

Until the open-space era few leaders could face the issue, being unable to use the same melting-pot rhetoric about uniting blacks and whites that they had used in talking about Italians and Scandinavians or, in fact, to point to any particular function that parks performed for society in regard to racial problems. The truth was that parks had been a battleground between the races since the late 1910s. In the open-space era, however, administrators began to claim that they could use them as a way to keep the city "cool"—to keep ghetto youths quiet and satisfied. This was no melting-pot rhetoric and involved no ideal nor practical aim of socialization. It involved nothing about white and black values melding. In a carry-over of the spirit of the recreation era, the park was simply a facility for the use of free time, in this case the free time of angry, potentially violent black youths.

One can easily characterize this maneuver cynically as still another undignified manipulation of images of the park to maintain the status quo. (When immigrants of a white racial stock are supposed to be assimilated into the dominant culture, the park socializes them; when the shorter workweek introduced in the late thirties gives people potentially disruptive time on their hands, then the park fills it up harmlessly; and when blacks riot, the park pacifies them.)

But indubitably the shift in images of the park signifies a genuine shift in the conception of it, from a rather intimate agent of socialization to a public service to be rendered bureaucratically, democratically, and in a spirit indifferent to local community standards or prejudice. If these words are reminiscent of the recreation facility, one of the hallmarks of the open-space era has been a renewed effort to conform to a democratic conception of public life.

In particular, and albeit partly in response to legal challenges, park administrators tried seriously to take a stand against racial discrimination. This was reflected by such small details as the use of photographs in the annual reports showing black and white children playing together rather than in their own separate play groups.[38] From one point of view such acts have been totems, but they have been pointed enough, at least, to bring down white backlash of the sort the Lindsay administration suffered in 1969. In fact, park administrators have been in a double bind: if they ignored blacks, they could be charged with complacency and discrimination; if they devised special activities for them, they could be accused of malicious social control.

In any case the black population had become an explicit and legitimate, if controversial, beneficiary of park programming by the beginning of the open-space era. But by the 1960s the new problematic minority in New York, at least from the vantage point of the dominant culture, was the Puerto Ricans. Accordingly, the revitalized programming of the open-space model included performing arts, music, and food calculated to appeal to Spanish-speaking people. Some advocated that park leadership, not only programming, be changed to accommodate Puerto Rican people, on the grounds that white middle-class supervisors could not easily communicate with or know the needs of residents in "underprivileged, inner-city neighborhoods"—the 1960s code word for poor ghetto residents, usually black or Puerto Rican. Self-styled community organizers would be more in touch with "nitty-gritty" problems.[39]

Women

The importance of the family to pleasure ground planners, and women's central role in the family, guaranteed that the parks of the era would be designed with women in mind.[40] "A large use of the park by families, by good women and dutiful children," would set a tone that would demand high standards for public behavior from everyone.[41] Accordingly, parks had to be respectable settings for middle-class women, safe resorts for unprotected ladies, women, mothers, wives, and children. Therefore refreshments were ideally nonalcoholic, although municipalites experimented with wine and beer to broaden the appeal of park restaurants; and prostitutes were automatically excluded from park life.

A woman's ideal role was as a stabilizing presence, not as a user of facilities for games and sports; but in fact, women, especially young women, were responsible for much of the burgeoning interest in athletics. In the 1890s they began to play lawn tennis, croquet, and basketball and to ride bicycles. Newspapers responded with disbelief and disdain but noted that women used park facilities more than men did.[42] Artists, like park planners, confirmed the ideal: their paintings and lithographs show women tied to the family and their men while extending a calming presence on the public scene. But in early photographs the ideal was betrayed by reality: women are seen in pairs, teaching each other how to skate or fixing their own bicyles and equipment without help from men.[43]

Reform park promoters wanted to use the park to assimilate immigrants, reduce nervousness, and fight delinquency, and park departments all around the country took special pride in the potential of the park movement to reduce juvenile delinquency. But since this problem was defined by and large as a male problem, park administrators did not even collect statistics for girl offenders. They pointed to the dramatic increase in the number of girls and women involved in active sports, but this was largely a matter of finally acknowledging what had long been going on and was now accelerating. Thus official policy edged toward treating women as users in their own right, not primarily as instruments through which to influence men's behavior.

The age and sexual segregation of the playgrounds of the reform era affected women's park experience. The outdoor gymnastic equipment for men and women was located at opposite ends of the park, with a building or trees, shrubbery, and lawns in between. A fence concealed by shrubbery enclosed the women's area. A recurrent specification in reform park reports was that areas of a park, and especially benches, should be reserved exclusively for the use of women and their children.[44] The public baths were available to women on a limited basis: "provision was also made for their use by women during certain restricted periods."[45] Generally, women had two days and nights each week, whereas boys and men got three days and nights. In the 1920s, when mixed bathing was finally allowed in pools, attendance increased.

Sexual segregation, sex-role stereotyping, and unequal treatment to the point of discrimination have always been closely linked. The theoretical rationale for separating boys and girls, that they were different, has guaranteed that treatment of the sexes would not be equal, that, for example, boys had a larger playground than girls. Thus the prevailing attitude that women's ultimate goal was marriage and motherhood meant that athletic activity for women and girls had to be justified in terms of improved health for the sake of motherhood. Even when the public record acknowledged that girls had a competitive spirit and might like to join in athletic contests, because of the widespread opinion that respectable girls could not appear in public without supervision their tournaments still had to be held under special conditions. This was the case even after World War I, when park planners began to recognize that girls needed more freedom to indulge in a wider range of sports.

But even though park programming reinforced stereotypes, it managed to threaten them. The sheer fact of accommodating females, separate or not, suggested that their need for recreation was similar to males', and the vigor with which they pursued activities must have laid many ideas about female passivity to rest.

Sex-role segregation began to wane in the era of the recreation facility. The practice of designing special sections of the park, playground, or bench for females dwindled, and planners included more types of females in more types of activities.[46] Park departments concluded that "co-recreation parties have greater appeal than when segregation of the sexes is enforced"—the pragmatic impetus toward sex-role integration was that park departments wanted to increase their attendance figures.[47] But ideology soon reinforced pragmatism: emphasis in the 1950s on family togetherness, the idea that Mom, Pop, and the kids must do things as a group, pushed the parks full circle back to pleasure garden attitudes toward the family, and recreation theorists came out for keeping the family together instead of separating it into skill and age groups.[48]

As women came to be perceived as less distinctive, less in need of protection, the literature no longer insisted that they should not go out alone in public. But apparently objective conditions did not change, for complaints regarding offenses against women became more frequent. Despite the decrease in sexual segregation, sex-role stereotyping did not, in fact, decline. By the end of World War II, for example, public relations had reached a peak, and programming a nadir; for example, to reverse the wartime image of women as workers, the first park publicity photographs of women in sexually alluring poses appeared at this time.[49]

Implicitly, the goal of central-city revitalization during the open-space era focused on middle-class users—the businessmen and -women on their lunch breaks from downtown offices and the suburban shoppers being courted back to the central business district. Thus the needs of middle-class women for a safe and attractive urban environment have had a large influence on recent park planning for adults. The concern for riot control in the late 1960s meant that ghetto youth were also a target population for park departments. Planners seldom needed to explain that ghetto youth were black adolescent males, and girls' recreational needs have not been enunciated clearly in this era. In general, although women's athletic needs have now been acknowledged by maintaining separate programs in volleyball, basketball, and softball and adding belly dancing and yoga classes, park programming has remained predominantly male oriented.

7

Benefits and Use

Social Benefits

The public park movement has been an experiment in collective reform and expenditure. Individual experience in the parks has ultimately been a means to collective ends. But, when park advocates describe the benefits of parks, they invariably dwell on concrete outcomes for specific types of users, not intangible ones for the social system as a whole. They point to a man in a park filling his lungs with fresh air to suggest to the taxpayers that they will not have to support as many hospitals if they support parks but are unlikely to explore basic public health questions much further, or systematically.[1]

This attachment to the tangible stems from conventional American individualism and the simple additive model of social life that goes with it. A more complex, interactive model would lead to a greater concern for intangibles. In the conventional American view, recreation is a good in itself, of value to the individual user of park services, and only thus of value to society— "in that the welfare of society is the sum of the welfare of its members."[2] The individual is conceptualized as a small circle within a larger set of circles—the small group, the neighborhood, the community, and in later years the world. Thus social welfare has largely been a matter of everybody or many benefiting, as in the Currier and Ives Culverhouse painting, "The Central Park, New York" (1871) by Charles Rosenberg, which depicts this additive formula visually: a bum, a black nanny with a white child, a family group of three adults and three children, a young couple, many groups in the background, two with walking sticks, some under a canopy. The social benefits of the urban park as depicted in park documents and pronouncements inevitably focus on the users and uses of park services.

The park programming of one era, carried on to the next without any objective change, sometimes contains a change in the meaning attributed to it. Baseball filled idle hours during the Depression, but during World War II it relieved tension, built morale, and created a feeling of solidarity. Changes in meaning of this kind usually have a systematic basis—they are symptoms of large shifts in the overall reckoning of the public good. But park officials have seldom been given to such overall assessment. The existing theory about the larger social purposes of parks, which has focused on the urban economy, public health, and socialization, has been naive and almost offhand.

Beautiful parks make a city more attractive, which is to say, they make a city more of an attraction. When what is attracted to the city is money, in one form or another, then the beauty of the parks can be argued to be of particular social benefit, and anyone to whom this money trickles down is likely to agree. During the pleasure ground era, it was a truism that a town beautified by parks would create a better working environment and thus be of legitimate benefit to business. But by the time of the recreation era the financial benfits to the city of parks had become dubious, and it was widely believed that parks might be more of a drain on the tax roll than an asset. In 1962 Jane Jacobs challenged even the long-standing assumption that parks increased or at least stabilized adjoining real estate values, arguing that a park in itself would not stabilize an otherwise declining neighborhood.[3] Nevertheless, ten years later new parks were still being advocated as a way to revitalize neighborhoods economically and stimulate the surrounding business district.[4]

The inflation of real estate values around new park sites has rightly been considered of benefit only to the real estate speculators who profit from it, but the stabilization of values around parks in declining neighborhoods, and the revitalization of those neighborhoods, clearly provides economic benefits for the city as a whole by holding, and attracting back to it, people with money to invest and spend. The nineteenth-century counterpart of this contemporary development was the role attributed to the big parks in holding and attracting wealthy residents to the cities. The rich of the last century often summered outside of cities, and some moved to Europe permanently. For this reason park reports presented parks as an inducement to "persons of wealth and leisure, from all parts of the world, to make the metropolis the place of their residence."[5] The economic benefits of keeping wealthy people in the city were savored by park advocates: thousands spent upon servants, carriages, livery, and maintenance.

Tourism was another great source of revenue for the city as a whole which parks could stimulate. As soon as Central Park was established, published tourist guides attest to the fact that it became a tourist attraction.[6] The San Francisco Conservatory housed the giant water lily Victoria Regina, a favorite tourist attraction. The elaborate floral displays along the main drives to Chicago's South Park system attracted throngs and added "to the already enviable reputation this boulevard has acquired as one of the most beautiful places of the country."[7]

Tourism was of benefit primarily to the business class. Despite the value of attracting and holding visitors, one newspaper cautioned against overdoing the thing and making a lower class of taxpayers feel that the parks were a burden on them for the benefit of the wealthy.[8] But some of the money presumably trickled down, and in any case this sort of admonishment has been rare. The Midwinter Fair of 1894 was welcomed because tourists would "leave at least $5,000,000 of their coin in California."[9] Chicagoans wanted their city to become one of the greatest Meccas in the

Opposite:
Replicas of Columbus's caravels from the World's Columbian Exposition of 1893 became permanent tourist attractions in the Jackson Park Harbor; Golden Gate Park offered a similar replica of a Norwegian explorer ship. Courtesy Chicago Historical Society.

Bottom:
The Lick Conservatory in Golden Gate Park housed these giant Victoria Regina lily pads, popular tourist attractions. Ca. 1900, Golden Gate Park. Courtesy Bancroft Library, University of California, Berkeley.

world for tourists, like Paris, New York City, and Berlin.[10] Attracting professional conventions was recognized as having comparable benefits, and, accordingly, park districts helped organize the activities and the traffic throughout the city and hosted large events and parades on park property itself. San Francisco's Storyland copied the original Fairyland in Oakland to keep tourists coming to San Francisco: the project would "invite, not repel, visitors, giving them cause to use the elaborate system of expensive freeways to come into San Francisco, not detour around them at 55 miles per hour."[11]

After the economic argument, the next most prominent argument in favor of parks has been that they improve public health: via the use of forests and trees to purify air and stop disease, via slum clearance to introduce light and air, via swimming to improve sanitation, and via physical exercise to improve soldiering and keep up morale.

Beyond this the mental health of park users has been the focus of pronouncements during all the eras of park design and programming, and it has been generally assumed that psychological well-being would diffuse and affect the entire population. Pleasure ground spokesmen hoped to establish a mental equilibrium for the public (and impressionable children) through music and the visual organization of landscape elements.[12] Reformers thought that they could achieve the same thing through a combination of vigorous exercise and inspiring moral supervision. Recreationists pointed to the psychological benefits of self-expression through physical activity and hobbies, and open-space advocates hoped to inspire the otherwise dispirited urban dweller with treats and delights.[13] In this intangible area of mental experience, debate is notoriously difficult. Olmsted said that no apothecary shop was as important to health as the nature provided by parks, but he would have been hard pressed to prove his point to a skeptic.

The park was one way to instill certain values related to political life in the young, the poor, and ethnic groups: good citizenship, social consciousness, and the sentiment of democracy. Building a stronger citizenry was a consistent theme through all the park eras. The reform park would accomplish more than the physical betterment of the children of the tenements; it would make children good and patriotic citizens "by teaching love of country in connection with the daily recreation of children."[14] Chicagoans added that the parks offered "the kind of training that assists materially in the development of good American citizens," namely, cooperation, subjection to proper authority, law, and order.[15]

Social consciousness, the opposite of selfishness, was essential to good citizenship and successful democracy. Park authorities asked how the American idea of "rugged individualism denoting selfishness [could] be changed to the ideal of service to society?"[16] In the pleasure ground era, the American Park and Outdoor Art Association argued that "to love trees and shrubs, and open fields, birds and flowers, rivers, lakes, and skies makes a man unselfish."[17] Team sports developed the habit of self-control for the sake of cooperation, solidarity, and mutual obligation. Later programmers claimed that competitive sports laid too much emphasis on personal ambition, narrowed loyalties, and lacked broader social consciousness, and so Chicagoans introduced community leagues to fuse individual and collective interests.

Nineteenth-century theorists like Alexis de Tocqueville believed that civilization worked against democracy because cities had a potential for extremes, which democracy could not tolerate. Thus democracy needed a place—parks—for the extremes to mix as equals. Recreationists construed democracy to mean equality of opportunity, opposition to special privileges for any individual or group, and freedom of choice within the bounds of what was in the interests of the community as a whole. Democracy was also equated with mass participation and with adaptation to existing recreational practices rather than the creation of new ones. It stood for loyal consensus among diverse social groups, "directly opposing foreign aims of 'class consciousness,' that we may render secure and unassailable those unities of purpose which underlie any strong or enduring democracy."[18] Self-control made possible the freedom of self-government. Robert Moses felt that a democratic civilization meant prudent control, regulation in the common interest, purposeful planning: "Parks are the outward visible symbols of democracy. That in my book is what they are for."[19]

Assessing Benefit

Use

Values are hard to measure since they are carried inside persons; they motivate behavior, but they cannot be touched. While self-control learned in a park might reduce the number of people in hospitals and penitentiaries, park advocates have been reluctant to rest their case on such empirical arguments. Partly no doubt to avoid the risk of being proved wrong, they have preferred to think that the social benefits of parks are immeasurable. Reform park advocates cast their pro-park propositions in business language: "every creative effort . . . becomes a paying investment, rendering dividends beyond computation in a useful, happy, contented people."[20] But they did not carry out the implied empirical tests. Even in the more mechanistic recreation era, park advocates liked to think that values, a chief benefit, were immeasurable: "see the professional man working beside the boilermaker . . . see the husband and wife enjoying a good laugh because they got tangled up in the 'allemande left' . . . the proud dad whose son is receiving a trophy for good sportsmanship . . . the paraplegics and polio victims regaining some use of their muscles in our natatoriums. What yardstick can measure these values?"[21] The difficulty of measuring change in a person's mind has undoubtedly led to the split between immeasurable moral influence and measurable changes in attendance or crime rates that characterizes park department thinking, and to the split between so-called passive and active recreation that characterizes park programming.

It has led as well to what seems a largely rhetorical employment of statistics having to do with actual park use. The extent of use has been assumed to be the chief measure of the social benefits of the parks, but, since the benefit is ultimately immeasurable, the actual measuring has been little more than a gesture. In the pleasure ground days Olmsted relied on close observation of people's conduct to determine whether or not the park was having the desired effects. The reputation of the pleasure grounds among tourists was another sign that the parks were successful. The use of attendance figures as a way to point to the effectiveness of an urban park did not emerge until the reform era. When it did, the figures were used uncritically. Park administrators assumed that attendance implied satisfaction and approval on the part of the public; they further assumed that attendance itself meant that the parks were having a beneficial influence on the people who came. Newspapers of the day also assumed that large numbers implied popularity, necessity, usefulness, and significance. Thus reporting an increase in figures of use was in itself reporting something meaningful. By the same token attempts to increase attendance, such as broadening the rules for involvement in competitions by including nature study and crafts as well as athletics, or supplying more particularly popular features like rose gardens or swimming pools, were equivalents to attempts to increase the quality of service. In fact, any attendance figure was a good one, because whoever attended a park benefited, so any figure at all implied some benefit.[22] The only questions had to do with the extent of the benefit.

Chicago was a case in point. In 1905 the liberal use of Chicago's parks confirmed the faith of park administrators in their effectiveness and demonstrated the necessity and the future usefulness of field houses.[23] In 1906 the Chicago Annual Report assumed that "figures speak with significance"[24] The reason that numbers alone were adequate was spelled out in the Chicago South Park Report for 1908:

Crafts, excluded in pleasure ground days as too similar to factory work, became a way for reform park theorists to integrate the unathletic into the local community. Ca. 1915, Chicago.

. . . one cannot read our statistical records and attempt to measure their relation to the civic problems of the day without a feeling of most serious responsibility. Such aggregations of people as are represented in the figures given herewith may not be expected to come and go without receiving definite impressions and without acting and reacting upon each other for good or evil. The very nature of the associations makes for positive rather than negative influences.[25]

The 1937 Chicago report retained these earlier assumptions. The fact that no park in the city has ever shown a falling off in attendance was evidence of constantly growing usefulness.[26] The National Recreation Association yearbooks also started reporting statistics on park use in the 1940s. But the national organizations, like the municipal departments, seldom used attendance figures rationally to sort out priorities among different activities, or as the basis for self-criticism, because their meaning was tied up with the assumption that large numbers were good in themselves.[27] The few exceptions to this rule only exemplify what they might well have done more frequently. For example, a 1912 Chicago report observed that the number of dance halls and poolrooms diminished when reform parks were created in their neighborhoods, and they reported a decrease in infant mortality rates where small parks were established.[28] Another Chicago report from 1937 compared the performance of boys and girls on physical education routines and concluded that children who attended parks did better than school children who did not.[29] For a short period during the Depression, in fact, the statistics were sometimes used imaginatively, as indicators of the more intangible qualities that the parks were meant to facilitate. For example, the Chicago Park District used statistics of clubroom use as their "best barometric index" to the attitude of a community toward itself. By analyzing their statistics according to where people lived, their age, sex, and race, the frequency and purpose of their visits, how long they stayed, and how long they came for what activities, they learned, for example, that people were willing to travel farther to swim in a pool than to participate in any other sport—over half a mile. The result surprised them. In other

the
fish-hawk.
and pigeon hawk.
Eagles
A, View, In the Central Park,
The po-lice Officer, genteelly and polite in his manners,

Left:
Parks have always required policing, despite present-day fear that crime in the parks indicates an unprecedented decline of civilization. The police officer of 1864 was a basic element of the social scene in Central Park.1864. Lewis Miller Collection, Museum of the City of New York.

Dog-walking services made use of Central Park, crystallizing the fear of the mid-1960s that Central Park was unfit for human use. New York City Department of Parks, *Report 1967*.

words, statistics gave rise to new knowledge; they did not merely confirm old myths.

More commonly, however, systematic empirical evaluation of park programming has carried less weight than political demands and pressures from interested groups. Parks have relied on political evaluation of their programs rather than broad-based user evaluation, if only because parks are more useful in the political patronage system than in the electoral process. Yet more than the patronage system, the chief reason for the relative absence of a systematic effort to conduct evaluative research has been a lack of imagination about alternative possibilities which has made such effort seem relatively pointless except as material for park promotion. The internal coherence of the park philosophies of park staffs has largely been its own criterion for success, regardless of whether or not the goods implied by these philosophies have come to pass in practice. A 1961 article in *Recreation* states that the aims and policies of the managing authorities, the money available, the quality of the professional staff, the quality of the recreation facilities, and the quality of the program offer the five criteria by which a program of recreation can best be measured.[30] Money is already quantified, but any effort to quantify the quality of staff, facility, or program is unlikely to get very far when the aims and policies of the managing authorities come first.

Nonuse

Not until the 1970s did people begin to worry that parks, such as Central Park, were being overused and that increasing use led to increased vandalism, even though it decreased the likelihood of the sort of crimes against persons that required a deserted setting.[31]In general use has been good, and more use better. In actual practice, however, parks have not always been used as much as planned, despite the publication of statistics revealing ever-increasing use. In all four park eras park spokespeople have occasionally noted that the parks were "not lived in, and delighted in by any large proportion of the population," and that enjoyment of the public reservations was "surprisingly limited."[32] At the turn of the century occasional comparisons of attendance at Golden Gate Park with attendance at other outdoor amusement areas reveal that the park got a total of 7,000 out of 35,000 pleasure seekers within the city, and the proportion would have dropped further if the numbers who went further afield for recreation had been included in the base.[33] A rare San Franciscan attempted to evaluate the effectiveness of the reform park empirically and concluded that

> . . . public recreation systems are quite ineffective. Not only are they often absent where the dance hall and other commercial amusements flourish, but at best they reach only 2 or 3 per cent of the population, while commercial dancing alone attracts 5 to 8 per cent. . . . The system as a whole offers nothing like the continuous opportunities of the dance hall for *habit forming.*[34]

These figures can be compared with the indirect evidence of where Chicago's ethnic groups celebrated their holidays. The Works Progress Administration Writer's Project translated the foreign language press in Chicago up to 1940; in my sample of six newspapers representing the major ethnic groups in Chicago, a clear pattern emerged: ethnic groups relied as heavily on a combination of private beer gardens, turnvereins, and cemeteries as the settings for holidays and ceremonial occasions as they did on public parks.[35]

In 1945 New York's entertainment magazine *Cue* noted that "people know Central Park and the entire park system are there, but the idea of using it seldom enters their heads."[36] In 1960 another lay critic called it "a source of deep amazement . . . that the park is so little used by the people of the city" except as an escape from heat in summer.[37] Recently, more systematic surveys by behaviorally oriented recreationists, such as Seymour Gold, have revealed that during any normal use period only 1 to 5 percent of the total possible users of a park are using it.[38]

One cannot discuss historical changes in park attendance without trying to assess the effect of crime. Yet sober assessment is next to impossible because reliable and comparable crime statistics were not collected by park departments over time. Most people assume park crime has increased, but no one knows if it has increased disproportionately to the general increase in crime. I suspect that it has not. Crime in parks is particularly troublesome because of the legacy of parks being solutions to and havens from urban problems. The split between real urban environments and ideal park environments makes park offenses outstanding.[39] The shock of unsafe parks is easily exploited by news media, but they cannot be held responsible either for the crime itself or the emotional impact it has, especially in this setting.

Parks were once objects of great interest in their own right. In the nineteenth century tourists made pilgrimages to them—Chicago's floral displays had to be protected from them by ropes—and bought stereopticon slides of them. They took home illustrated music programs as souvenirs.[40] Newspapers regularly covered park events, especially social ones; in San Francisco a Sunday paper had a regular column called "Sunday at the Pleasure Places." Magazines like *Harper's*, *Scribner's*, and *Overland Monthly* liked to print illustrations of park activities and vistas.[41] Clearly, those days are over; interest, not to mention attendance, has shifted. Yet, although Gold rightly criticizes the profession for not looking seriously at the reasons people go elsewhere for entertainment, the relative nonuse of parks is not a social evil in itself. In the nineteenth century illustrations of parks in tourist guides and popular literature typically depicted activities and population diversity—use and users—whereas modern illustrations (like the photograph of Central Park on the 1973 UN Christmas card) show the landscaping of the park, perhaps one of the buildings on its border, and people, if at all, in patterns at a remote distance.[42] This reflects a decline in direct park use. It also reflects a new place that parks have assumed in popular consciousness, as a sort of urban asset or resource, a space permanently full of potential, whether it is put to use or not, for contributions to urban well-being.[43] Many people who use the parks only rarely, "just like to know they are there," would be disturbed if parks were not there, and they consider their lives enhanced because of parks.[44]

A great deal of the sense of well-being is made up of judgments of this kind, especially in the city with its superabundance of amusements, interesting objects, and opportunities. The benefits of the urban park are not only a function of its direct use but also of its place in the consciousness of urban dwellers—one of its indirect uses. Such intangible use could be quantified, measured by surveys, and taken into consideration by planners and policy makers, in the context of a positive and comprehensive vision of the city that encompasses the complementary nature of its various competing attractions, including the parks, and the particular contribution of each to urban well-being.

8

The Role of Parks in the City

The history of the American urban park movement has been considered as a succession of responses to changing ideological currents and as a decline—in the power of park leaders to command resources and in the interest of the general public in the parks themselves (chapter 7). Three other tendencies are also apparent in park history. They reveal the social, political and institutional roles of the park in city life, in turn, useful in formulating policy and guiding action in the near future. The first tendency is another decline in the range of social functions performed by parks. A second is the practice of elites using parks deliberately as mechanisms for solving urban problems, and a third is the dialectical character of the transformation of one park type to another. The decline in the range of functions needs to be appreciated by anyone interested in identifying the territory left to the parks and the functions they can usefully perform in the future. The social control function should be acknowledged so that discussion can focus on the kind of leadership and planning desirable in our time. The dialectical character of park history should also be appreciated, for it indicates the need for park planners to view their own working definitions of park use critically and to develop a fuller comprehension of the interplay between urban groups.

Dialectic Adjustment

The dialectic of park history begins with the ideal of the pleasure grounds to serve all elements of society. Upper- and middle-class domination of the pleasure gardens was the reality, despite lip service to the ideal and the pious hope that the mingling of the classes in the parks would result in the elevation of lower-class manners and morals. This comes out most clearly in contemporaneous discussions of the comparative number of riders and pedestrians in the parks and the means of transportation to and from the parks. In New York, according to a commissioner's report, "From the number of users on foot and in carriages on ordinary days and on Sundays and holidays, it is clear that a great many citizens find the park difficult to access."[1] In San Francisco William Hammond Hall kept statistics on the number of people who came to the park in vehicles, on horseback, or by foot from 1873 through 1880 and concluded that the number of pedestrians was limited because of inadequate public transportation to the park.[2] Since over 90 percent of the 300,000 people in San Francisco were pedestrians rather than horsemen or wheelmen, in 1894 a local newspaper criticized the park commissioners for spending too much for the convenience of vehicles and too little for the comfort of pedestrians. Admitting that "the horses and the carriages and the bicycles are a part of the show that the people on foot go to see," it still judged the one-fourth of the total park area devoted to roads excessive.[3]

Much of the pleasure ground planning simply did not take the details of working-class life into account. For example, the fare to get to the peripheral park locations was exorbitant for working-class families: if a man went to the park with his wife and four children, that could cost each of them 15¢ each way, altogether as much as a day's wages. That limited park usage to special occasions. Further, when people worked six days a week, the time necessary to get out to these locations and back limited excursions to Sunday. Concerts and "fast driving days," however, were often

Unable to justify spending public funds on a clubhouse at the racetrack, the social elite of Chicago built this one with private funds adjacent to Washington Park. Chicago. Courtesy Chicago Historical Society.

Fashionable turnouts could not resist using the fine park roads and boulevards for horse racing. First, fast driving days within the pleasure grounds satisfied them, but soon the social elite agitated for special speedtracks. Derby Day 1903, Washington Park. Courtesy Chicago Historical Society.

scheduled on Thursdays or Saturdays, dictating elite, not mass usage. In 1872 the New York commissioners observed that "except on Sunday and Saturday afternoons and general holidays, the number of residents of the city who come to the park in carriages is larger than of those who come by streetcar or on foot. The value which the mass of community finds in it is, therefore, yet to be seen mainly in its use on other than working days."[4]

Even on Sunday, when the parks were accessible, they could be a source of humiliation. The San Francisco *Report* pointed out that the Sunday assembly in the park was

> also the weekly dress parade of the populace. When it is considered how few opportunities the San Francisco woman, with daily duties to perform, has to show her best clothes, except by a tiresome and unpleasant parade on the streets, and how convenient it is to those thinking of having new clothes made to have a place to go, where all that is latest and prettiest, up to a certain standard in cost, is to be seen, the large attendance in the park concourse can readily be accounted for.[5]

John McLaren worried that this custom of fine dress made the park psychologically out of reach for those people who could not afford the finest clothes: "The immense Sunday crowds which throng the music grounds and immediate neighborhoods of Golden Gate Park are not of poor or distinctly poor working classes . . . They are, by far the larger part, well dressed, even richly dressed in many cases, and the people who most need a park do not feel at ease in such assemblage."[6]

Beyond humiliation there was also an essential lack of appeal. Park commissioners forbade the kinds of athletics and other popular entertainment that enjoyed mass popularity—gambling, animal fighting, vaudeville, minstrels, roller skating. Such prohibitions limited park use by entire ethnic groups, such as the Germans who liked music, dancing, and beer and wine in shady groves. Park policy would not tolerate such celebrations and festivities on Sundays, even though the Germans toiled hard and long on the other six days of the week, so German gymnastic societies countered by constructing buildings with gymnasiums, bars, meeting rooms, and swimming pools.[7] Effectively, if not intentionally, they created their own reform park field houses before the reform era. However seriously the pleasure ground was intended as a melting pot, the immigrants were going elsewhere, and in large numbers refused to melt in.

The evidence of a dialectical process is simply that the reform park was aimed primarily at working-class and immigrant children and was sited in their immediate neighborhoods; the excluded class of one era became the focus of park programming in the next. The principal means of their exclusion—distance from the parks—was addressed directly by the concept of the neighborhood park. To put it another way, the ideal of the pleasure ground era—parks to reach the masses—became the reality of the reform era. Two groups effectively excluded from the reform park—middle class and adults—in turn became the focus of recreation facility programming. When the Chicago field houses were first installed, park reports proudly stated that they served the poorest, least educated members of society. Unwittingly, the focus on poor children had the consequence of discouraging middle-class children from using park facilities. In Chicago, even in the recreation era, annual reports revealed that middle-class children stayed away from some parks and from organized activities and game rooms.[8] They did go skating, but probably because skating lacked the taint of the organized, indoor activities oriented toward molding the needy. The very emphasis on molding went with a playground mentality and a focus on children's programming that tended to exclude adults from the reform parks. Heavy adult use of San Francisco reform parks on weekends, in fact, was cause for comment in commission records.[9]

Effectively excluded from the reform park, the middle class, especially middle-class adults, became a focus of recreation facility programming. The service mentality of the era, the mentality of "something for everyone," had to recognize adult and middle class demands for park services. The recreation facility was a way of taking the idea of the neighborhood park, the park for the whole neighborhood, to its logical conclusion, just as the reform park had been a way of actually implementing the pleasure ground aim of reaching the laboring masses.

"Something for everyone" in turn exposed another exclusion and thus another contradiction. Racial segregation had gone unchallenged in park thinking until after World War II, so in practice equality of park service had meant separate parks, or separate areas in parks. Even segregated facilities, of course, were inadequate in proportion to the black population, and, instead of integrating blacks and whites, or even facilitating coexistence, parks became arenas for racial tensions, as in the Chicago race riots of 1919.[10] Park literature published its first articles on "Playground for Colored Americans" in 1920, and by 1933 Chicago had a "Negro Day" in Soldier Field.[11] The park servicemen's centers of World War II were for whites only, so a special one was added for black service men and women.[12] Throughout the recreation era separate park publicity photographs showed black and white children engaged in their separate activities, and not until the open-space era were black and white children shown together. Accordingly, open-space policy, such as that of Mayor Lindsay's New York City parks, focused on the needs and demands of blacks, principally young black males, at times to the extent of provoking a white backlash. Open-space programming has been hip, in the fashion of black street culture, and open-space design has incorporated or imitated the street itself. It remains to be seen if excluded elements of the urban population will force another revolution in park typology, and what the new type will be.

This kind of dialectic adjustment is a sign of vitality, but it is paralleled by a potentially deadening transformation from crusade to bureaucracy noted by analysts of other urban institutions such as the YMCA, jails, and public hospitals. The pull toward renewal may win, judging by the ideology of the open-space system which has de-emphasized fixed planning standards and emphasized experience, hence the general idea that recreation is wherever one finds it. This fourth phase of park planning suggests that bureaucratic ossification is not inevitable, that organizational regeneration and revitalization can continue.

Park planners' responsiveness, however delayed, to new definitions of their clientele is matched by an adjustment in how they define city problems and cities generally. If the pleasure ground was an antidote, the reform park was a mechanism of social progress, the recreation facility a public service, and the open-space park a stimulant; this is because these were appropriate responses to park planners' changing perceptions of the city. As the president of the American Recreation Society, V. K. Brown, said, "a park system needs a city to serve. How otherwise . . . can parks, like veritable reflector basins, mirror contemporary life and times. Mirror them they must, apparently, that's their history."[13]

In general the changing conceptions of park functions reveal an increasingly positive and optimistic view of cities. Initially, the park elite viewed cities as a necessary evil, a poison to which an antidote was necessary. Only occasionally were the early parks promoted as suitable adornments for the city conceived of as an admirable expression of human activity.[14] Olmsted was characteristically disturbed about views of architecture and commercial life around the periphery of the park. In the park the city was not supposed to exist.[15]

Around the turn of the century park departments began to reveal a more conciliatory tone: "How to reconcile man's late advantages in rural community life with his recent disadvantages of life in the city wilderness are questions which earnest citizens in every large city are pondering . . . the new park facilities spell hope of at least a partial solution of many of these problems."[16] In fact, inasmuch as the reform park was a social center, it would restore the rural sense of community to urban living itself, so that people would no longer need breaks from urbanity.

Meanwhile a new consciousness of the city found its way into reform park pageants. In dance, music, and song children acted out the great waves of immigration, the impact of the great inventions, political high points, and even the development of urban infrastructure, its water supply, rapid transit, and commerce.[17] When the City Beautiful movement codified the idea that cities were perfectable, if only visually and in one place in town, this attitude stimulated park departments to foster the creation of garden clubs which promoted and improved landscaping around homes, private yards, and streets.

During the recreation era parks were used mechanically, to complete the definition of a neighborhood. The enlarged idea of the parks system, rather than individual parks, contributed to the evolution of comprehensive, community-based city planning.[18] The basic outlines of the city were accepted as they were, and the city began to take on a new meaning, as a vehicle for the advancement of national well-being. Parks became a primary conduit for federal funds.[19] Park-planning theory assumed that parks could be distributed throughout the city according to some uniform standard. Planners assumed that they could add and subtract parts of a city of which they had, for the first time, a bird's-eye view, and that mere equal distribution itself was a worthy goal.[20] Parks, if assembled together in the proper proportion with other urban elements—housing, business, sewage, streets and other transportation networks, schools, hospitals—would yield a neighborhood.

What with reduced park maintenance and the urban crime problem after World War II, critics noticed that the parks were dying, and park professionals picked up on the idea that the rejuvenation of the big city parks would depend on the rebirth of the city itself. This reflected a growing awareness that the public park, more than any other component of the city, reflects the life and vitality of the city and its people.[21] Thus along with a grim assessment of the current urban scene a more organic and, in the long run, optimistic idea of the city was emerging. This new, increasingly comprehensive idea of the city surfaced in the mid-1960s, as the open-space ideology. It was in this new spirit that in 1964 President Lyndon Johnson could invoke Aristotle: "Men come together in cities in order to live, but they remain in order to live the good life."[22] The good life uniquely possible in the city encompassed social groups larger than the family, the target of pleasure ground policy, or the neighborhood which was the focus of the reform park and recreation facility. The idea of networking not only ruled the spatial organization of open-space planning but also its vision of social organization. The open-space system was premised on a new version of the old idea of public man. And the new park was specifically a place to be "in public," where we are related to other people even though we do not necessarily know them personally nor even feel some bond of neighborhood or mutuality with them.[23] But though the new parks were public spaces, they were hardly forums, and public man was not meant to be as he had been in ancient Athens, conversing, debating, and contending for public honor. Public man was more of a contemplative, and the city was now conceived of as an art form in itself. Social life, civilization itself, had become an object of appreciation, and the intricate forms and juxtapositions generated by an active industrial and commercial culture came to be judged according to aesthetic criteria. With this new appreciation of the city as an artifact, Central Park became significant in a new way, in that it was the only place "from which the dream of Manhattan is wholly visible because the eye has room to embrace it and the heart the distance to love it."[24]

A dream of Manhattan suggests a nostalgic reverie, and the fact that the goal of open-space planning has characteristically been specified as revitalization points to the centrality of nostalgia in the spirit of the movement. Nowhere has park literature revealed a flowering of mature satisfaction with urban life, and a skeptic might well argue that we should now be speaking of the possibility of urban vitality, since it is a stage that we so far have overlooked. In other words, the wishful positives of much current park thinking can sometimes seem fairly empty. Park thinking from this vantage point has reverted, with nostalgia for the city that never was replacing nostalgia for nature uncorrupted by cities and the aestheticizing of the city replacing the aestheticizing of terrain and vegetation. This reversion is in keeping with the fact that park thinking about the city has never changed fundamentally. Park thinking has never really questioned, or engaged critically, the drive for short-term profits associated with a capitalist social organization, or the urban realities resulting from it. The pleasure ground was a moderate reform; it was stronger than simply beautifying streets through a tree-planting program but weaker than regulatory zoning regarding housing and land use, which would have been possible only if the power of private capital had been radically limited. If the reform park was more integrated with working-class culture than the pleasure ground had been, it was never intended to be entirely integrated. The new neighborhood parks were close enough to the people to reach and reform them but not close enough to be fully assimilated into working-class life and become an expression of working-class consciousness. No modern park planner has advocated abandoning efforts to create parks until everyone has clean, well-ventilated, spacious housing, even though modern technology makes that goal a realistic one. Happy litanies about the continuity of human activities in parks—children watching squirrels, mothers and couples dotting the landscape, games of baseball—remind us that one hundred years makes no difference to a park, and that city life too is timeless; but this sort of reverie tends to close the horizon of the mind to speculations about what cities might have been, or might be, if they were the expression of a different kind of social system.[25]

Whatever optimism is justified by the parks' responsiveness to urban problems and changing conceptions of the city has to be guarded. Parks may be responsive, but they are extremely slow in their adjustments to social change. To be considered relevant to politics and planning, they should respond more quickly, and they might incorporate citizen demand and evaluation in a more participatory mode of planning. The issue of planning style is tied up with the history of attempts to use parks as a mechanism of social control.

Social Control and Policy

The term social control was coined by the sociologist Edward Ross in 1901, and it crystallized an attitude toward social planning that had been developing since the Civil War. It was contrasted against laissez-faire individualism, on the one hand, and strictly authoritarian, despotic rule, on the other. This middle ground meant rule by knowledgeable leaders. It never occurred to these experts that the people knew best, or that the relevant contrast was with an ascendant popular culture flourishing in a participatory democracy. The early park leaders felt no doubt or shame about elite stewardship and proudly accepted the responsibility. The proper role of the rich was to take care of the poor, and in the words of New York's Mayor Kingsland in 1851, parks would benefit the "poorer classes entrusted to our keeping."[26] The American Social Science Association stressed the "responsibilities of the gifted and educated classes toward the weak, the witless, and the ignorant" in its charter, and Olmsted himself was one of founders of this association.[27]

The genteel reformers of the nineteenth century believed, as Geoffrey Blodgett has put it, "adequate structures of social and political intercourse could be defined for the popular mass by a cultured elite hovering above."[28] Olmsted, according to Thomas Bender, "combined a sincere feeling for the less fortunate with a somewhat manipulative concern for raising them up to middle-class standards."[29] Today this same attitude is condemned as condescending, and contemporary social scientists often use the term social control in opposition to a number of positives: freedom, individuality, growth, social improvement, emancipation, the use of intelligence in response to a fluctuating universe, a proliferation of competing voluntary organizations, social governance, justice, opportunity, democracy, and enlightenment ideals.[30]

This change in how we evaluate social control means that actions, once considered acceptable and laudable by most intellectual and political leaders, are now criticized. The exclusion of political organizing and activism, for example, is now considered antidemocratic. At the turn of the twentieth century Central Park's reputation for "serious and continued misuse" stimulated the citizens of Los Angeles to pass an ordinance to prohibit the use of parks for political rallies or discussion altogether. They claimed that "crowds of idlers have gathered there . . . for the 'discussion of all sorts of questions' to the inconvenience and disgust of thousands."[31] During the Depression the Chicago park commissioners reported that in certain parks "bad traditions had developed," but that "the way to combat antidemocratic tendencies in a community is to make other subjects more interesting than radicalism, rather than to conduct a series of lectures on the evils of radicalism."[32] Accordingly, a printing press was offered to the neighborhood boys with gratifying results: employment and elimination of destructive mischief and delinquency.[33] The park department could proclaim success: "In times of general irritation and unrest, the parks have been a steadying influence. No radical or revolutionary movements have gained foothold among those boys in park schedules of recreation. Prejudices, exploited elsewhere for sinister ends, here vanish as the people join in united purpose to serve their common needs."[34] This is control by diversion. Similarly, park documents have ignored the use of parks like Chicago's Bughouse Square or New York's Thompkins Square for speechmaking, and such consistent underemphasis is as manipulative as overt exclusion.

The Lindsay administration tried to involve blacks in New York City's park activities to keep them off the streets, and the fact that the city did not blow up, that the programs did not aggravate racial tensions, comforted park administrators. The following, from San Francisco, spells out the species of manipulation involved:

> To avoid being caught up in the eddies of unrest that have swept other cities, every resource of the public recreation services has been used to the fullest. Local and federal funds have been sought and obtained to provide jobs for youth in our parks and recreation centers, to provide buses for free transportation to public swimming pools, day camps, and excursions; free amusement rides were arranged at the San Francisco Zoo and Golden Gate Park playgrounds; youth groups are admitted free to baseball games at Candlestick Park; free jazz rock concerts for youngsters are held at the Band Concourse and a series of summer teenage dances have been most successful in every neighborhood. In the crowded industrial section, vest-pocket playgrounds and playcourts were installed and operated in alley ways and vacant lots, providing safety and open space away from heavy traffic.[35]

If one accepts and values social change, not all "eddies of unrest" are bad, if they stimulate desired changes. This example demonstrates how the transformation of the term social control from enlightened, progressive democratic leadership to top-down manipulation reflects changes in popular ideas about the meaning of democracy and governance. Beginning in the 1960s, largely in response to U.S. involvement in Vietnam, there was a notable upsurge of citizen interest in reclaiming governance from elected and appointed leaders by participating directly. Among planners this translated into community involvement and advocacy planning, both based on the premise that people should express or be served in terms of their own needs rather than be given what experts had determined they needed. In tandem, the direct popular programming rationale of the open-space era was participation in park activities. Thus crafts, festivals, and street theater were valued because they offered people an opportunity to participate. But participation in park activities was not participatory planning, nor was the phenomenon of park leaders responding to some aspect of popular culture because it was popular.

This response, elaborated into policy, might better deserve to be called populist planning, and populist planning, because of its similarity to traditional modes of social control, seems to be the best realistic hope for American urban parks. Beyond populist planning is participatory planning, which, to have any substance, would have to presuppose participatory financing—possibly a voucher system.

A voucher system implies transfer payments which, because they benefit the individual directly and the larger community only indirectly, counter the historical tendency of park policy. If authorities in charge of disbursing funds earmarked for recreation offered some form of transfer payment to individuals, families, schools, or workplaces, the money might be spent on trips to the countryside, drinks at the local bar, dune buggy rides, roller skates, beautiful landscaping, instructions in kinesthetics, a hot tub, or plots of land for vegetable gardens; or it might be pooled and spent on basketball or tennis courts, or swimming pools for the neighborhood or workplace. Businesses might be inspired to supply such services, as, in fact, they have to capture some of people's discretionary funds. If public spending on recreation had started as a uniformly distributed transfer payment, we might have an even wider proliferation of recreational environments than we see today. Parks as such would be scarcer but more special and radically different from one another.

The Functions of Parks: Past and Future

The functions that parks have aimed to fulfill are not natural or inevitable; the distinctiveness of the ideas they embodied can be clarified by speculating about what might have happened to parks if different ideas about cities and social problems reigned. Pleasure grounds were devised by moral elites who sometimes liked to think they would have preferred to live in the country, perhaps as gentlemen farmers. In contrast, some rural migrants idealized the city for the entertainment it provided, for its bright lights, its sense of importance, the freedom it offered from semifeudal relationships in agrarian communities, and, most of all, for its wages. To them the city was a golden opportunity, not a necessary evil. Perhaps parks designed to express their hopes and attractions would have been more like fairs or amusement parks. During the reform era machine politics was the reality: an order was being formed but not the detached and dispassionate rule of law of the reformers. Perhaps reform parks based on an ideology that actually condoned the reality of personal favoritism would have been more like the clubs, beer gardens, turnvereins, cemeteries, and churches that ethnic groups were organizing then. From the 1930s on planners operated as if city planning was merely a problem of systems management, where in reality the city was becoming a collection of competing bureaucracies and overlapping jurisdictions. If this reality had been elevated to an ideal, planners might have had to compete more on the merits of each park proposal. Fewer parks might have made it through the competition, but each might have had a more distinct character and been better geared to the needs of a particular group. The underlying ideology of the open-space system is that the city is an art form worth saving. But rioters did not act as though they felt the urban fabric worth saving; it already had been wrecked and vandalized by urban renewal, narrow municipal boundaries, and a tax structure that enabled the suburbs to seem independent of the city center. If we had the money to spend on parks that we spend on highways and defense, would the city's beauty lie only in the perceptual gymnastics now necessary to see harmony where others see only disfigurement?

Our future situation will be the same, in that whatever is decided about the function of parks will largely derive from some vision of the city, and it is by no means obvious how the city, as a set of problems and opportunities, is to be viewed. This is so even though two basic aspects of the meaning of parks would seem to be independent of, or more fundamental than, any function related to some particular characterization of the social order. First, while parks are

The pleasure ground was meant to replace the commercial amusement park which violated all its principles, showing construction ("the hand of man"), relying on buildings to shape space along a uniform setback, showing off electric lighting, and generally maximizing the stimulating effect of the rides and environment. Luna Park, Seattle. Undated. University of Washington Library.

mechanisms of social control, they manage to express a life force independent of social order. Plants subliminally represent the uncontrollable nature of the life force; no one can make a plant grow, even though manipulation of the environment can promote or hinder its growth. House plants, urban greenery, and park planting alike remind people, whether consciously or not, that they too have an irrepressible life force within them. Second, in a similar way, the very setting aside of ground for park activities is a collective recognition of the need for play, even though the urban park offers very little true play, and parks will always be associated with the related ideas of spontaneity and freedom. In Jungian terms parks will invariably represent the shadow side of our work-oriented culture.

Beyond these two timeless archetypes, however, park design and policy will continue to be a function of the historical consciousness of cities—of ideas about what cities have been, can be, and ought to be. Parks will continue to present a special obstacle to the clarity of this sort of consciousness, in that one of their functions has apparently been to represent the continuity of urban culture, but their continuing physical existence has often achieved this end at the price of softening the edges of urban history.

Needed clarity is obscured by the layering which comes from deliberate preservation and from a more thoughtless eclecticism. Layering can be seen in most cities that have examples of all four park types. Sometimes in the same park evidence of several models coexist.[36] Some cities have tucked newer park types into the edges of old ones, without altering the basic scheme of the original.[37] The pleasure grounds are particularly susceptible to modification because they are large enough so that part of them could be changed without changing the character of the whole and because landscape is easier to raze than buildings. In one of the most common modifications of the pleasure ground, the installation of a playground on its periphery, an actual synthesis of the two park types is typically not attempted. Swings are not installed under trees, nor are pleasure gar-

Special play equipment for children was not a typical feature of pleasure ground design, but it was often inserted later. The separate slides for boys and girls anticipated the sex segregation of the reform park. Golden Gate Park, 1890s. Courtesy the Bancroft Library, University of California, Berkeley.

den ponds open to wading. One type exists inside or beside the other encapsulated and immune.

Layering is often a matter of consciously preserving a park type associated with one era during a later one; as would be expected, this has applied in particular to the pleasure grounds. During the Depression federal funds were used to restore and renovate special features of the pleasure grounds such as the bird sanctuary and the Japanese temple in Chicago's Jackson Park. The resistance to modifying Central Park has been continuous, organized, and literate. Despite the rise of the new park types, pleasure grounds continue to be valued for their original purposes—a soothing contrast to the city. Popular literature still refers to Central Park as a great medicine.[38]

Layering, as has been said, softens the outlines of history even as it preserves the sense of it. The design implication of this pattern of accumulation has all too often been a thoughtless eclecticism: landscaping for beauty, field houses for indoor activity, parking lots and swimming pools with extra lighting for night use, kinetic sculpture. There is nothing intrinsically wrong with eclecticism if elements from different models are put together in a new way, with a new set of meanings implied in the relationship between these elements. But when elements are picked without reference to their original meaning, and sit next to one another without creating a new meaning system, the entire composition loses an inner tension and vitality; it becomes banal. This happens too often in the standard bread-and-butter solutions visible almost everywhere in all kinds of landscapes. It may be understandable in cases where the building accounted for the major part of the designer's fee, but it is not excusable.

Today an eclectic jumble of styles and services obscures the real movement of the history of urban parks, the gradual reduction in the range of social functions performed by the parks. This new status needs to be acknowledged to identify the actual choices available to park departments in the

Besides the accumulation of park types over time, park departments have deliberately recreated park types. Middle-sized cities which only started their departments in the twentieth century create a large pleasure ground at the same time they build reform-style parks, and new towns typically establish recreational facilities, field houses, and naturalistic grounds simultaneously.

near future. This decline is from a great height. Parks were one of the first services for which municipal governments were willing to take responsibility, and one of the first services able to set a wide range of tasks for themselves. The steady rise of social service agencies, which paralleled the gradually increasing division of labor in society generally, left parks with fewer and fewer of the reasons for existence they had at their beginning. By 1957 the U.S. census reported that recreation competed with public safety, education, highway, hosptial, sewage disposal, transportation, housing, and community development functions for a mere 4.7 percent of the money borrowed by the nation's forty-one largest cities.[39]

The history of the relations between park and city-planning departments epitomizes the decline.[40] Park administrators claimed that zoning was a natural outgrowth of their work, since parks presented the first major commitment to a relatively fixed land use. Charles Eliot, landscape architect, represented common opinion when he claimed that parks should be used as the basis for city planning. (After securing open areas and replacing derelict structures, Eliot recommended multiplying playgrounds and open landscaped areas and, above all, providing every family dwelling with a piece of arable or garden ground.[41]) But after 1930 urban-planning departments become part of the municipal-governing apparatus. At first they cooperated with park departments, using parks as a mechanism of urban renewal. Chicago's park department supplied data to the planning commission regarding the location of parks and the park design standards and criteria used in locating them.[42] The first exhibit presented at the annual convention of the American Institute of Planners was a map of Chicago showing the location of new parks and before-and-after photographs of the new sites.[43] Park departments in turn took inspiration from city master plans which integrated parks into a larger system of urban elements and in the 1950s developed master plans for their own overall development.

Eventually, however, cooperation turned into formal constraint. By 1962 in Chicago a law required referrals to the Department of City Planning for projected work.[44] Planning became so important in San Francisco that the Department of City Planning, rather than the Department of Parks and Recreation, took on the responsibility for designing the recreation and open-space element of the city's comprehensive plan.[45]

This development led inevitably to another: state and federal sponsorship of municipal park plans. The increasingly minor role of park departments in urban planning was paralleled by the planners' decreasing interest in them. For example, the 1949 index to *The American City*, a journal that reached all types of professionals, bureaucrats, and managers working in an urban context, listed thirteen articles on parks, thirty on active recreation but nearly as many, twenty-seven, on parking facilities and parking meters. The topics of planning, zoning, and public works programs captured 102 articles and notes. Parks continued to be important to urban planners considering urban renewal schemes, but planners did not invariably propose substituting a park for a cleared slum. Other land uses were likely candidates. City planners increasingly took responsibility for including parks in their plans, but park organizations did not necessarily extend their vision to urban planning.[46] Parks continued to be one, but only one, of the physical elements that a planner could use to help give identifiable shape to a community.[47]

As a rule park departments are still saddled with a mental outlook that goes with their glory days as an all-purpose reform agency for society, and they have not sharpened their focus in proportion to the number of functions they have lost. They have not taken the measure of their own decline. It is as if their own eclecticism has befuddled their reading of history. Yet with a few functions park leadership should be taking particular pains to clarify them. The actual choices remaining to park departments can be distilled from history and others extrapolated from it.

As it stands, the only uncontested function parks retain, beyond the archetypal suggestions mentioned earlier, is as a mechanism for social integration. This function derives in part from the imagery of continuity provided by their eclectic layering. The value of parks, like that of works of art, increases as they become older, for parks provide a tangible link with the past, unify the culture across time, and register its successive attempts to cope with its problems.[48]

Another integrative problem the park pursues is the creation of consensus. Today parks still try to integrate different social groups physically and intellectually by excluding the issues that divide them: "the recreative arts can serve powerfully as integrative forces in community life. Boys of all classes can play together on the neighborhood baseball team; different neighborhoods can play together. People can come together to hear music; to see plays. People can sing together and yell together."[49] When people do activities together, get to know each other better, they are "welded together in the consciousness of common interests."[50] The purposely apolitical character of parks is justified in terms of its integrative function: "The parks have suffered in the past whenever they were drawn into partisan politics. It is to be hoped that public opinion will insist that they be kept out of the partisan arena. They are our own secular social institution dedicated to neighborly friendliness, to the healing of those sharp differences of opinion that divide us into opposing factions."[51]

Finally, parks have served as an aesthetic mechanism of integration by sustaining values threatened by the facts of city life. The park keeps them "on hold" until the culture can reincorporate them. For example, the old pattern of organic beauty deriving from an internal agreement among the component parts of the preindustrial town is unavailable in the raucous, unevenly developed industrial city, but a park can be a perfect world in miniature, one that provides norms for the larger world to live up to. It can be what Manfredo Tafuri calls a utopian space, or what Colin Rowe calls a garden, a place framed off that shows the difference between itself and ordinary reality.[52] The pleasure ground landscape shows the ideal of freedom of choice within the context of industrial order, the reform park the ideal of orderly industrialization in the context of a chaotic city, the recreation facility the ideal of apolitical machinelike efficiency in the context of a society fighting for economic and political hegemony, and the open-space system the ideal of vitality and viability in the context of a city threatened by a shift to suburbia.

Each of these aspects of the park's integrative function—historical, political, aesthetic—needs to be defined conceptually and operationally. Lack of definition regarding park purposes is a particularly vexing problem to designers, administrators, and citizens who have to make policy decisions about how to design, manage, and support parks. It enters a vicious cycle: parks, for lack of definition, are banal; the public loses interest; the number of intended functions declines; the budget allocation is reduced; the park functions have even less to do with societal needs. The way out of the circle is to have a clear understanding about what parks can and should do for cities and their populations.

While clarity of conception is the first and most important goal, the question of planning style is critical. More realistic than a voucher system is populist planning, which in practice must include a planning style as well as a number of key planning issues. A society can hardly plan without some of its members planning for others. One model of a viable planning style might be developed from our experiences of parenting. A populist planner must be responsible to the population rather than patronize it, but retain inspiration and care. Mutual aid may be the appropriate beginning for an image of this delicate balance, since genuine helpers are permissive, tolerant, caring, loving—and incapable of falling into indifference.[53] Mutual aid may be the best way to think of and judge all collective activities, even bureaucratic ones.

Some specific planning issues are essential to parks' successful accommodation to the near future. Populist planning has several implications for park programming. Along with a greater responsiveness to popular culture it could produce significant regional variation in park type.[54] So far, despite regional variation in climate and topography, all four models of the urban park have shown a remarkable nationwide homogeneity in form and programming.[55] They have been diffused from city to city and region to region through such media as annual reports, congresses, manuals, national professional associations, and universities. The process had led to design criteria with little living relation to particular cultures, climates, or people. Its antithesis, design with local roots, could introduce regional character into the line of park design options.[56]

Parks might respond more directly to the demographic group now most overlooked by park programming: women. Today many existing facilities are usually overcrowded after 5 P.M. by working women of all ages who understand the value of exercise for their appearance, physical health, and mental well-being, especially since most of their jobs are sedentary. Women need to organize to demand better and more extensive hours for swimming pools and gymnasiums. Parks could be considered in terms of the human potential movement, since many women are struggling for self-actualization and fulfillment in a male-oriented society. Along these lines, for example, they could become holistic health centers.[57]

One of the most pressing needs of society today is for day-care centers, and parks could become a setting for private and governmental experimentation with different types of day-care facilities. The buildings and landscapes are there, although not the money for staffing. That will come with the attitude that child rearing is a social, not only an individual and family, function.

Community gardens, so popular with both sexes during both world wars, should be re-established. Vegetable and flower gardening offers activities that all ages have enjoyed.

Vegetable gardens were revived during both world wars as victory gardens for adults. Demonstration garden in the heart of downtown Manhattan, Union Square, 1916.

Demand exceeded supply for these twenty foot square victory gardens in Golden Gate Park. 1943. San Francisco Public Library.

It is educational for children and relaxing for many adults; it involves exercise and yields a useful product. Whenever park departments issued permits for allotment gardens, the demand was always greater than the space allocated. The fact that gardening has been ousted from parks unless defined as educational, or necessary because of war, suggests a basic split between production and consumption. In all eras the park has been kept free of connotations of work, to serve as a balance to ugly, stressful work environments. But the use of environments exclusively for artistic experience is really an instance of conspicuous consumption. Once only the wealthy could afford to maintain flower and sculpture gardens, so public parks copied this example to the ultimate detriment of the principles on which they were based. Greater integration between the useful and the beautiful could enhance our experience of work, leisure, streets, and nature. As American society becomes ever more urbanized, work-pleasure becomes ever more important to urban life.

Visions

Contemporary attitudes toward urban parks fall into three levels of sophistication. The first, the most naive assumption, is that parks are just plots of land preserved in their original state. If asked to discuss the issue at all, many laymen have maintained this much, that parks are bits of nature created only in the sense that some decision was made not to build on the land. Many are surprised to learn that parks are an artifact conceived and deliberated as carefully as public buildings, with both physical shape and social usage taken into account. The second, a little more informed, is that parks are aesthetic objects and that their history can be understood in terms of an evolution of artistic styles independent of societal considerations. The third is the view that each of the elements of the urban park represents part of planners' strategy for moral and social reform, so that today, as in the past, the citizen visiting a park is subject to an accumulated set of intended moral lessons.

The naturalistic landscaping of the nineteenth-century pleasure grounds was always man-made, imposed on land such as Golden Gate Park's sand dunes, for which few other uses were possible. Undated. Courtesy the Bancroft Library, University of California, Berkeley.

In considering the history of the parks, it is tempting to pin down park planners' strategy as essentially classist or reactionary and call for sweeping changes. But thoughtfulness about how parks could be used is actually more useful than a line on how the instrument has been used. Action requires decisions, and there is no universal formula for deciding how broadly based a decision-making process should be. Sometimes citizens want to be directly involved; sometimes they want to rely on representatives. Some elite, expert judgments are appropriate to all; some are class biased. Mass taste is sometimes an enlivening source of programming and design; sometimes it contradicts people's own long-term goals. The potentiality of parks to shape and reflect social values is still by no means fully appreciated or understood. Those with an interest in the character of urban life should seize on parks as one of the vehicles for the realization of their particular visions, and debate about parks should revolve around those visions.

Notes

Notes to Chapter 1

1. *San Francisco Herald*, March 13, 1854, p. 2.

2. "Central Park," *Scribner's Monthly*, vol. 6 (September 1873), pp. 526–527.

3. "A Ramble in Central Park," *Harper's New Monthly Magazine*, vol. 59 (October 1879), p. 690. Even earlier, Melville's *Moby Dick*, completed in 1851, described this sense of being stifled by New York's density.

4. William McMillan, "The Care of Urban Parks," *Garden and Forest*, vol. 8 (February 27, 1895), pp. 82–83. Active sports, like baseball, bicycling, and tennis, boomed in the 1880s, but even before then simpler park pursuits were active.

5. See Galen Cranz, "Changing Roles of Urban Parks: From Pleasure Garden to Open Space," *Landscape*, vol. 22 (Summer 1978), pp. 9–18. I am indebted to Charles McLaughlin, March 1978, for this interpretation.

6. Walter Creese, *The Search for Environment, The Garden City: Before and After* (New Haven: Yale University Press, 1966). Nationally, the American Park and Outdoor Art Association tried to limit billboards in both urban and rural areas. *Journal of APOA Association*, 1879–1903.

7. In San Francisco property owners along City Hall Avenue accused public officials of "threatening to beautify the avenue." *San Francisco Examiner*, May 22, 1901.

8. "A Ramble in Central Park," p. 692.

9. New York State, *Documents of the Senate,* vol. 1, no. 18, 84th sess., 1861, p. 51.

10. Richard M. Gibson, "Golden Gate Park," *Overland Monthly,* vol. 37 (March 1901), pp. 762–763.

11. "Central Park: Part II," *Scribner's Monthly,* vol. 6 (October 1873), p. 681.

12. The *San Francisco Examiner* covered a debate about what should be played on the concert bill around the time of the Midwinter Fair. The debate focused on popular versus classical music, that is, a good time versus instruction. People sent in programs that they themselves would like to hear played, and, although most people submitted suggestions for popular compositions, Park Commissioner Hammond feared that erring on the side of popular programs might prompt eastern visitors—who went to San Francisco park concerts just so that they could write home that they sat outdoors in sunshine in January or February—to write something unflattering about the city's "jay" taste in music (January 4 and 5, 1894).

13. *San Francisco Call,* May 19, 1895, and *San Francisco Chronicle,* June 7, 1894.

14. "Central Park: Part II," p. 680.

15. New York City, Department of Parks, *Report 1871*; and Clay Lancaster, "Central Park: 1851–1951," *Magazine of Art,* vol. 44 (April 1951).

16. *San Francisco Call,* March 13, 1893; "The Great Exhibition and the Central Park," *Harper's Weekly,* vol. 24 (December 11, 1880).

17. Frederick Law Olmsted, Jr., "Public Advertising," *American Park and Outdoor Art Association,* vol. 4, part 1 (1900), p. 5.

18. "Signs in Golden Gate Park," *San Francisco Call,* March 30, 1900, p. 12.

19. San Francisco, Park Commission Minutes, 1896, p. 17. This distaste for signs in parks was extended to other parts of the city through the logic of the City Beautiful movement. The American Park and Outdoor Art Association felt that "billboards nullify the efforts of the city to produce beautiful parks and boulevards." "The Billboard Nuisance," *American Park and Outdoor Art Association,* vol. 5, part 2 (1901), p. 30.

20. Charles D. Lakey, *The Public Grounds of Chicago: How to*

Give Them Character and Expression (Chicago: Charles D. Lakey, 1869); "Central Park: Part II," p. 689.

21. J. B. Jackson, in *American Space* (New York: Norton, 1972), pp. 214–219, explains the initial resistance to museums as part of class conflict regarding the definition of a park: the lower class wanted athletics, betting, and mass spectacles whereas the upper class wanted cultural enlightenment and a greater refinement of manners. Because the elite thought a park should serve such didactic purposes, they had no objections to, in fact promoted, museums in parks, according to Jackson. I have found, however, that at least some of the elite were sensitive to an overbearing instructive mode, so they tried to separate enjoyment from both amusement and instruction. Jackson credits the emergence of a third option, opposed both to athletic fields and museums, to Olmsted, who insisted that scenery had primacy over the other two visions because it best offered mental refreshment. This is precisely what Olmstedians like Sargent called enjoyment.

22. C. S. Sargent, "Playgrounds and Parks," *Garden and Forest*, vol. 7 (June 6, 1894), p. 221.

23. O. C. Simonds, "Appreciation of Natural Beauty," *American Park and Outdoor Art Association, Second Report*, vol. 2 (1898), p. 79.

24. MacMillan, "Urban Parks."

25. C. S. Sargent, "Keep Off the Grass," *Garden and Forest*, vol. 7 (July 25, 1894), p. 291.

26. For a fuller discussion of the discrimination against popular culture, see Donna Dumont et al., "San Francisco's Park Policy in the Nineteenth Century: Goals versus Outcomes," Working Paper 342 (Berkeley: Institute of Urban and Regional Development, University of California, 1981).

27. William Hammond Hall, in the *San Francisco Call*, November 16, 1886, p. 7.

28. *San Francisco Examiner*, November 2, 1900.

29. *San Francisco Bulletin*, November 3, 1900.

30. *San Francisco Newsletter*, November 17, 1900.

31. Sargent, "Proposed Speedway," p. 109.

32. Ibid.

33. C. S. Sargent, editorial comment, *Garden and Forest*, vol. 5 (April 20, 1892). Sargent devoted a series of articles and editorials to this controversy: March 9, March 30, and April 20, 1892, *Garden and Forest.*

34. New York City, Department of Parks, *Report 1898.*

35. Boston, City Council, "Fifteenth Annual Report of the Board of Commissioners of the Department of Parks," *Documents of the City of Boston for the Year 1890,* Document 15 (Boston: Boston Public Library, 1890).

36. The main driveway of Golden Gate could be used by troops until 9:00 a.m., and the use of side drives and the open areas around the music stand were permitted at all times. *San Francisco Call,* May 28, 1898, p. 14.

37. C. S. Sargent, "Military Parades in Central Park," *Garden and Forest,* vol. 6 (June 7, 1893), p. 241.

38. Dieter Hennebo, *Geschichte der deutschen Gartenkunst* (Hamburg: Alfred Hoffman, Broschek Verlag, 1963). The contribution of Americans to the evolution of the picturesque is part of the evidence that the American municipal park is more indigenous than English or European.

39. *San Francisco Call,* February 9, 1893.

40. *San Francisco News,* August 10, 1901.

41. "Central Park: Part II," p. 674.

42. *San Francisco Alta,* March 25, 1851, p. 2.

43. *San Francisco Alta,* July 19, 1850, p. 2.

44. New York State, *Senate Document,* 1861, p. 8.

45. "Coney Island for Battered Souls," *New Republic,* November 23, 1921, pp. 372–374. Recently the contrast has been drawn between Coney Island and the Chicago park system at the time of the 1893 Columbian Exposition; see John F. Kasson, *Amusing the Million: Coney Island at the Turn of the Century* (Canada: McGraw Hill, 1978). The opposition of the municipal park to the amusement park continued after scientific recreational facilities were introduced. In this regard Moses claimed that regenerating Coney Island as a year-round residential community was merely complementing the amusement park. *New York Times,* June 25, 1939. Even Olmsted, in protecting his definition of a park as primarily for mental refreshment, distinguished it from other types of outdoor spaces for sports and entertainment such as playgrounds, plazas, athletic fields, and public flower gardens. Although his firm designed an amusement park, he saw the park per se as opposed to amusement, and some reformers hoped to oust amusement parks altogether.

46. *San Francisco Alta*, September 9, 1854, p. 1.

47. "A Ramble in Central Park," p. 692.

48. Joseph Kirkland, *The Story of Chicago*, vol. 1 (Chicago: Dibble Publishing Co., 1892), p. 374. The difference between the ideal site (periphery of city) and the actual sites alerts one to an ideological contradiction which could be interpreted in various ways. Perhaps stated ideals obscured real motivations. Or perhaps once park advocates won, they emphasized the practical side and the low cost of their endeavors. Most likely the contradiction means that business was against removing land from the marketplace, while progressives were for it, and so they had to reach a compromise—a remote, and hence inexpensive, site. Although initially a weak victory, in the long run it was the wedge for continued public spending in recreation, and, after population growth brought the city up to the edge of the park, proponents realized their hopes for an accessible pleasure ground.

49. New York State, *Senate Document*, vol. 3, no. 82, 1853.

50. Discussed in Lakey, *Public Grounds of Chicago.*

51. San Francisco, *Nineteenth Annual Report of the Board of Park Commissioners of San Francisco, for the year ending June 30, 1890*, p. 10. In San Francisco separate park, playground, and recreation commissions existed until their consolidation in 1950 (hereafter all park report titles cited as *Report* with the year).

52. San Francisco, Park Commission, *Report 1889.*

53. Chicago, South Park Commission, *Report 1873*, p. 18.

54. "A Ramble in Central Park," p. 694.

55. William Hammond Hall, San Francisco, Park Commission, *Biennial Report 1872–1873*, appendix C.

56. F. E. Fanset (landscape gardener), *San Francisco Star*, July 22, 1893, p. 29. McLaren's most criticized practice was piling small rocks, bricks, and broken concrete into mounds, coating them with colored cement and tooling them to represent massive rocks, in keeping with his scale of design.

57. Hall, quoted in Gibson, "Golden Gate Park," p. 751.

58. Referring to encroachments, Samuel Parsons noted, "There seems to be something about the design of a park that tempts the incompetent, the dreamer, the visionary, to attack it in the most light-hearted manner." Quoted in *New York Herald*, January 20, 1964.

59. Thomas E. Will, "Public Parks and Playgrounds: A Symposium," *Arena*, vol. 10 (July 1894), p. 274.

60. San Francisco, Park Commission, "Engineer's Report," *First Biennial Report 1870–1871*, appendix B. In the second biennial report, Hall associated straight lines and shade with the Persian garden that needed the seeming as well as veritable coolness to counteract the burning sun. Reprinted in *Overland*, vol. 11 (December 1873), p. 533.

61. For example, Mel Scott, *American City Planning since 1890* (Berkeley: University of California Press, 1969), and N. T. Newton, *Design on the Land* (Cambridge: Harvard University Press, 1971).

62. New York State, *Senate Document*, vol. 63, 1860, p. 41.

63. Good drainage and pure drinking water were prime ingredients of the park's healthfulness in cities still without adequate sewerage and water systems.

64. A mechanical pump returned the water back up to the top of the waterfall. The dry bed can still be seen today.

65. San Francisco, Park Commission, *Report 1902*, p. 12.

66. San Francisco, Park Commission, *Report 1895*.

67. F. L. Olmsted and C. Vaux, in Chicago, South Park Commission, *Report 1871*.

68. Chicago, South Park Commission, *Report 1906*, p. 32. In Chicago this practice was not abandoned until the 1930s.

69. San Francisco, Park Commission, *Biennial Report 1872–1873*.

70. The records are contradictory about the technique that finally succeeded in rooting plants into sand. The *Overland Monthly's* 1901 account claimed that yellow lupine and barley were planted along with all varieties of grass, but with little success. It credits the strong, fibrous roots of the sea-bent grass with finally accomplishing the goal. Hall's unpublished manuscript claims that sprouted barley with lupine seeds did the trick. Beatty's recent account credits a mixture of spreading rooted plants (imported sand grass from France) and tap-rooted lupine. The confusion probably results from the different treatments of the east and west sides of the park: mat grass was used on the east end, and the lupine-barley combination on the beach side. Years later Hall noted wryly that "he who replaced the finer growth will get credit for 'making' the park," an allusion to the fact that McLaren often gets credit for reclamation, but McLaren was not yet even working for the parks department (Hall, unpublished manuscript). See Russell Beatty, "Metamorphosis in Sand," *California Horticulture Journal*, January 1970, pp. 41–46, and L. C. Lane, "The Golden Gate Park—Its Evolution," lecture at Cooper Medical College, reported in *San Francisco Bulletin*, January 5, 1901. Lane's is the most technically detailed account and conforms to Hall's own explanation that the barley protected the lupine as well as some acacia and pine seed. Both Beatty and Lane mention the different treatment of each end of the park, but their descriptions of which plants were used still conflict.

71. C. S. Sargent, "Tender Bedding Plants in Public Parks," *Garden and Forest*, vol. 6 (September 6, 1893), p. 371.

72. C. S. Sargent, "The Use of Color in Our Parks," *Garden and Forest*, vol. 7 (July 18, 1894), pp. 281–282.

73. C. S. Sargent, "The Architectural Attack on Rural Parks," *Garden and Forest*, vol. 8 (September 4, 1895), p. 351.

74. New York City, Department of Parks, *Report 1898*.

75. *San Francisco Call*, March 10, 1896, p. 5.

76. *New York Times*, August 9, 1960.

77. Gibson, "Golden Gate Park," p. 758.

78. *San Francisco Call*, July 9, 1895, p. 8.

79. The residential area surrounding a park, if park designers of the 1890s had their way, would also be self-consciously styled. Riverside Park in New York stimulated the development of upper-class dwellings, the architecture of which was "happily in keeping with the contemporary work of a more public character shown in such examples as Grant's Tomb, Columbia College, the Cathedral of St. John the Divine, and St. Luke's Hospital." These comparisons assume a favorable assessment of the neoclassic revival. New York City, Department of Parks, *Report 1898*.

80. San Francisco, Park Commission, *Report 1890*, p. 16.

81. Chicago, South Park Commission, *Report 1873*, p. 19.

82. Mrs. Herman J. Hall, "Park Inconsistencies," *American Park and Outdoor Art Association*, vol. 7, part 4 (July 1903), p. 19.

83. "Central Park: Part II," p. 675.

84. *San Francisco Call*, August 12, 1901, front page.

85. *San Francisco Call*, November 14, 1895, p. 11.

86. *The First Report of the [American] Park and Outdoor Art Association* in 1897 was a review of the papers presented at that convention, and their titles show a balance between the two. The titles were: "The True Purpose of a Large Public Park," "The Use and Management of Public Parks," "Parks and Municipal Art," "Rural Parks in a Prairie State," "Parks as Investments and Educators," "Park Design and Park Planting," "Ornamental Planting for Public Parks and Grounds," "The Metropolitan Park System of Boston," and "Park Development of the City of New Orleans."

Notes to Chapter 2

1. Educators generally assumed the businessman's outlook and shaped the school system according to the principles of profit-making, economic institutions. This influence was especially revealed by the emphasis placed on efficiency, by more and more educators as they spoke out about their objectives and techniques. Merle Curti, *The Social Ideas of American Educators* (New York: Scribners, 1935), p. 230. Curti also refers to Jane Addams's early description of the impact of commercial and industrial needs for legible handwriting, quick and accurate arithmetic, punctuality and orderliness, and prompt and unquestioning obedience.

2. Howard Braucher, "A National Recreation Magazine Established Thirty-Five Years Ago," *Recreation*, vol. 36 (April 1942), p. 1, reported this finding.

3. U.S. Department of Housing and Urban Development, *Urban Recreation* (Washington, D.C.: Government Printing Office, 1974), p. 24.

4. In Morton and Lucia White, *The Intellectual versus the City, from Thomas Jefferson to Frank Lloyd Wright* (Cambridge: Harvard University Press, 1962), p. 156.

5. Thomas E. Will, ed., "Public Parks and Playgrounds: A Symposium," *The Arena*, vol. 10 (July 1894), p. 275.

6. *San Francisco Call*, July 14, 1897, p. 6, and December 28, 1899, p. 1.

7. For example, *San Francisco Call*, May 20, 1900, p. 20.

8. New York City, Department of Parks, *Report 1913*, p. 167.

9. Joseph Lee, *Play and Education* (1907), quoted in "Philosophies upon Which We Built," *Recreation*, vol. 49 (June 1956), p. 269.

10. Leon Rosenthal, "Open Spaces," *Park International*, September 1920, p. 187. Translation of chapter 2 in "Villes et Villages Francais apres la Guerre" (Paris: Payot, 1918).

11. Chicago, South Park Commission, *Report 1905*, p. 47.

12. Theodore J. Smergalski (superintendent of playgrounds, West Chicago Parks), "The Relation of Supervision to Play and Recreation," *Parks and Recreation*, vol. 1 (July 1918), p. 13.

13. F. L. Olmsted and John Nolen, "Experts' Report on Civic Center," *Preliminary Reports on the City Planning Commission of the City of Milwaukee* (Milwaukee: Phoenix Printing Company, 1911), pp. 19–24.

14. Chicago, South Park Commission, *Report 1908*, p. 114.

15. Chicago, South Park Commission, *Report 1906*, p. 56.

16. Chicago, South Park Commission, *Report 1911*, p. 29.

17. C. H. Meeds, "Should Playgrounds Be Landscaped?" *Parks and Recreation*, vol. 7 (September-October 1923), p. 74.

18. Smergalski, "The Relation of Supervision," p. 17.

19. Will, "Parks and Playgrounds: A Symposium," p. 287.

20. Chicago, South Park Commission, *Report 1909*, p. 37.

21. Chicago, South Park Commission, *Report 1905*, p. 48.

22. San Francisco, Playground Commission, *Report 1928–1929*, p. 13, and Chicago, South Park Commission, *Report 1913*, p. 72.

23. B. D. Stoddart, "Recreative Centers of Los Angeles," March 1910, quoted in Rainwater, *Play Movement*, p. 105.

24. Chicago, South Park Commission, *Report 1916*, p. 61; and Rainwater, *Play Movement*, p. 189.

25. New York City, Department of Parks, *Report 1916*, p. 63.

26. New York City, Borough of Brooklyn, Department of Parks, *Report 1915*, p. 161. In New York City consolidation of separate borough park departments took place in 1934, with the first report of the consolidated districts published in 1940.

27. Rainwater, *Play Movement*, p. 91.

28. Mayer N. Zald, *Organizational Change: The Political Economy of the YMCA* (Chicago: The University of Chicago Press, 1970), p. 33.

29. Chicago, South Park Commission, *Report 1909*, opp. p. 21.

30. Chicago, South Park Commission, *Report 1907*, p. 72; *Report 1906*, pp. 52–53; *Report 1908*, p. 119.

31. Chicago, South Park Commission, *Report 1907*, p. 65.

32. Chicago, South Park Commission, *Report 1911*, p. 44.

33. "Louisville Convention Proceedings," *Parks and Recreation*, vol. 4 (October 1920), p. 82.

34. New York City, Bureau of Recreation, *Report 1912*, p. 47.

35. New York City, Department of Parks, *Report 1913*, p. 125.

36. The circus came to San Francisco in 1905, when permission was granted to Barnum's to erect tents in Mission Park. The circus in Chicago was held in its central Grant Park from 1919 to 1923; part of the proceeds was assigned to philanthropy, presumably to justify the unheralded change in policy which allowed a profit-making organization to use park property.

37. Chicago, South Park Commission, *Report 1908*, p. 115.

38. Chicago, South Park Commission, *Report 1920*, p. 40.

39. Judith Oliver, "Newspapers Vital to Parks," *Park International*, November 1920, pp. 263–264.

40. San Francisco, Park Commission Minutes, April 23, 1908, p. 764. Permission was temporary, but this did not mollify indignant newspapers.

41. San Francisco, Park Commission Minutes, July 6 and 20, 1906, pp. 674–675.

42. San Francisco, Park Commission, *Report 1924*, p. 18.

43. Unspecified author, "Boyhood and Lawlessness, His Playground," p. 11.

44. Letter from Theodore Roosevelt in Howard Braucher, "A National Recreation Magazine . . . ," *Recreation* (April 1942) p. 2.

45. San Francisco, Playground Commission Minutes, June 10, 1915.

46. E. T. Attwell, "Playgrounds for Colored America," *Park International*, November 1920, p. 218.

47. San Francisco, Park Commission, *Report 1902*.

48. *San Francisco Star*, April 13, 1901; *San Francisco Post*, May 8, 1901, editorial.

49. San Francisco, Park Commission, *Report 1902*, p. 7.

50. Nevertheless, its size did have a lower limit. Shurtleff of Boston wrote that large playgrounds were more efficient than small ones because of too much cost in the perimeter, the loss of privacy, and too much contact with street traffic. The New York City Police Department reported that the over ninety acres of backyard space in the most crowded part of Manhattan were relatively useless, since they were broken up into "tiny plots and cubby holes of somewhat less than 1,000 square feet each." See Arthur Shurtleff, *Future Parks, Playgrounds and Parkways* (Boston: Boston Park Department, 1925), and Rowland Haynes, "How Much Playground Space Does a City Need?" *The American City*, vol. 16 (March 1917), p. 243.

51. F. L. Moulton et al., "Proposed West Side Playground Sites," *The City Club Bulletin*, vol. 4 (1911), pp. 103–105.

52. "Report of the Committee on Park Census for 1901," *American Park and Outdoor Art Association*, vol. 5, part 1 (1901), pp. 5–9.

53. Editorial Notes, *Park International*, May 1921, p. 273.

54. Franz J. Herding (architect and city planner), "Block Interior Parks," *Park International*, March 1921, p. 124.

55. Edna Farrier, "Utilizing the City's Waste Spaces for Recreation," *Park International*, May 1921, pp. 248–253.

56. New York City, Department of Parks, *Report 1916*, p. 65, and *Report 1915*, p. 33.

57. Park officials may have turned to centralized constructions because they realized their efforts on behalf of social reform had failed, but their motivations were probably not so direct. Seldom did the same people follow both courses of action. Rather social reformers pursued a line of settlement house work and supervised play in small parks, victory gardens, or vacant lots, while a completely different group pursued urban design, City Beautiful ideals, and the like. The diversion from the efforts to use the playground as an agent of social reform to the reliance on physical reform may have been functional to the system as a whole, but it does not seem like self-delusion or a lie. Rather two competing ideologies were attached to two separate social groups, each pursuing its own ideals honestly. The reform movement failed in its effect the future but not because it was directly opposed by City Beautiful advocates. Rather the energy of the urban designers was channeled to another target, undermining and detracting from the settlement house orientation toward playgrounds and small parks as a result.

58. Chicago, South Park Commission, *Report 1907*, p. 9, and Edward Bennett, "Grant Park, The Frontispiece of Chicago," *Park International*, November 1920, pp. 205–216.

59. George E. Kessler, *A City Plan for Dallas* (Dallas: Board of Commissioners, 1911), p. 25.

60. C. S. Sargent, "Playgrounds and Parks," p. 221.

61. The power of the social and ideological context in which designers work is indicated by the work of the Olmsted Brothers as consulting landscape architects for the City of Chicago during the reform era. The same firm which years before had produced the picturesque pleasure grounds all around the nation could now produce neoclassical, rectangular plans.

62. New York City, Department of Parks, *Report 1916*.

63. J. Haslett Bell, "A Typical Neighborhood Park."

64. New York City, Department of Parks, *Report 1914*, p. 36.

65. Clarence Rainwater, a recreation worker and sociologist, chronicled both the programming and design stages of reform park evolution up to 1922 in Chicago, which he and most practitioners considered the most advanced system in the country. Rainwater, *Play Movement*, p. 91; J. F. Foster, "An Article on Small Parks Read before the Chicago Society for School Extension" (Chicago Historical Society, 1902), pp. 9–10; and Henry G. Foreman, "Chicago's New Park Service," *Century Magazine*, vol. 69 (February 1905, pp. 611–612.

66. Golf courses could usually not be accommodated, so instead they were inserted into pleasure grounds or built in new regional parks or near suburban parks where land costs were not prohibitive.

67. New York City, Department of Parks, *Report 1913*, p. 176.

68. The world's largest outdoor pool, 1,000 feet long and 150 feet wide, was donated to San Francisco by Herbert Fleischhacker, president of the Park Commission, and opened in 1925.

69. Belinda Gerry, "The Spider Web Motif in Park Design," *Park International*, September 1920, pp. 164–166.

70. Phelps Wyman, "Without Views, No Park," *Parks and Recreation*, vol. 8 (March-April 1925), p. 361.

71. Chicago, South Park Commission, *Report 1905*, p. 59.

72. New York City, Department of Parks, *Report 1913*, p. 107, and *Report 1914*, p. 32.

73. New York City, Department of Parks, *Report 1913*, p. 180.

74. San Francisco, Playground Commission, *Report 1929–1930*, p. 8.

75. National Recreation Association, *Recreation and Park Yearbook: Mid-Century Edition, A Review of Local and Country Recreation and Park Developments 1900–1950* (New York: National Recreation Association, 1951), p. 5.

76. Rainwater, *Play Movement*, p. 216.

77. Seattle, Park Department, *Report 1912*.

78. Editorial Notes: "Field and Community Houses," *Park International*, September 1920, pp. 169–170.

79. "Park Architecture: Fieldhouses," *Park International*, September 1920, p. 136.

80. San Francisco, Playground Commission Minutes, October 10, 1923.

81. Horace Peaslee, "Park Architecture: Bathing Establishments," *Park International*, July 1920, p. 27.

82. Henry G. Foreman, "Chicago's New Park Service," *Century Magazine*, vol. 69 (February 1905), p. 613.

83. The field house was the architectural innovation of this era, but museums in neoclassical styling were also prominent. According to Henry Hope Reed, the first curator of Central Park (interview, 1974), museums were a cult of the 1920s; parks did not create a demand for them. At the same time that social workers were trying to introduce recreation centers into neighborhoods, a social elite was insinuating museums into many downtown parks—parks sited, in some cases, in response to pressure from the elite leadership of the City Beautiful movement. Building dates in Chicago confirm Reed's typification of the twenties: the Field Museum opened in 1920; the Art Institute, in Grant Park, was granted an extension the same year; the fine arts building in Jackson Park began conversion to the Museum of Science and Industry in 1925; at the same time citizens were promoting the establishment of Shedd Aquarium and Adler Planetarium; and the Chicago Historical Society was sited at the entrance to Lincoln Park in the late 1920s.

84. Chicago Bureau of Public Efficiency, *The Park Governments of Chicago* (Chicago, 1911), p. 8. See also San Francisco, Park Commission Minutes, November 17, 1907, p. 720, and Editorial Notes, *Park International*, September 1920, pp. 168–169.

85. San Francisco, Park Commission Minutes, 1916, p. 632.

86. San Francisco, Playground Commission Minutes, February 21, 1923. Park guardians were willing to accommodate vehicular and delivery traffic within the parks, to their detriment. Not until World War II did the commissioners in several cities abandon this policy for the sake of the Interstate Highway Defense Act and yield park territory for efficient freeway connections.

87. Editorial Notes, "Night Riders to the Rescue of Park Scenery," *Park International*, January 1921, pp. 72–76. Commemorative sculpture and statuary was not so much excluded from the reform park as it was withheld from it. Donors were interested in more impressive settings, and continued to plague the larger pleasure grounds up to the 1920s. Most statues in Golden Gate Park date from the period 1885 to 1920 and were presented to the city as gifts in memory of the subject or to honor his ethnicity. Because memorials were not always satisfactory artistically, the New York Park Commissioners thought about different means of controlling them. One was to map available space in the city into zones, each for a different type of honored leader; another was to require full-sized models in stucco or wood to be put up in the proposed site in order to judge the proportions and setting. After World War I designers admonished that parks should not be turned into war memorials unless the donated object or building completed the design of the park. They tactfully suggested flagpoles, water fountains, and even plaques as more appropriate memorials than portrait sculpture. See New York City, Department of Parks, *Report 1915*, p. 59, and *Report 1916*, p. 75; Frederick Law Olmsted, "Parks as War Memorials," *Parks and Recreation*, vol. 2 (July 1919), p. 31; Howard Walker, "Memorials in Parks: Flagpoles," *Park International*, January 1921, pp. 53–56; and subsequent issues of *Park International* and *Parks and Recreation*.

88. "Sandwich Men to Grace Parks," *San Francisco Call*, April 24, 1908.

89. San Francisco, Park Commission Minutes, February 5, 1925, p. 85. *Park International* offered designers measured drawings of display posts, road signs, and sign brackets; see *Park International*, July 1920, pp. 83–86.

90. D. L. Mackintosh, "Are Our Public Parks Edifying?" *Parks and Recreation*, vol. 3 (July 1920), p. 40.

91. *San Francisco Call*, July 6, 1901.

92. Chicago, South Park Commission, *Report 1908*, p. 89.

93. Chicago, South Park Commission, *Report 1910*, p. 12.

94. *San Francisco Chronicle*, May 19, 1904.

95. Chicago, South Park Commission, *Report 1936*, p. 178.

Notes to Chapter 3

1. New York City, Department of Parks, *Six Years of Park Progress* (1940), p. 3. This was the first annual report published in New York after Moses became president of the Park Commission in 1934. Most cities stopped publication of annual reports during the Depression and resumed sometime during the war.

2. C. P. Keyser, "Parks and Cities," *Parks and Recreation*, vol. 20 (February 1937), p. 264.

3. Raymond C. Morrison, and Myrtle E. Huff, *Let's Go to the Park* (Dallas, Tx.: Wilkinson Printing Company, 1937), p. 7.

4. Sal J. Prezioso, "My Philosophy of Recreation," *Recreation*, vol. 54 (December 1961), p. 509.

5. New York City, Department of Parks, *Twenty Years of Park Progress* (1954), p. 4.

6. Alfred K. Eckersberg, "Planning, Acquiring, and Building Chicago Parks," *Recreation*, vol. 49 (October 1956), p. 392.

7. Kevin Mosley, "Our Parks, People Keep Out!" *Chicago Land Magazine*, vol. 7 (December 1969), pp. 40–44.

8. San Francisco, Playground Commission Minutes, September 16, 1931.

9. V. K. Brown (superintendent of playgrounds and sports, South Park Commissioners, Chicago), "What Shall We Do With This New Leisure?" *Parks and Recreation*, vol. 17 (May 1934), p. 363.

10. San Francisco, Recreation Commission, *Supervised Recreation* (1939).

11. Chicago, Park District, *Report 1935*, p. 57.

12. The continuity in park ideology from the Depression through World War II into the postwar years may surprise those who were alive at the time and experienced the otherwise sharp changes

between those periods, but from the point of view of the historical record these years of park history are bound together.

13. In 1943 Chicago was proud that it had not requested the postponement of induction for any of its employees, but by the next year the park police department had to secure deferments for its men. Chicago, *Report 1943*, p. 29, and *Report 1944*, p. 95.

14. New York City, *West Side Improvement*, October 12, 1937 (published on the occasion of the opening).

15. The annual reports and minutes of Chicago and San Francisco show disproportionate attention to regulations, hardware, and accounting, while New York's reports under Moses placed a premium on efficacy.

16. New York City, Department of Parks, *Six Years of Park Progress, 1939–1940.*

17. Minutes of the San Francisco Recreation Commission, January 15, 1942.

18. Chicago, *Report 1941*, p. 210.

19. Day Camp and child care were allied with the industrial question. See *Recreation and Other Activities in the All-Day School Program* (Leaflet 7, U.S. Office of Education, 1943), cited in Martin H. Neumeyer, "Wartime Trends in Recreation," *Recreation*, vol. 38 (January 1945), pp. 535–536.

20. Physical fitness was in part only a new label for traditional sports of the pleasure ground and for the gymnastic activities of the reform park, but, because the program originated in a war-preparedness mood, because it was designed to appeal to adults of all ages and both sexes, and because it was viewed as a special program by the bureaucracy itself, it was a contribution of the recreation facility era. Physical fitness clubs introduced a social component to the program. Later these programs received a shot in the arm from President Kennedy's call to the nation to improve the physical condition of its young people. For example, see San Francisco, Park Department, *Report 1961–1962*, p. 5.

21. V. K. Brown, "The Place of Parks in a World at War," *Parks and Recreation*, vol. 26 (March-April 1943), p. 152.

22. Chicago, Park District, *Report 1941*, p. 212. In San Francisco the Civil Defense Council described what the Recreation Department could contribute: moral service, evacuation service, use of its facilities, and use of their trained personnel to protect citizens (first aid, home nursing, nutrition).

23. In Sag Harbor, Long Island, children spent one day under an imaginary dictatorship as part of the Bill of Rights Week program. By the end of the day, many of them had been arrested by storm-troopers and sent to concentration camps. "World at Play," *Recreation Magazine*, vol. 35 (June 1941), p. 202.

24. For examples of writers who viewed these activities as self-expression, see L. H. Weir, "Parks and Their Use, Part II," *Parks and Recreation*, vol. 24 (June 1941), p. 451, and San Francisco, *Supervised Recreation*, 1939. For an example of writers who viewed these same activities as a way to make group association more enjoyable, see Chicago, Park District, *Report 1938*, p. 144. Even after the war social workers continued to view games as a way to meet groups' needs for social power, competence, and sharing. Brian Sutton-Smith and Paul Gump, "Games and Status Experience," *Recreation*, vol. 48 (April 1955), pp. 172–174.

25. Chicago, South Park Commission, *Report 1936*, p. 188.

26. Chicago, South Park Commission, *Report 1938*, p. 144.

27. Chicago, South Park Commission, *Report 1936*, p. 179.

28. Chicago, South Park Commission, *Report 1935*, p. 147.

29. Chicago, South Park Commission, *Report 1935*, p. 158, and *Report 1936*, p. 187.

30. M. N. Walsh, M.D. (of the Mayo Clinic), in Carlos E. Cummings, M.D., "How the Museum Serves in Wartime," *Recreation*, vol. 36 (July 1942), p. 222.

31. Ruth Norris, "The Human Values in Recreation," *Recreation*, vol. 55 (November 1962), p. 443.

32. Chicago, South Park Commission, *Report 1939*, pp. 158, 161.

33. San Francisco, Park Commission Minutes, March 12, 1942.

34. San Francisco, Park Commission Minutes, July 1934, p. 44, and San Francisco, Playground Commission Minutes, June 7, 1933.

35. San Francisco, Park Commission Minutes, December 1934, p. 86, and San Francisco, Playground Commission Minutes, January 17, 1934.

36. New York City, Department of Parks, *Sixteen Years of Park Progress, 1934–1939.*

37. New York City, Department of Parks, *Eighteen Years of Park Progress, 1934–1952.*

38. Chicago, Park District, *Report 1945*, p. 100.

39. San Francisco, Playground Commission Minutes, January 15, 1942. (The Commission published its name as Recreation rather than Playground during its later years.)

40. Robert Moses, "New York City after the War," *Recreation*, vol. 38 (October 1944), p. 373.

41. New York City, Department of Parks, *Eighteen Years of Park Progress, 1934–1952*.

42. Robert Moses, "Recipe for Better Parks," *Parks and Recreation*, vol. 48 (November 1965), p. 661.

43. New York City, Department of Parks, *Report 1940*, p. 10.

44. Chicago, South Park Commission, *Report 1940*, p. 228.

45. Harvey S. Crass, "Parks—Now and 25 Years Hence," *Parks and Recreation*, vol. 31 (December 1948), p. 711.

46. Chicago, South Park Commission, *Report 1939*, p. 21.

47. Robert B. Nichols, "New York City's Park-Design Controversy," *Landscape Architect*, vol. 53 (July 1963), p. 286.

48. Garrett Eckbo, "Man and Land," *Proceedings of the Sixty-fourth Annual Conference of the American Institute of Park Executives*, Kansas City, Mo., September 23–27, 1962, p. 87.

49. John B. Cabot, "Architecture in Parks," *Parks and Recreation*, vol. 42 (April 1959), p. 156.

50. J. R. Lawwill, "A Philosophy for Park Structures," *Parks and Recreation*, vol. 31 (August 1948), p. 428.

51. Robert Nichols, "New Concepts behind Designs for Modern Playgrounds," *Recreation*, vol. 48 (April 1955), p. 155.

52. New York City, Department of Parks, *Eighteen Years of Park Progress, 1934–1952*.

53. Ada Louise Huxtable, "Just a Little Love, A Little Care," *New York Times*, December 9, 1943. Ironically, Moses is known for having appointed highly qualified professional designers: Gilmore Clarke, Aymor Embury, Earle Andrews, Allyn Jennings, Stuart Constable, Francis Cormier.

54. Alfred B. LaGasse, "Design of Park and Recreation Areas of Approximately 10 Acres," *Parks and Recreation*, vol. 38 (April 1955), p. 4.

55. Chicago, Park District, *Report 1935*, p. 140.

56. Wilhelm Beckert, "Maintenance Mart," *Parks and Recreation*, vol. 42 (April 1959), editorial, pp. 202–203.

57. Chicago, South Park Commission, *Report 1945*.

58. Keith A. MacDonald, "Color in Parks and Playgrounds," *Parks and Recreation*, vol. 39 (May 1956), p. 5.

59. Robert B. Nichols, "New Concepts," p. 155.

60. William Penn Mott, Jr., "Dress Up Your Play Areas with Inexpensive Play Sculptures," *Parks and Recreation*, vol. 39 (May 1956), p. 4.

61. Chicago, South Park Commission, *Report 1957*, p. 29.

62. William Penn Mott, Jr., "Magic Key to Your Park's Story," *Parks and Recreation*, vol. 42 (May 1959), p. 220; William Penn Mott, Jr., "Designing Parks for Children," *Parks and Recreation*, vol. 41 (September 1958), p. 37; Edward C. Davenport, "New Ideas for Making the Playground Attractive," *Parks and Recreation*, October 1951, p. 19; *San Francisco Chronicle*, October 29, 1959.

63. Nichols, "New Concepts," p. 157.

64. Sam Bornstein, "Rides," *Proceedings of the Second Annual Conference on Revenue-Producing Facilities*, Wheeling, W.Va., March 11–14, 1962, p. 58.

Notes to Chapter 4

1. Lindsay hoped by his leadership to bring about a renaissance of parks; see John V. Lindsay, *White Paper on Parks and Recreation* (issued by Fusion Candidate for Mayor), October 8, 1965.

2. Open-space thinking was foreshadowed in the recreation era by city planners interested in green belts and garden cities, and even earlier by Olmsted's own efforts to create interconnected systems of parks in most cities where he worked, including greater New York City, Boston, Minneapolis, and Seattle. The post-1965 era is unique for its interest in small fragments of the cityscape as well as larger networks of space.

3. *Proceedings of the Sixty-seventh Annual Conference of the American Institute of Park Executives, Inc.*, Milwaukee, Wisc., September 19–23, 1965, pp. A6–A7.

4. Chicago, Park District, *Report 1966*, p. 2.

5. Personal communication, 1974.

6. Young adults who grew up in New York City during the 1950s

report that there was nothing to do, that the parks were just there (personal interviews with graduate sociology students, CUNY, 1974). One of the most astute landscape designers observed, "It was felt in many quarters that as an institution, the Parks Department had become seriously bogged down . . . or at any rate was reflecting an era no longer with us. The current regime dates largely from the 1930s." Robert B. Nichols, "New York City's Park-Design Controversy," *Landscape Architecture*, vol. 53 (July 1963), p. 285.

7. Dan Kiley (landscape architect), quoted in the *Chicago Sun Times*, January 26, 1969.

8. "A Summer Night's Dream: The Arts in Central Park," *New York Times*, August 9, 1972.

9. New York City, Department of Parks, *Report 1967*, p. 4.

10. New York City, Department of Parks, *Report 1967*.

11. "Central Park Buffs Mark Designer's Birthday," *New York Times*, May 1, 1972. See also files of the design firm which created the cake, Haus-Rucker, Inc., New York City.

12. My emphasis. See Donald G. Brauer, "Park Planning for the Future," *Parks and Recreation*, vol. 7 (November 1972), p. 14. Herbert Gans, in *People and Plans* (New York: Basic Books, 1968), drew on the adage that you can lead a horse to water but you can't make him drink in arguing that a planner could provide facilities but could not actually guarantee a leisure experience.

13. A historic site reveals "diverse urban elements as the traditional urban park reveals nature, and they both serve as social gathering places." Paul M. Bray, "Preservation Helps New Parks Take Shape," *Kite*, December 6, 1978, p. 1.

14. Personal interview with Don Simon, curator of Prospect Park, 1974. The preservation of public open space became part of San Francisco's 1972 improvement plan, and in Chicago private open-space groups welcomed similar refinements in park programming.

15. Mary Maxine Boyd, "Parks for All Seasons . . . and for All People," *Parks and Recreation*, vol. 5 (May 1970), p. 23.

16. *Proceedings of the Sixty-seventh Annual Conference of the American Institute of Park Executives, Inc.*, Milwaukee, Wisc., September 19–23, 1965, p. A7.

17. Another example of such a struggle over visibility comes from *People's World*, August 28, 1965. Three hundred persons met in

Merritt Park's bandstand in Oakland to reaffirm their opposition to the Vietnam War in 1965. They met in defiance of a police order which sought to banish them to a smaller and less conspicuous locale.

18. Personal interviews, Henry Hope Reed, Doris Freedman, and Thomas Hoving, New York City, 1974. Similarly, when the National Park Service established parks adjacent to urban centers, old-line naturalists only reluctantly shifted from a policy of conservation to active service.

19. Edwin L. Weisl, Jr., pp. 1–6 of a written speech to the City Club, New York City, undated 1974. One fine point against intense use of the park was that overlapping generates too many things in complex relationships to one another, inappropriate when life itself cannot be so planned. (Leticia Kent, Weisl's assistant, present at personal interview, 1974.)

20. Lindsay, *White Paper*, p. 3.

21. The rationale for expanding the National Park Service closer to metropolitan areas was the same.

22. Streets were not only where the action was, but also they provided less costly sites. The San Francisco Department of City Planning went so far as to suggest that, because of the high cost of land in high-density areas, sidewalk widening with planting and seeding be substituted for conventional park development. *Recreation and Open Space Programs: Recommendations for Implementing the Recreation and Open-Space Element of the Comprehensive Plan of San Francisco.* Department of City Planning, July 1973.

The pragmatic side of site selection always accompanied the ideal. By the mid-1970s community development block grants to improve housing allowed cities to make parks out of vacant lots—these sites can hardly be said to have been selected at all. Further, worries about money were so severe that park departments, reluctant to add to their overall acreage, called these parcels lot improvements instead of parks and hoped to sell them to individuals or community organizations after improving them. They had little interest in insuring that the lots played a role in a network of open spaces.

23. Several cities experimented with installing play equipment underneath freeways, but Seattle was the first to sponsor an over-the-freeway park. See Hans A. Thompson, "Seattle's Over-the-Freeway Park," *Parks and Recreation*, vol. 7 (June 1972), pp. 36–38. Lawrence Halprin, "Landscape Between Walls," *Architectural Forum*, vol. 3 (1959), pp. 148–153, describes interstices, and Jacques Simon and Marguerite Rouard, *Children's Playspaces* (New York: Overlook Press, 1977), enumerate "hidden spaces." Karen Engstrom, "Lake Union Park—A Back-to-Nature Site," *Seattle Times Pictorial*, December 16, 1973, pp. 32–37, describes the reclamation of an abandoned industrial site.

24. Interview with Bill Hodgson, June 19, 1974, New York City.

25. Donald G. Brauer, "Park Planning for the Future," p. 14.

26. Lindsay, *White Paper*, p. 10.

27. August Heckscher's letter of transmittal, New York City, Department of Parks, *Report 1967*.

28. The Drunk Park in San Francisco is a rare example of a more revolutionary design for a vest-pocket park. A city lot has been filled with seven-foot sections of galvanized sewer pipes for winos to sleep in. Designers and, more to the point, funders, seldom tolerate this kind of radical empiricalism, but a church sponsored this design for the actual behavior of drunks. In only its first year of use, it is so popular that a second is being planned. Tom Coles, "Sixth Street Park," *Archetype*, vol. 2 (Autumn 1980), p. 47.

29. Jane Jacobs, *Death and Life of Great American Cities* (New York: Vintage Books, 1961); Ruth Leeds Love, "The Fountains of Urban Life," *Urban Life and Culture*, vol. 2 (July 1973), pp. 161–209; William H. Whyte's film and book *The Social Life of Small Urban Spaces* (New York: The Conservation Foundation, 1980). Paley Park was designed by the firm of Zion and Breen.

30. Brauer, "Park Planning for the Future," p. 14.

31. *Chicago Sun Times*, June 25, 1968.

32. The decorative use of fountains also exemplified the affinity between the old City Beautiful movement and the open-space system. In the European version of the adventure playground water was a plastic element important to children's play, but in America lack of supervision and maintenance problems curtailed its use.

33. The multilayered, terraced, and multifaceted point of land which extended into Lake Michigan in Chicago, even though designed in the 1930s, offers contemporaries a worthy example of a physical structure which could accommodate the copresence of diametrically opposed social groups: black bongo players, retired Jewish swimmers, university students, gay men, teenyboppers, football players, families, serious swimmers, weekend sunbathers. This place works much like the Portland fountains studied by Love, "The Fountains of Urban Life."

34. *San Francisco Examiner*, December 2, 1968.

35. Ray L. Tribble, "Trends in the Design of Community Centers," *Proceedings of the Twentieth Annual Conference of the Great Lakes Training Institute*, Indiana University, Bloomington, 1966.

36. Only one innovation in the use of plant material was adopted nationwide during the era: gardens for the blind composed of raised beds of flowers with strong fragrances.

37. For example, see the cartoon reprinted in Seymour M. Gold, "Urban Parks: An Endangered Species," *California Parks and Recreation*, vol. 33 (February-March 1977), p. 28. Seymour M. Gold, "Social and Economic Benefits of Trees in Cities," *Journal of Forestry*, February 1977, pp. 84–87, and *idem*, "Social Benefits of Trees in Urban Environments," *International Journal of Environmental Studies*, vol. 10 (1977), pp. 85–90.

38. The only welcome building type was the indoor recreation center, which Lindsay pledged himself to give high priority in slum areas. Lindsay, *White Paper*, p. 4.

39. Mosley, "Our Parks, People Keep Out!" pp. 40–44.

40. When twenty stables were built without a city building permit in San Francisco, they were torn down. *San Francisco Progress*, City Central Edition, March 24, 1976.

41. *San Francisco Examiner*, September 1, 1975; *San Francisco Progress*, September 5, 1975; *San Francisco Daily Commercial News*, December 13, 1968.

42. Ada Louise Huxtable, "Just a Little Love, A Little Care," *New York Times*, December 9, 1973, and "Parks Department Offers a Building for a Museum," *New York Times*, July 19, 1966.

43. Kevin Starr, "Man Who Grew Golden Gate Park," *California Living Magazine, San Francisco Sunday Examiner* and *Chronicle*, November 7, 1976, p. 33.

44. *San Francisco Chronicle*, December 20, 1968. Thomas Devine, Letter to the Editor, *New York Times*, July 7, 1967.

45. Henry Raymont, "For Art, Fifth Avenue is a Two-Way Street," *New York Times*, June 5, 1970, p. 18.

Notes to Chapter 5

1. The secure place of parks among urban institutions stems in part from the fact that the same groups who have occasionally opposed them—idealists, civic organizations, newspapers, landowners, and government agencies—have also promoted them. No social group has consistently thrown its weight against parks, and they are not a divisive issue. To the contrary, they function as a mechanism of tension management by being an arena for consensus between groups with conflicting interests in other spheres of life. Ultimately, the true opposition to parks lies in the limits imposed by functioning in this way. While no group consistently opposes parks, no one vigorously defends a particular vision of parks either, for fear of alienating others. Parks are defeated not by any social group but by the contradictions between consensus and integration, on the one hand, and action on the other.

2. For example, see the account in Chicago, South Park Commission, *Report 1908*, p. 72.

3. Lois Wille, *Forever Open, Clear and Free* (Chicago: Henry Regnery Co., 1972).

4. John C. Olmsted, "The True Purpose of a Large Public Park," *Park and Outdoor Art Association*, 1897, p. 11.

5. *San Francisco Alta*, May 29, 1866, p. 1.

6. David L. Wiemer, *Private Funds for Parks and Recreation* (Long Island City, N.Y.: Playground Corporation of America, 1969), pp. 29, 31; and Rainwater, *Play Movement*, p. 133. Private foundations, especially the Russell Sage Foundation, established in 1907, and the Harmon Foundation, established in 1922 (specifically for the purpose of acquiring land for permanent play space while costs were low and desirable locations available), promoted recreation, the use of schoolyards, and research on community conditions.

7. "Andrew Jackson Downing, Father of American Parks," *Park International*, July 1920, p. 48.

8. San Francisco, Park Commission, *Report 1890*. San Francisco's Commissioner Stowe "believes that the generous gifts of philanthropic citizens should enrich and beautify the park." *San Francisco Examiner*, June 11, 1894. After the commissioners had secured money for the construction of a lake, they started looking for "generous citizens to buy for the park the bronze cider press and vase" left from the Midwinter Fair of 1894. "The commissioners are constantly on a keen lookout for rich men with generous impulses. Such must expect to yield or to keep out of the track of W. W. Stowe." Park Clipping File, McLaren Lodge, San Francisco, ca. 1895.

9. See, for examples, the *San Francisco Alta*, June 15, 1876, p. 1 and San Francisco, Park Commission Minutes, July 1, 1909, p. 111, respectively.

10. Through the Chamber of Commerce, San Franciscans urged Congress to lease the Presidio Reservation lands to the city as a public park. *San Francisco Alta*, February 20, 1874, p. 1. The merchants association of San Francisco was organized in 1894 for the improvement of the city, which focused on street cleaning, street paving, lighting, and parks. Kiwanis and Lions Clubs continued this tradition of businessmen functioning as civic organizations up until the present day. Robert H. Weibe, *Businessmen and Reform* (Cambridge: Harvard University Press, 1962).

11. William Hammond Hall, unpublished manuscript. This set of commissioners were E. L. Sullivan, C. J. Brenham, William Alvord, Louis McLane, and Oliver Eldridge.

12. For example, one commissioner worked on the behalf of the condemned anarchists eventually executed after the Haymarket Riots in Chicago.

13. After Chicago's devastating fire of 1873, the commission was financed privately by two members—Chauncey Bowen and L. B. Sidway—until they ran out of money and access to it. Their New York friends on the American Exchange Bank, and philanthropist Robert Bayard, came to their rescue "due largely to the personal relations between them." Chicago, South Park Commission, *Report 1908*, p. 60.

14. J. D. Redding, appointed in 1892. *San Francisco Call*, July 9, 1895, p. 8.

15. C. S. Sargent, "Parks, Parkways and Pleasure-Grounds," *Garden and Forest*, vol. 8 (May 15, 1895), p. 192.

16. The Boston park commissioners similarly suffered charges of negligent, corrupt management, extravagance, gross waste, incompetence, and corruption, simulating the commission's own investigation in 1900. See Nathan Matthews, Jr., *The Investigation of the Boston Park Department* (Boston Municipal Printing Office, 1900).

17. New York State, *Documents of the Assembly*, vol. 2, no. 131, 80th sess., 1857.

18. Judges, who "would rank considerably above average men," were likely to represent the different political parties, and would be in a position to know a lot about the men from whom they would make a selection. Chicago, South Park Commission, *Report 1908*, p. 66.

19. In Seattle an analysis of the years 1890 to 1904 shows that twenty-four park commissioners sat on a board of five and that few served their full term, many resigning after a little more than a year of service. Clarence B. Bagley, "Municipal Parks," *History of Seattle*, p. 274. Sargent made the same complaint about New York City in "The Need for an Efficient Park Service," *Garden and Forest*, vol. 9 (May 6, 1896), p. 181.

20. F. E. Fantset (landscape gardener), *San Francisco Star*, July 22, 1893.

21. C. S. Sargent, "Park Lands and Their Boundaries," *Garden and Forest*, vol. 9 (October 21, 1896), p. 421.

22. *Chicago Globe*, March 12, 1888.

23. C. S. Sargent, "Park Boards and Their Professional Advisors," *Garden and Forest*, vol. 7 (November 21, 1894), p. 461.

24. C. S. Sargent, "Work for the Municipal Art Society," *Garden and Forest*, vol. 7 (January 10, 1894), p. 11.

25. Sargent, "Park Boards," p. 462.

26. Charles W. Eliot, "The Need of Conserving the Beauty and Freedom of Nature in Modern Life," *National Geographic*, vol. 26 (1914), p. 68. Professional associations for landscape architects included the Municipal Art Association, the Society of American Artists, the National Academy of Design, the Architectural League, the American Institute of Architects, the Art Students League, the Sculpture Society, and the American Fine Arts Society.

27. Although recreation workers have different kinds of work to do than social workers, work with a different client, and work for a different bureaucracy, recreation has always been a subfield of social work.

28. "In the Field . . . John W. Faust," *Recreation*, vol. 42 (October 1948), p. 327.

29. Smergalski, "Relation of Supervision," p. 17.

30. L. H. Weir, "Historical Background of the Recreation Movement in America," *Parks and Recreation*, vol. 29 (July-August 1946), p. 242.

31. Arthur Williams, "An Organization Is Born," *Recreation*, vol. 40 (June 1946), p. 261.

32. National Recreation Association, State and Federal Recreation Service, Publication 2: "The Role of the Federal Government in the Field of Public Recreation" (New York: National Recreation Association, 1953), p. 51.

33. San Francisco, Playground Commission Minutes, January 25, 1928.

34. San Francisco, Park Commission Minutes, October 1937, p. 59.

35. Richard M. Baker, "Public Relations in Recreation," *Recreation*, vol. 50 (October 1957), p. 300.

36. New York City, Department of Parks, *Report 1916*, pp. 27, 29.

37. Ibid., p. 63.

38. Brown, "This New Leisure," p. 363.

39. Hall mentions this observation of Olmsted's in his memoirs, and the original is in F. L. Olmsted, *Walks and Talks of an American Farmer in England* (New York: George P. Putnam, 1852).

40. Chicago, South Park Commission, *Report 1912*, pp. 44–45.

41. See George Hjelte, "City Parks . . . Amenity or Necessity?" *Recreation*, vol. 53 (May 1960), p. 213.

42. The New York senate report on Central Park stated that it was not proper for a municipal corporation to purchase lands on speculation, but it acknowledged that it "could not be concealed that the Central Park has been, and will be, in a merely pecuniary point of view, one of the wisest and most fortunate measures ever undertaken by the City of New York." New York State, *Senate Document*, vol. 1, no. 18 (1861), p. 18. The park had already more than quadrupled the value of much of the property in its vicinity by 1861.

43. Heriot C. Hutchins, "An Approach to Recreation Planning," *Recreation*, vol. 43 (September 1949), p. 275.

44. See table 7, "Amount and Share of General Expenditures, City Park and Recreation Activities, 1955–1970," in U.S. Department of Housing and Urban Development, *Urban Recreation* (Washington, D.C.: Government Printing Office, 1974), p. 58.

45. Editorial Notes, "Tax-Free Areas," *Park International*, July 1920, pp. 71–72.

46. For a review of these alternative methods of gaining land, see Hjelte, "City Parks," pp. 213–214. The New York annual report for 1954 also summarized the sources of land: transfer from other departments by acquisition of tax liens, condemnation, and donation; joint programs with schools and semipublic, public, and private housing agencies; projects in connection with parkways and expressways, civic centers, reclamation, waterfront and other neglected areas.

47. In Chicago, for example, the Public Works Administration (PWA) and the Works Progress Administration (WPA) made possible extensive paving of the park and boulevard driveways, especially the outer drive and the bridge between north and south Chicago, the construction and renovation of both the landscaping and the field houses in many neighborhood parks like Riis Park, and the creation of park beaches.

48. New York City, Department of Parks, *Six Years of Park Progress, 1934–1940*, p. 19.

49. The Trust for Public Land has spearheaded such maneuvers across the nation. Lowell, Massachusetts, and other urban cultural parks have involved unprecedented coordination of local, state, and federal funding sources.

Notes to Chapter 6

1. *San Francisco Call*, October 6, 1912, p. 5. Olmsted felt that the landscape itself, not only the intermingling of the classes, would inspire communal feelings among them and mute resentments over disparities of wealth and fashion: Geoffrey Blodgett, "Frederick Law Olmsted: Landscape Architecture as Conservative Reform," *Journal of American History*, vol. 62 (March 1976), p. 878. Bender argues that Olmsted's generation considered the nation's most urgent social program to be the development of urban institutions that would bring all social classes together; Bender, *Toward an Urban Vision*, p. 178.

2. L. E. Holden, "Parks as Investors and Educators," *First Report of the [American] Park and Outdoor Art Association*, 1897, p. 48.

3. "Olmsted Will Be Honored around the Country," *New York Times*, January 15, 1972.

4. New York State, Senate Document, vol. 3, no. 26 (1884), p. 86.

5. San Francisco, Park Commission, *Report 1897*, pp. 18–19.

6. *Chicago News*, October 17, 1900.

7. *San Francisco Bulletin*, November 3, 1900.

8. J. Horace McFarland, "Parks and the Public," *Parks and Recreation*, vol. 6 (September-October 1922), p. 12.

9. Chicago, South Park Commissioners, *Report 1921*, p. 69.

10. Conrad L. Wirth, "Related Park and Recreational Problems," *Parks and Recreation*, vol. 20 (December 1936), p. 173.

11. *San Francisco Call*, May 1, 1900, p. 1. For a fuller discussion of the Children's Quarter, see Galen Cranz, "The Sharon Building: The Transformation of Women's Recreational Needs in the Late Nineteenth Century," *Heresies 11*, vol. 3 (1981), pp. 77–79.

12. *San Francisco Call*, March 8, 1887, p. 5. The children's building and its display facilities were enormously popular, but its fees made it inaccessible to poor children. The populist *San Francisco Examiner* fought to reduce charges for donkey rides from 5¢ to two for 5¢. This increased business and yielded a thousand-dollar profit, which was used to pay for a free day for poor kids.

13. But not day care. The Golden Gate Kindergarten Association asked the commission to cooperate in joint sponsorship of a kindergarten to take care of small children whose mothers worked in the morning, but the department put the issue into abeyance—permanently (San Francisco, Playground Commission Minutes, December 29, 1926)—and a year and a half later the same commission voted to eliminate the kindergarten department from the playground organization altogether. Park departments have nearly always drawn the line at day care, although not, after the reform period, at all kinds of custodial arrangements.

14. The Right Rev. Nicholas H. Wegner (director of Father Flanagan's Boys' Home in Nebraska), "The Significance of Play," *Recreation*, vol. 48 (October 1955), p. 358.

15. Special groups of children were singled out for federal attention, among them juvenile delinquents, children of migrant families, bedridden children, mentally retarded or disturbed children, and children in foster homes and institutions.

16. "A Children's Play Area with Some New Ideas Is Started in Central Park," *New York Times*, September 29, 1972.

17. C. Gilbert Wren and D. L. Hanley, "Time on Their Hands," *Recreation*, vol. 35 (September 1941), p. 364.

18. R. T. Harbo, "Recreation Has a Job to Do," *Recreation*, vol. 38 (July 1944), pp. 201–204. The first national conference on the prevention of juvenile delinquency was held in 1947.

19. *San Francisco Recreation*, November 1944.

20. Chicago, Park Commission, *Report 1944*, p. 5. In New York, Moses was not interested in these more refined appeals to adolescents. His cure for juvenile delinquency was old fashioned: "Keep young folks occupied in their spare time, give them plenty of elbow room for play, stimulate competitive sports, and half at least of the youth problem is solved." *Recreation Bulletin*, February 4, 1946.

21. See Graenum Berger, "Human Problems of Old Age," *Recreation*, vol. 39 (October 1945), pp. 373–374, 386–387.

22. *San Francisco News*, October 31, 1957.

23. Richard Wade, "Problems and Possibilities in Urban History" (unpublished paper, The University of Chicago, 1969), p. 29.

24. Chicago, South Park Commission, *Report 1908*, pp. 110–111.

25. Rainwater, *Play Movement*, p. 109.

26. New York City, Department of Parks, *Report 1914*, photograph entitled "The Melting Pot;" San Francisco, Playground Commission, *Report 1928–1929*, "Where 37 Varieties Play," also calls playgrounds "melting pots," p. 24. This ideal was hard to realize, according to an account from the 1930s: "In Chicago at least, parks and sectors within larger parks like Lincoln were so rigidly staked out as were the ethnic, racial, and class neighborhoods from which the people came. One would no more venture into 'other people's' area within Lincoln Park as venture into their home neighborhoods." Personal correspondence, John C. Pock, January 8, 1981.

27. "Saving the Parks," *Chicago Tribune*, November 7, 1948.

28. Chicago, Park Department, *Report 1953*, p. 7.

29. New York City, Park Commission, *Report 1913*, p. 124.

30. Ibid., p. 178.

31. Ironically, acknowledging the recreational uses of the streets

in the late 1960s became a way for park departments to show they were "hip" and aware of and willing to meet the "real" recreational needs.

32. A. Attwell, "Playgrounds," p. 217.

33. Ibid., p. 218. Results of a survey of municipalities made by the Playground and Recreation Association of America, ca. 1919.

34. Nash, "Playgrounds," *Encyclopedia of the Social Sciences*, 1932, p. 163.

35. "Facilities Available to Colored Citizens," *Recreation*, vol. 35 (October 1941), p. 439.

36. Florence Jansson, "Give Them Something to Do," *Recreation*, vol. 38 (January 1945), pp. 525–526, 550.

37. Chicago, Park Department, *Report 1947*, p. 64.

38. For example, Chicago, Park Department, *Report 1966*, p. 20.

39. Dave Warner, "Totlots," *Parks and Recreation*, vol. 5 (July 1970), pp. 32–33.

40. For a fuller discussion of women's roles see Galen Cranz, "Women in Urban Parks," *Signs*, vol. 5 supplement (Spring 1980), pp. 79–95, and Galen Cranz, "Women and Urban Parks: Their Roles as Users and Suppliers," in *Building for Women*, Suzanne Keller, ed. (Lexington, Mass.: Lexington Press, 1981), pp. 151–171. For a more specialized discussion of a building built especially for women and children in Golden Gate Park in 1886, see Galen Cranz, "The Sharon Building: The Transformation of Women's Recreational Needs in the Late Nineteenth Century," *Heresies 11*, vol. 3 (1981), pp. 77–79.

41. Boston City Council, "Annual Report of the Board of Commissioners of the Department of Parks," *Documents for the City of Boston for the Year 1890*, document 15 (Boston, 1890), p. 30.

42. For example, "San Francisco Belles Gain Health and Muscle on Stowe Lake," *San Francisco Call*, October 11, 1896, p. 15.

43. New York, Museum of the City of New York, "Central Park File, Photos and Lithos pre-1900," vertical files.

44. A small park might be divided by a fence, within which women and girls and little children would be allowed, while boys and men would be seated outside (New York City, Park Commission, *Report 1913*, p. 7). As late as 1922, the San Francisco Park Commission received a request for more benches in Hunting Square with signs to read, "These Benches and This Part of This

Square is Hereby Reserved for Ladies and Children." The motion passed (San Francisco, Park Commission Minutes, April 1922, p. 620); and in August 1926 the Department of Health similarly requested that a portion of Columbia Square be fenced or roped off for the use of women and children, and again the park commission complied. Only in the 1930s did this kind of protective segregation wane.

45. New York City, Park Commission, *Report 1904*, p. 19.

46. The last reference to a special area for women and children on a San Francisco beach was in the minutes of the San Francisco Park Commission for May 1934.

47. Chicago, Park Department, *Report 1939*, p. 150. Charles A. Bucher, "Family Recreation: Foe of Juvenile Delinquency," *Recreation*, vol. 50 (February 1957), pp. 46–48.

48. Ben Solomon, "Preventive Recreation," *Recreation*, vol. 49 (March 1951), p. 566.

49. Of the few new activities developed just for women, all were sexually stereotyped. Toward the end of the Depression women decorated the lounge rooms in the local Chicago field houses. They hung wall hangings and draperies at the windows and brought in furniture and rugs (Chicago, Park Department, *Report 1939*, p. 153). Recreation programming during the war was oriented exclusively to servicemen—since only men were drafted into military service, the one female activity was preparing entertainments for the men.

Notes to Chapter 7

1. Nevertheless, advocates from the pleasure ground era insisted on discussing benefits to the social system such as moral influence and the decline of nervousness. In their minds, proper socialization would create better workers and parents who would raise better children. The system as a whole would gain strength and resilience.

2. Wren and Hanley, "Time," p. 366.

3. Jane Jacobs, *Death and Life*, p. 92.

4. For example, Thompson, "Over-the-Freeway," pp. 36–38. The Heritage Conservation and Recreation Service and the National League of Cities renewed this claim in the late 1970s.

5. New York State, Senate Document, vol. 1, no. 18, (1861), p. 18.

6. *Pocket Map and Visitors' Guide to Central Park,* 1859; T. Addison Richards, "The Central Park," 1866, and T. Addison Richards, "The Central Park Explained and Illustrated in Familiar Form," 1871. These were part of the appeal to tourists detailed in American Scenic and Historical Preservation Society, *Sixteenth Annual Report,* 1911, pp. 381–489.

7. Chicago, South Park Commission, *Report 1883,* p. 16.

8. *San Francisco Alta,* February 27, 1878, p. 1.

9. *San Francisco Examiner,* July 10, 1893.

10. Chicago Plan Commission, *Chicago Can Get Fifty Million Dollars for Nothing!* (Chicago: Chicago Plan Commission, 1916).

11. *San Francisco Chronicle,* December 14, 1955. Today city parks are seldom tourist attractions; only the most famous ones like Central Park and Golden Gate Park attract foreign visitors. Parks are not self-conscious about urban society—the pleasure grounds turn their backs on it, the reform parks try to fix it, the recreation facility serves it, and the open-space system integrates with it—so they cannot sustain the touristic function, which MacCannell has defined as turning a social process into an object of appreciation; see Dean MacCannell, *The Tourist: A New Theory of the Leisure Class* (New York: Schocken, 1976). When parks are viewed less as nature, less as part of the urban backdrop, and understood more as deliberate social experiments, they may regain the appeal to tourism that they had earlier when their status as experiments was clearer in the public mind.

12. A Chicago newspaper detailed in a surprisingly modern way the mechanisms through which experiencing the park was processed by the mind of an infant: "The baby is busy taking in, correlating, and putting away in its inner consciousness impressions of the universe. So that sometimes—twenty years hence—there will flash into its mind a scene made up of leafy trees, sparkling grees grass, and a cool, blue sky, the result of its mental photography of yesterday." "Sunday in the Park," *Chicago News,* July 9, 1888, p. 2.

13. Relaxing activities were defended in times of war: "They are nature's own nerve tonics. . . . By encouraging everybody to encourage his own recreation, his own saving hobby, we can beat all the Hitlers, and all their campaigns, in any war of nerves that they may launch!" Brown, "The Place of Parks," p. 154. Yet as soon as the war was over park propaganda, with characteristic obviousness, reintroduced the idea that park activities were fun rather

than a means to an end. "Industrial workers, constituting the larger membership of our older teams, played through their competition in the name of physical fitness and plant morale. They hesitated to admit that an interval of honest fun relieved the monotony of serving in production lines. Such admissions were apparently avoided as being unworthy of the boys at the front who couldn't permit themselves the luxury of recreation." Chicago, Park District, *Report 1945*, p. 67.

Recreation was superior to psychotherapy: "all of our group work and recreational organizations have done and are doing a great deal toward the prevention of later difficulties, emotional in origin, which may otherwise end in an individual having to seek special and expert help because of nervous or personality difficulties." Evelyn Spencer, "The Wheel Has Turned Full Circle: The Relationship of Group Work, Recreation and Mental Health," *Recreation*, vol. 44 (November 1950), p. 311.

14. New York City, Parks Department, *Report 1904*, p. 15.

15. Chicago, South Park Commission, *Report 1905*, pp. 58–59.

16. R. C. Morrison, "Rugged Individualism and Community Beautification," *Parks and Recreation*, vol. 17 (July 1934), p. 387.

17. O. C. Simonds, "Appreciation of Natural Beauty," *Second Report of the American Park and Outdoor Art Association*, 1898, p. 79.

18. Chicago, Park Department, *Report 1939*, p. 163.

19. Robert Moses, "The Moses Recipe for Better Parks," *Recreation*, vol. 49 (May 1956), p. 215.

20. San Francisco, Playground Commission, *Report 1928–1929*.

21. Chicago, Park Department, *Report 1951*, p. 93.

22. Thus, for example, the early park reporters estimated that Central Park attracted 10 million visitors in 1860 and 15 million a year in the 1870s. Similarly, in Chicago 20,000 to 30,000 were reported visiting Lincoln Park on Sundays. These figures had meaning in and of themselves.

23. Chicago, South Park Commission, *Report 1905*, p. 6.

24. Chicago, South Park Commission, *Report 1906*, p. 46.

25. Chicago, South Park Commission, *Report 1908*, p. 114.

26. Chicago, South Park Commission, *Report 1937*, p. 25. Today low attendance figures are used as a selling point by promoters of National Parks and wilderness areas.

27. Although park departments reported a consistent increase in use—for example, the National Recreation Association reported a twelvefold increase in playground use from 1910 to 1950 and a thirty-three-fold increase in use of indoor centers, and in San Francisco a comparison between 1912 and 1954 showed a fivefold increase—in no case were the figures compared to percentage increases in population growth. A rare critic of the idea that attendance figures were the ultimate measure of adequate recreational service noted, "the idea that participation in a recreation activity—in any recreation activity—is an end in itself dies hard. It is still held by many who do not see where it leads, and it puts recreation leaders in the position of having to evaluate their movement in terms of numbers and nothing else." Harold Williams, "Can Recreation Have an Ulterior Motive?" *Recreation*, vol. 51 (September 1958), p. 228.

28. Chicago, South Park Commission, *Report 1912*, p. 45.

29. Chicago, Park Department, *Report 1937*, p. 146.

30. Prezioso, "My Philosophy," p. 509.

31. One of the earliest to call attention to the possibility of overuse was David L. Wiemer, *Private Funds for Parks and Recreation* (Long Island City, N.Y.: Playground Corporation of America, 1969), p. 22.

32. Charles W. Eliot, "Popular Utilization of Public Reservations," *American Park and Outdoor Art Association*, vol. 6, part 2 (1903), p. 6.

33. On a Sunday in San Francisco 11,000 people went to the various theatres, 10,000 to the circus, 4,000 to a baseball game, and 3,000 to the coursing grounds—in all, an "afternoon army of 28,000 pleasure seekers." Others went to dancing pavilions, to the baths at the Cliff (Sutro Baths), to harbor-viewing spots, and across the bay to picnic grounds and shooting parks. *San Francisco Chronicle*, September 2, 1901.

34. "The Public Dance Hall: The Problem as Dealt with by San Francisco Committee," *Parks and Recreation*, vol. 7 (July-August 1924), p. 596.

35. WPA Writer's Project, *Foreign Language Press Survey* (Chicago, 1940). The papers, listed in the bibliography, were German, Polish, Bohemian, Jewish, and Italian. The index to the survey does not even list parks or recreation, further evidence of the remote connection between municipal parks and ethnic groups. In the absence of indexing I checked "Avocational and Intellectual Contributions and Activities," "Aesthetic," "Theatrical," "Festivals, Pageants, Fairs, Expositions," "Athletics and Sports," "Permanent Memorials," "Benevolent and Protective Institutions," "Settlement Houses and Community Centers," "Assimilation," "Segregation," "Nationalistic Societies and Influences," "Youth Organizations," and "Representative Individuals."

36. *Cue*, July 14, 1945, p. 8.

37. M. Mannus, "The New York I Know: II. Central Park," *The Reporter*, January 21, 1960, p. 22.

38. Seymour M. Gold, "Neighborhood Parks, The Nonuse Phenomenon," *Evaluation Quarterly*, vol. 1 (May 1977); and Seymour M. Gold, "Nonuse of Neighborhood Parks," *Journal of the American Institute of Planners*, vol. 38 (November 1972), pp. 369–378. The most effective way to assess changes in attendance would be to compare statistics on city park use as a percentage of urban population through the four eras of park history, but such figures are not readily available.

39. For a fuller discussion of issues related to crime in parks, see Galen Cranz, "Crime in Heaven: An Historical Perspective on Crime and Delinquency in City Parks," paper presented at the Pacific Sociological Association meeting, Portland, Oregon, March 18–21, 1981.

40. New York City, Park Department, *Report 1903*, p. 29.

41. For example, "A Ramble in Central Park." *The New Yorker*, with its changing weekly covers, has often returned to Central Park for its subject matter in this century. In contrast, television did not often turn to park life for its programming. It turned instead to other more exotic environments which pleasure grounds had been for most people in the nineteenth century. Television eliminated part of the impetus to take a trip to a special local landscape and thereby contributed to the park's loss of standing in urban culture.

42. See Steve Dotterer and Galen Cranz, "The Picture Postcard: Its Development and Role in American Urbanization," *Journal of Popular Culture*, in press.

43. Empty pleasure grounds are good backdrops for movie scenes supposedly set in the historical past or a foreign land because they are so neutral as to time and place, and they are often unused. In the nineteenth century the pleasure grounds were picturesque, but travel, television, and the movies have jaded the appetite for the picturesque today, and the old parks seem less strongly contrasted to the surrounding city than they must have originally; that is to say, they seem more neutral.

44. This position has a design implication: if people only need to know that park land is held open and in public trust, then the designs of parks could become much more variable. Maintenance, in particular, could vary; Gold suggests that some parks could go to weeds, both as a money-saving tactic and to appeal to children and naturalists; see Seymour M. Gold, "The State of Urban Parks," *Parks and Recreation*, vol. 11 (October 1976), pp. 13–19.

Notes to Chapter 8

1. New York City, Department of Parks, *Report 1872.*

2. This must have been an important point to Hall: some of these figures are published in his engineer's report in the third biennial report of the San Francisco Commission for 1874–1875 and included in his unpublished memoirs.

3. Editorial from an unidentified newspaper, September 28, 1894, Park Clipping File in McLaren Lodge, Golden Gate Park, San Francisco.

4. New York City, Department of Parks, *Report 1872.*

5. San Francisco, Park Commission, *Report 1895.*

6. San Francisco, Park Commission, *Report 1870–1871*, p. 4.

7. *Staats Zeitung* (Illinois), October 22, 1867. Germans actively pressured West Chicago park commissions to build sports places within the municipal parks. *Abendpost*, June 26, 1895, WPA translation, Chicago Historical Society, and *San Francisco Call*, May 17, 1901.

8. Chicago, Park District, *Report 1939*, pp. 151–152. A college professor of sociology recounted his middle-class boyhood recollections of Lincoln Park between the years 1930 and 1942: "Although I was aware of Park-Bureau-sponsored 'activities,' I don't recall ever participating in any of them or exactly what they were—I think I now know why—I recall something called the 'fresh-air' or 'open-air' program and a vague image of kids taking naps in a screened-in area/structure somewhere in the park—associated with TB campaign and feeling left out." Not only the association of the park with the poor, but also the exclusivity of its ethnic patrons discouraged his involvement in organized activities. He remembered "large clumps of different ethnic groups with signs marking out territorial controls for Sunday picnics scattered at 'safe' distances from each other—with picnic tables pushed together that remained all week—I used to peer at them and the kids—and again the feeling of being left out." Personal correspondence from John C. Pock, January 8, 1981.

9. For example, the record book of the San Francisco Playground Commission (1920–1925 inclusive) for the date January 28, 1920, reveals heavy adult use of playgrounds on Saturday afternoons and Sundays.

10. See Joseph V. Lohman, *Police and Minority Groups* (Chicago: Chicago Police Department, 1947); and Allan H. Spear, *Black Chicago: The Making of a Negro Ghetto 1890–1920* (Chicago: The University of Chicago Press, 1967), pp. 116, 205–206.

11. Ernest Attwell, "Playgrounds for Colored Americans," *Parks International*, November 1920, pp. 217–224.

12. Chicago, Park District, *Report 1942*, p. 15.

13. V. K. Brown, "Now and Then in Our Park Systems," *The American City*, vol. 64 (April 1949), p. 75.

14. One of the few examples of a prourban sentiment in this period: Lakey, a park booster, said parks "are to form conspicuous ornaments of a city whose magnificence will result from the fact that she is to be the eastern portal of a region whose wealth and power cannot be measured by anything the world has yet seen" (Lakey, *The Public Grounds of Chicago*, 1869, p. 20).

15. Bender has offered an alternative interpretation. He has argued that for the nineteenth-century park advocates the city was as much respected as the country, and the reformers of that era hoped to be able to bring the two values into a counterpoint relationship rather than an antidote. "The interpretation offered challenges the notion that American thinkers of that period were simply antiurban. . . . Many Americans gradually, but definitely, abandoned agrarianism in favor of a more complex environmental vision. By midcentury they were seeking a new understanding of city and country, art and nature, that would allow them to hold key values identified with each" (Bender, *Toward an Urban Vision*, p. xi). My judgment is based on language as well as my reading of the meaning of these nineteenth-century writers. They used the term "antidote" or its synonyms more frequently than "counterpoint" and its equivalents.

An Italian analyst has viewed American parks as representing an urban-rural link, again the implication being that the city was not entirely to turn one's back on (Manfredo Tafuri, "Olmsted and the Origins of Planning in the United States," Conference, Massachusetts Institute of Technology, Cambridge, 1975).

16. Chicago, South Park, *Report 1908*, pp. 110–111.

17. New York City, Park Commission, *Report 1913*, p. 125.

18. Herbert Hare, "Trend of Park History," *Parks and Recreation*, vol. 5 (1970), p. 61.

19. In San Francisco, New York, New Orleans, and Seattle parks received the greatest amount of money spent on public works, and in Chicago, Cincinnati, Minneapolis, and Newark highways received the greater amount; but always one or the other was a major category for receiving funds. (Works Progress Administration, *WPA Projects: Analysis of Projects Placed in Operation Through June 30, 1937*, Washington, D.C.)

20. Chicago, Park District, *Report 1935*, p. 35.

21. Jere Stuart French, "The Decline and Deterioration of the American City Park," *Parks and Recreation*, vol. 5 (August 1970), p. 41.

22. Quoted at University of Michigan in Mel Scott, *American City Planning Since 1890* (Berkeley: University of California Press, 1969), chap. 8, "The Search for a New Comprehensiveness."

23. Thus social critics of the 1960s, from feminists to architects, viewed coffee houses and restaurants as a public service for bringing people together in this public way, allowing them to relate indirectly to one another through their mutual interest in a third event, object, or subject.

24. Marya Mannes, "The New York I Know: II. Central Park," *The Reporter*, January 21, 1960, p. 20.

25. "Park at 100 Finds City Life Timeless," *New York Times*, July 21, 1953.

26. Edward A. Ross, *Social Control: A Survey of the Foundation of Order* (Reprint of 1901 edition, New York: Johnson Reprint Corporation, subsidiary of Harcourt, Brace, Jovanovich, Inc., 1970). In sociological writing since Parsons, social control sometimes means latent or unintended control, sometimes the self-regulation of the masses, and sometimes the power of popular will. The term, as it is used in this study, has its narrower original meaning.

27. Attributed to New York City's Mayor Kingsland, April 5, 1851.

28. Cited in Geoffrey Blodgett, "Frederick Law Olmsted: Landscape Architecture as Conservative Reform," *The Journal of American History*, vol. 62 (March 1976), p. 875. In California the attitude of *noblesse oblige* was no less strong than in the east and midwest. Hall wrote in *Overland Monthly* regarding urban parks that it was "the duty of every wealthy community to foster such elements of refining influence as will tend toward a cultivation of the feelings of its least favored members." William Hammond Hall, "Influence of Parks and Pleasure Grounds," *Overland Monthly*, vol. 11 (December 1873), p. 529.

29. Blodgett, "Olmsted," p. 889.

30. Bender, *Toward an Urban Vision*, p. 179.

31. Samuel P. Hays, *Conservation and the Gospel of Efficiency 1890–1920* (Cambridge: Harvard University Press, 1959); C. W. Mills, *White Collar: The American Middle Classes* (New York: Oxford University Press, 1951); Julia and Herman Schwendinger, *The Sociologists of the Chair* (New York: Basic Books, 1974); Constance Perin, "Social Governance and Environmental Design," in *Responding to Social Change*, Basil Honikman, ed. (Stroudsberg, Penn.: Dowden, Hutchinson and Ross, 1975); Robert H. Wiebe, *Business and Reform* (Cambridge: Harvard University Press, 1962); and Robert H. Wiebe, *The Search for Order: 1877–1900* (New York: Hill and Wang, 1967).

32. *Los Angeles Times*, March 19, 1901.

33. Chicago, Park District, *Report 1936*, p. 193.

34. Chicago, Park District, *Report 1937*, p. 161.

35. San Francisco, Park Department, *Report 1966–1967*.

36. This reference is to New York City's Washington Square Park. Robert B. Nichols, "New York City's Park-Design Controversy," *Landscape Architecture*, vol. 53 (July 1963), pp. 286–287. Layering has proceeded not just from nostalgia and expediency but also from the developmental nature of park history: park authorities feel that each of the four historical types is necessary to have a complete recreational system. Thus cities that did not even exist in the mid-nineteenth century, when pleasure grounds were being built, reproduced this stage when their own park planning began in the early twentieth century.

37. One rare example of a park's being completely redesigned comes from Kansas City, where in 1908 a reform park with pergola and shallow pool complex was completely leveled and the pool filled with debris and covered with asphalt. It served in this way as an open playground next to an elementary school for many years. In 1970 it was redesigned according to the aesthetics of the open-space era, with a sculptural play unit. This park is unusual for having been completely changed from a reform park to a recreation facility to an adventure playground. E. F. Corwin, "Rebirth of a Park," *Parks and Recreation*, vol. 7 (October 1972), pp. 17–18.

38. For example, R. Clary, *The Making of Golden Gate Park* (San Francisco: California Living Books, 1980), and Edward S. Martin, "A Philosopher in Central Park," *Harpers*, February 1914. The transcendental value of communion with nature has never diminished but rather tends to move from the older pleasure grounds to the country, state, regional, and national parks.

39. George Hjelte, "City Parks . . . Amenity or Necessity?" *Recreation*, vol. 53 (May 1960), p. 214.

40. The relationship between parks and schools is another case in point. Reform parks sometimes tried to compete with schools directly, claiming to be a more effective agent of socialization since play worked through both mind and body and playgrounds were not limited to school hours. This expansive attitude was soon deflated, and park administrators had to settle for claiming that parks could be an important adjunct to the public school system.

41. Eliot, "The Need of Conserving the Beauty and Freedom of Nature in Modern Life," p. 69.

42. Chicago, Park District, *Report 1953*, p. 25.

43. Chicago, Park District, *Report 1950*, p. 70.

44. Chicago, Park District, *Report 1962*, p. 14.

45. Allan Jacobs, *Making City Planning Work*, p. 279.

46. This is the opinion of C. R. Dineen, "Parks and Planning," *Parks and Recreation*, vol. 29 (November-December 1946), p. 361.

47. Department of Planning, City of Chicago, *Basic Policies for the Comprehensive Plan of Chicago*, 1964. Physical facilities such as transportation lines, schools, and parks helped citizens to define and identify with their communities; "parks and recreation spaces can be brought into congested communities, to give more meaning to leisure."

48. Central Park is a symbol of historical continuity as a kind of time machine back to nineteenth-century New York City in the novel by Jack Finney, *Time and Again* (New York: Simon and Schuster, 1970).

49. Harry A. Overstreet, "Recreation: New Obligations—New Approaches," *Recreation*, vol. 38 (February 1945), p. 588.

50. New York City, Park Commission, *Report 1914*, p. 36.

51. Chicago, Park District, *Report 1937*, p. 143.

52. Colin Rowe and Fred Koeter, *Collage City* (Cambridge: The MIT Press, 1978).

53. Another way of looking at this is to say that process may be the answer: a mechanism, not a fixed solution, is the way in which planning achieves its ideals. This is a widespread dilemma of general significance. How is planning possible without planning *for*? Without the widespread use of democratic decision-making techniques at the grass-roots level, what can be done?

54. Historically citizens have pressured for more active sports, but this does not mean spaces for tranquility and serenity need be abandoned. We might consider giving up large meadows to active sports and securing smaller enclosed gardens for contemplation and meditation. More restaurants and eating places close to or within parks could also spring up in response to the popularity of eating out as recreation.

55. Some regional variation within the United States attests to the influence of geology, climate, and culture on parks and commons before the rise of the municipal park movement. The southern Atlantic style derived from plantations, dispersed settlement patterns, and reliance on river fronts; see Newton, *Design on the Land*. The New England style derived from a stony area of austere morality and no tradition of display, one whose towns were small, operationally compact, and near highways, with a common cow-pasture tradition and a tradition of drilling local militia which required a common open space. The south was generally slower to establish parks than the east, midwest, and far west, because it was not as industrialized as the other parts of the country and had a warm climate and tradition of outdoor life; parks were unnecessary.

56. These proposals have been published in Cranz, "Women in Urban Parks," and Cranz, "Women and Urban Parks."

57. Galen Cranz, "The Beautiful and the Useful: Urban Parks in China," *Landscape*, vol. 23 (1979), pp. 3–10.

Bibliography

Methodological Overview

The sources used in doing this study can be understood and used by others in the context of its general structure.

Each of the four chapters in part I followed the same general procedure. First, I described the social problems of the period as perceived by park planning theorists. I drew these pictures in the language of the day, using the terminology and categories of thought preferred by the writers of the time, to place each model in the intellectual order of its era. How people have understood urban problems has shaped their ideas about what parks should accomplish for society, and their ideas have been realized in the favored activities and forms of the urban park. Accordingly, each chapter described the activities planned for the park type it treats—what architects today call the program—and then characterized the ideal form of that type in regard to a cascade of physical variables: site selection and transportation, overall composition of the plan, the use of landscape elements, including water, land, trees, shrubs, lawn, paving, flowers, architecture, sculpture, signage, and equipment. Only when social context, physical form, and social program all changed, did I conclude that a new "type" had emerged (If only one of these dimensions changed I judged this a variation within the existing type. Thus the shifts in architectural style in the nineteenth century—from rustic to Richardsonian Romanesque to neoclassical—did not create a new type, nor did an elaboration of reform philosophy into "group social work" in the 1920s in one city; even dramatic historical events like World War II did not create a new model, since the program, form, and ideology behind them did not change, nor have recent changes in the kinds of support from the federal government, including the new mixtures of private and governmental financing, created a new "type.") This formulation of ideal park types took park ideology at face value.

Part II placed each model in its sociopolitical context by describing and analyzing its promoters and its intended and actual beneficiaries. A distinctive aspect of this study is its shift in point of view from the actor's to the analyst's, the subjective to the objective, the overt to the covert, the manifest to the latent, the ideal to the real, the descriptive to the theoretical, the emic to the etic. In order to understand our fore-planners' motivations from the inside, I wanted to feel what those decision makers felt and to assume their logic. Yet a change in ideological styles would not be a satisfactory explanation of changes due to underlying structural forces. Therefore I took two viewpoints, the first a description of parks and their goals in the terms people at the time used to justify their actions. Then I stepped back and put these ideologies into a context of social structure: Who was promoting these ideas for whom? An analysis of the social groups dispensing and receiving park services helped reveal the interests behind these actions. Those involved at the time eventually recognized discrepancies between the ideal and the real, and adjusted their plans accordingly. Thus the alternation between ideology and social reality created a dialectic from which new models for park usage emerged. Stepping back yet again to look at the relationships between parks, other urban institutions, and the city as a whole helped me assess their function even more broadly, at the institutional level of analysis. Because both insiders and outside analysts have made active, if differing, uses of the concept of social control in describing the purpose of parks, the concept recurs continuously throughout the book.

Evaluating Sources

Studying change over time—longer than one person's life—demands the use of archives rather than direct observation. Park professionals have written reports, articles, and books about the physical and social planning of city parks. Frederick Law Olmsted, and Andrew Jackson Downing before him, were prolific writers. Olmsted never published a book, but his reports were often published in the public documents of the agency his firm worked for, and since then enough of them have been collected in anthologies to provide a readily accessible explanation of his planning theories. Substantial collections are in Frederick Law Olmsted, Jr., and Theodora Kimball (ed.) *Forty Years of Landscape Architecture* (Cambridge: The MIT Press, 1973); S.B. Sutton (ed.), *Civilizing American Cities: A Selection of Frederick Law Olmsted's Writing on City Landscapes* (Cambridge: The MIT Press, 1971); Albert Fein, *Landscape into Cityscape: F.L. Olmsted's Plans for a Greater New York City* (Ithaca, N.Y.: Cornell University Press, 1968); Charles McLaughlin (ed.), *The Papers of Frederick Law Olmsted, Vol. 1. The Formative Years 1822–1852* (Baltimore, Md.: Johns Hopkins University Press, 1977).

Published conference proceedings and the official journals of professional societies are also important sources because practitioners from all over the country report on theory in practice. Further, those journals reprint pertinent articles from journals in related fields.

The most basic source for information about what park administrations did, and why, comes from their public documents—published annual reports and unpublished minutes. These documents are not without limitations: they do not always state the assumptions made about social context, requiring knowledge of local history. For example, *Report of the South Park Commissioners to the Board of County Commissioners of Cook County for the Year 1880*, p. 8, referred to legislation "so recently and so widely known as not to need comment."

Over time the quality of reports from the same department might vary, but that is information in itself useful in corroborating changes in era. Some departments consistently published better reports than others. For example, in Chicago the South Park Commission wrote much longer, more philosophically oriented reports than either the Lincoln or West Park Commissions, or the other small districts which existed in obscurity until consolidation of all the districts in 1935. Since even contemporaries recognized that the other districts had "not been so aggressively brilliant as the South Park Board," research today can rely disproportionately on the reports from one district (Chicago Bureau of Public Efficiency, *Park Government of Chicago*, Chicago, Illinois: Chicago Bureau of Public Efficiency, 1911, p. 11).

Their greatest drawback is that they suppress conflict. Thus no hint of the shortcomings of one park type is indicated until a new one is inaugurated, and no self-criticism is published until the problem has been resolved. For example, the Chicago South Park Commission's *Report 1921* was self-congratulatory about attendance figures being back up, but they did not criticize themselves in print when figures were down immediately after World War I (1919 to 1920). Similarly, the Chicago Park District's *Report 1939* revealed that the community council idea adopted from Rochester, New York, had not been working only when they had an exception, the Back of the Yards Council, to discuss.

Newspapers are a major compensation for this deficiency since some specialized in scandal and conflict, while others routinely supported establishment practices. Further, newspapers are one of the few ways to gauge popular reactions to official park planning. Unhappily, few newspapers are indexed, and those few have inadequate listings for articles on parks. For example, no newspaper index exists at the Library of the University of California, Berkeley, but one exists at the state library in Sacramento. That index, however, lists only a tiny portion of those articles—not even the most important—which were actually written about San Francisco's park system. Relevant clippings have been collected in scrapbooks for the years around the turn of the century in McLaren Lodge, park administration headquarters in Golden Gate Park. A similar collection (the Ambler Scrapbooks) at the Chicago Historical Society can help reduce the number of hours at microfilm reading machines.

Photographs, lithographs, and artwork of parks are also useful for assessing popular usage and for analyzing differences between artistic and real images of parks. When personal memoirs and oral histories refer to the parks in a city, they too are a source of data about the salience of parks; oral histories or biographies of non-elites are not common, however, limiting this source severely. My personal observations of park usage and design were obviously useful for the present era and, in fact, motivated this study. More systematic observational studies of park usage have been done by some researchers in the environmental behavior field (for example, Ruth Leeds Love, "The Fountains of Urban Life," *Urban Life* vol. 2 (July 1973), pp. 161–209, and Clare Cooper-Marcus, *People Places* (Berkeley, Calif.: Department of Landscape Architecture, 1976). Nevertheless, the usefulness of direct observation—whether personal or systematic—is limited when the analysis is institutional rather than behavioral.

Secondary sources offer useful guidelines to how someone else interprets parks, and, depending on when and from what perspective they were written, they can become primary sources themselves. For example, Henry S. Curtis, *The Play Movement and Its Significance* (New York: Macmillan, 1917), Clarence E. Rainwater, *The Play Movement in the United States* (Chicago, Illinois: The University of Chicago Press, 1922), and L.H. Weir (ed.) *Parks: A Manual of Municipal and County Parks, Vols. I and II* (New York: A.S. Barnes and Co, 1928) tell histories of the playground movement or the park and recreation movement, offering a summary of facts and a reliable chronology, but their purposes in writing make their analyses evocative of their own time and perspective. Local city histories which contain sections on parks share with park documents an unwillingness to expose issues that "divided or embarrassed particular cities" (C. N. Glaab and A. Theodore Brown, *History of Urban America*, New York: Macmillan, 1961, p. 231). Secondary sources are often primary because so many park scholars have been simultaneously a part of the park movement. Notable exceptions include social historians Geoffrey Blodgett, Thomas Bender, Paul Boyer, cultural geographers J. B. Jackson, Richard Walker, landscape architecture historians Albert Fein, Charles McLaughlin, N. T. Newton, and Walter Creese.

Books

Adams, William Howard, ed. *The Eye of Thomas Jefferson.* Washington, D.C.: National Gallery of Art, 1976.

Andrews, Wayne. *Architecture, Ambition and Americans: A Social History of American Architecture.* New York: The Free Press, 1964.

Aronowitz, Stanley. *False Promises: The Shaping of American Working-Class Consciousness.* New York: McGraw-Hill, 1974.

Bagley, Clarence B. *History of Seattle.* Vol. 1. Seattle, Wash.: Clarke, 1916.

Banfield, Edward C., and James Q. Wilson. *City Politics.* Cambridge, Mass.: Harvard University Press, 1963.

Beard, George M. *American Nervousness.* New York: Arno Press/ *New York Times*, 1972. (Originally published 1881.)

Bender, Thomas. *Toward an Urban Vision: Ideas and Institutions in Nineteenth-Century America.* University Press of Kentucky, 1975.

Benevolo, Leonardo. *The Origins of Modern Town Planning.* Cambridge: The MIT Press, 1967.

Bennett, Joseph W. *Vandals Wild.* Portland, Or.: Bennett Publishing, 1969.

Bernert, E. "Local Community Fact Book of Chicago." *Chicago Community Inventory.* Chicago: The University of Chicago Press, 1949.

Blumenson, J. J. G. *Identifying American Architecture.* Nashville, Tenn.: American Association for State and Local History, 1977.

Boyer, Paul. *Urban Masses and Moral Order in America, 1820–1920.* Cambridge: Harvard University Press, 1978.

Breines, Simon, and William J. Dean. *The Pedestrian Revolution: Streets Without Cars.* New York: Vintage Books, 1974.

Burnap, George. *Parks: Their Design, Equipment and Use.* Philadelphia: Lippincott, 1916.

Burns, Allen T. *Relation of Playgrounds to Juvenile Delinquency.* New York: Russell Sage, 1907.

Chadwick, George F. *The Park and the Town.* New York: Praeger, 1966.

Chapin, F. S. *Contemporary American Institutions.* New York: Harper, 1935.

Chase, I. W. U. *Horace Walpole: Gardenist.* Princeton, N.J.: Princeton University Press, 1943.

Chermayeff, Serge, and Christopher Alexander. *Community and Privacy: Toward a New Architecture of Humanism.* Garden City, N.Y.: Doubleday and Company, 1963.

Childhood and Government Project, University of California, Berkeley. "Wednesday's Child: Bearing the Costs of Post-War America." First draft of report, June 27, 1977.

Churchill, Henry S. *The City Is the People.* New York: W. W. Norton, 1962.

Clary, R. *The Making of Golden Gate Park.* San Francisco: California Living Books, 1980.

Clawson, Marion. *Statistics on Outdoor Recreation.* Washington, D.C.: Resources for the Future, 1958.

Cook, Peter. *Architecture: Action and Plan.* New York: Reinhold, 1967.

Counts, George S. *School and Society in Chicago.* New York: Harcourt, Brace and Company, 1928.

Counts, George S. *The Social Composition of Boards of Education: A Study in the Social Control of Public Education.* (Supplementary Educational monographs, published in conjunction with *The School Review and The Elementary School Journal,* Number 33, July 1927.)

Cranz, Galen. "Women in Urban Parks: Their Roles as Users and Suppliers of Recreation Services." In *Women and Land Use.* S. Keller, ed. Lexington, Mass.: Lexington Books, 1981.

Creese, Walter L. *The Search for Environment, The Garden City: Before and After.* New Haven: Yale University Press, 1966.

Curti, Merle. *The Social Ideas of American Educators.* New York: Scribners, 1935.

Curtis, Henry S. *The Play Movement and Its Significance.* New York: Macmillan, 1917.

Davis, Allen F. *Spearheads of Reform: The Social Settlements and the Progressive Movement 1890–1914.* New York: Oxford University Press, 1967.

Doell, C. E., and G. B. Fitzgerald. *A Brief History of Parks and Recreation in the U.S.* Chicago: Athletic Institute, 1954.

Doell, C. E., and L. F. Twardzik. *Elements of Park and Recreation Administration.* 3rd ed. Minneapolis: Burgess Publishing, 1963.

Donajgrodzki, A. P., ed. *Social Control in Nineteenth Century Britain.* Totowa, N.J.: Rowman and Littlefield, 1977.

Downing, Andrew Jackson. *Rural Essays.* New York: 1853.

Duffy, John. *A History of Public Health in New York City 1625–1866.* New York: Russell Sage, 1968.

Duhl, Leonard J., ed. *The Urban Condition.* New York: Basic Books, 1963.

Dunham, Allison. "Preservation of Open Spaces: A Study of the Nongovernmental." In *Forever Open, Clear and Free.* Lois Wille, ed. Chicago: Henry Regnery, 1972, appendix B.

Eliot, C. W. *Charles Eliot, Landscape Architect.* Boston: Houghton Mifflin, 1902.

Fabos, Julius Gy., Gordon T. Wilde, and V. Michael Weinmayr. *Frederick Law Olmsted, Sr.: Founder of Landscape Architecture in America.* Amherst, Mass.: University of Massachusetts Press, 1968.

Fein, Albert. *Frederick Law Olmsted and the American Environmental Tradition.* New York: Brazillier, 1972.

Fein, Albert. *Landscape into Cityscape: F. L. Olmsted's Plans for a Greater New York City.* Ithaca, N.Y.: Cornell University Press, 1968.

Fiske, Donald, and Salvatore Maddi. *Functions of Varied Experience.* Homewood, Illinois: Dorsey Press, 1961.

Fitch, James M. *Architecture and the Esthetics of Plenty.* New York: Columbia, University Press, 1961.

Fredrickson, George M. *The Inner Civil War: Northern Intellectuals and the Crisis of the Union.* New York: Harper and Row, 1965. (Especially chapter 7, "The Sanitary Elite: The Organized Response to Suffering," pp. 98–112.)

Fried, M. "Grieving for a Lost Home." In *The Urban Condition.* Leonard Duhl, ed. New York: Basic Books, 1963, pp. 151–171.

Friedberg, M. Paul. *Playgrounds for City Children.* Washington, D.C.: Association for Childhood Education International, 1969.

Funnel, Charles E. *By the Beautiful Sea: The Rise and High Times of That Great American Resort, Atlantic City.* New York: Knopf, 1975.

Gans, Herbert J. *The Levittowners.* New York: Vintage, 1967.

Gans, Herbert J. *People and Plans.* New York: Basic Books, 1968.

Garnsey, Morris E., and James R. Hibbs, eds. *Social Sciences and the Environment.* Proceedings. Boulder, Colo.: The University of Colorado Press, 1967.

Gilbert, James. *Designing the Industrial State: The Intellectual Pursuit of Collectivism in America 1880–1940.* Chicago: Quadrangle Books, 1972.

Gilbert, Katherine. "A Study of Architectural Semantics." In *Architecture in America: A Battle of Styles.* William A. Coles, ed. New York: Appleton-Century-Crofts, 1961, pp. 108–113.

Gilliam, Harold. *The Natural World of San Francisco.* Garden City, N.Y.: Doubleday and Company, 1967.

Glaab, C. N., and Theodore A. Brown. *A History of Urban America.* New York: Macmillan, 1961.

Goffman, Erving. *Behavior in Public Places: Notes on the Social Organization of Gatherings.* New York: The Free Press, 1963.

Goodman, Cary. *Choosing Sides: Playground and Street Life on the Lower East Side.* New York: Schocken Books, 1979.

Gusfield, Joseph. *Symbolic Crusade.* Urbana: University of Illinois Press, 1963.

Haber, Samuel. *Efficiency and Uplift: Scientific Management in the Progressive Era, 1890–1920.* Chicago: The University of Chicago Press, 1964.

Hall, Edward. *The Hidden Dimension.* Garden City, N.Y.: Doubleday and Company, Inc., 1966.

Hall, Edward. *The Silent Language.* New York: Premier Books, 1959.

Hanford, C. H. *Seattle and Environs 1852–1924,* Vol. 1. Chicago: Pioneer Historical Publishing Co., 1924.

Hansen, Gladys, ed. *A Guide to the Bay and Its Cities.* American Guide Series. New York: Hastings House, 1973.

Harlean, James. *Romance of the National Parks.* New York: Macmillan, 1939.

Harris, John, ed. *The Garden: A Celebration of One Thousand Years of British Gardening.* The Exhibition at the Victoria and Albert Museum May 23 to August 26, 1979. London: New Perspectives Publishing Ltd., 1979.

Harris, Neil. *The Artist in American Society: The Formative Years 1790–1860.* New York: Braziller, 1966.

Hawes, The Hon. Kirk. *A Condensed History of Dearborn Park and the Efforts That Have Been Made During the Past Eight Years to Secure the Right to Erect a Public Library Building and a Soldiers' and Sailors' Memorial Hall on the Same.* Chicago: The Chicago Public Library and the Grand Army Hall and Memorial Association of Illinois, 1891.

Hayden, Dolores. *Seven American Utopias: The Architecture of Communitarian Socialism, 1791–1975.* Cambridge: The MIT Press, 1976.

Hays, Samuel P. *Conservation and the Gospel of Efficiency, 1890–1920.* Cambridge: Harvard University Press, 1959.

Hecksher, August. *Open Space: The Life of American Cities.* New York: Harper and Row, 1977.

Hennebo, Dieter. *Geschichte der deutschen Gartenkunst.* Hamburg: Alfred Hoffman, Broschek Verlag, 1963.

Hitchcock, H. R., Jr., et al. *The Rise of an American Architecture.* New York: Praeger, 1970. Published in association with the Metropolitan Museum of Art.

Holland, Laurence, ed. *Who Designs America?* Garden City, N.Y.: Doubleday and Company, 1966.

Hoover, Edgar M., and Raymond Vernon. *Anatomy of a Metropolis.* Garden City, N.Y.: Anchor Books, 1962.

Hoyt, Homer. *One Hundred Years of Land Growth in Chicago: The Relationship of the Growth of Chicago to the Rise of Its Land Values, 1830–1933.* 1933. Reprint. New York: Arno Press, 1970.

Hunt, John Dickson, and Peter Willis, editors. *The Genius of the Place: The English Landscape Garden 1620–1820.* New York: Harper and Row, 1975.

Hyams, E. D. *Capability Brown and Humphrey Repton.* New York: Scribner's, 1971.

Jackson, John Brinckerhoff. *American Space: The Centennial Years 1865–1876.* New York: W. W. Norton, 1972.

Jacobs, Allan B. *Making City Planning Work.* Chicago: The American Society of Planning Officials, 1978.

Jacobs, Jane. *The Death and Life of Great American Cities.* New York: Vintage Books, 1961.

Johnson, Elvin R. *Park Resources for Recreation.* Columbus, O.: Merrill, 1972, p. 132.

Johnson, Johnson, and Roy. *A Progress Report on the Future of Chicago's Lakefront.* Ann Arbor, Mich.: Johnson, Johnson, and Roy, Inc., 1968.

Jones, Dorsey Dee. *Edwin Chadwick and the Early Public Health Movement in England.* Iowa City: University of Iowa, 1931.

Kando, Thomas M. *Leisure and Popular Culture in Transition.* St. Louis, Mo.: Mosby, 1975.

Kasson, John F. *Amusing the Million: Coney Island at the Turn of the Century.* Toronto: McGraw-Hill Canada, 1978.

Kirkland, Joseph. *The Story of Chicago,* Vol. I. Chicago: Dibble Publishing, 1892.

Klein, Maury, and Harvey A. Kantor. *Prisoners of Progress: American Industrial Cities, 1850–1920.* New York: Macmillan, 1976.

Lakey, Charles D. *The Public Grounds of Chicago: How to Give Them Character and Expression.* Chicago: Charles D. Lakey, 1869.

Lane, Roger. *Policing the City: Boston 1822–1885.* New York: Atheneum, 1971.

Laurie, Michael. *An Introduction to Landscape Architecture.* New York: Elsevier, 1975.

Ledermann, Alfred, and Alfred Trachsel. *Creative Playgrounds and Recreation Centers.* New York: Praeger, 1959.

Lee, Joseph. *Constructive and Preventive Philanthropy.* New York, 1902.

Lubove, Roy. *The Urban Community, Housing and Planning in the Progressive Era.* Englewood Cliffs, N.J.: Prentice-Hall, 1967.

Lynch, Kevin. *The Image of the City.* Cambridge: The MIT Press, 1960.

McLaughlin, Charles, ed. *The Papers of Frederick Law Olmsted, Vol. 1. The Formative Years 1822–1852.* Baltimore, Md.: Johns Hopkins University Press, 1977.

MacCannell, Dean. *The Tourist: A New Theory of the Leisure Class.* New York: Schocken, 1976.

Mann, Arthur. *Yankee Reformers in the Urban Age: Social Reform in Boston, 1880–1900.* Cambridge: Harvard University Press, 1954.

Marx, Leo. *Machine in the Garden: Technology and the Pastoral Ideal in America.* New York: Oxford University Press, 1967.

Mayer, Harold M., and Richard C. Wade. *Chicago: Growth of a Metropolis.* Chicago: The University of Chicago Press, 1969.

Mead, George Herbert. *Mind, Self, and Society.* Chicago: The University of Chicago Press, 1934.

Meeker, Arthur. *To Chicago With Love.* New York: Knopf, 1955.

Meller, H. E. *Leisure and the Changing City, 1870–1914.* London: Routledge and Kegan Paul, 1976.

Mellor, J. R. *Urban Sociology in an Urbanized Society.* London: Routledge and Kegan Paul, 1977.

Melville, Herman. *Moby Dick or The White Whale.* New York: Dodd, Mead and Company, 1923.

Michelson, William. *Man and His Urban Environment.* Reading, Mass.: Addison-Wesley, 1970.

Miller, Norman P., and Duane M. Robinson. *The Leisure Age.* Belmont, Calif.: Wadsworth, 1963.

Mills, C. W. *White Collar: The American Middle Classes.* New York: Oxford University Press, 1951.

Moore, Charles. *Daniel H. Burnham.* Boston: Houghton Mifflin, 1921.

Morrison, Raymond, and Myrtle E. Huff. *Let's Go to the Park.* Dallas, Tx.: Wilkinson, 1937.

Mumford, Lewis, "The Renewal of the Landscape." In *The Brown Decades: A Study of the Arts of America 1865–1895.* New York: Dover, 1955.

National Recreation Association. State and Federal Recreation Service. Publication 2: "The Role of the Federal Government in the Field of Public Recreation." New York: National Recreation Association, 1953.

Newton, N. T. *Design on the Land: The Development of Landscape Architecture.* Cambridge: Harvard University Press, 1971.

Olmsted, Frederick Law. *Walks and Talks of an American Farmer in England.* Parts 1 and 2. New York: George P. Putnam, 1852.

Olmsted, Frederick Law, Jr., and Theodora Kimball, eds. *Forty Years of Landscape Architecture.* Cambridge: The MIT Press, 1973.

Park, Robert, Ernest Burgess, and Roderick McKenzie. *The City.* Chicago: The University of Chicago Press, 1967.

Perin, Constance. "Social Governance and Environmental Design." In *Responding to Social Change.* Basil Honikman, ed. Stroudsberg, Penn.: Dowden, Hutchinson and Ross, 1975.

Pierce, Bessie L. *A History of Chicago: 1871–1893. Vol. III, The Rise of a Modern City.* New York: Knopf, 1957.

Pinkney, David H. *Napoleon III and the Rebuilding of Paris.* Princeton, N.J.: Princeton University Press, 1958.

Platt, Anthony M. *The Child Savers.* Chicago: The University of Chicago Press, 1969.

Porter, C. H. *Chicago Beautiful, Parks and Boulevards.* Chicago: Charles H. Porter, 1915.

Poulsen, Charles. *Victoria Park.* London: Journeyman Press and Stepney Books, 1976.

Rainwater, Clarence E. *The Play Movement in the United States: A Study of Community Recreation.* Chicago: The University of Chicago Press, 1922.

Ranney, Victoria Post. *Olmsted in Chicago.* Chicago: Donnelley and Sons, 1972.

Real, Michael R. "The Disney Universe: Morality Plan." *Mass-Mediated Culture.* Englewood Cliffs, N.J.: Prentice-Hall, 1977, pp. 46–89.

Reed, Henry Hope. "Landscape Architecture." In *The Brittanica Encyclopedia of American Art.* New York: Chanticleer Press, 1973, pp. 330–334.

Reed, Henry Hope, and Sophia Duckworth. *Central Park: A History and a Guide.* New York: Clarkson N. Potter, 1976.

Reiss, Albert J., Jr. *Louis Wirth on Cities and Social Life.* Chicago: The University of Chicago Press, 1964.

Reps, John. *The Making of Urban America.* Princeton, N.J.: Princeton University Press, 1965, chapter 12.

Riis, J. A. *How the Other Half Lives.* 1890. Reprint. New York: Hill and Wang, 1966.

Roper, Laura. *A Biography of Frederick Law Olmsted.* Baltimore, Md.: Johns Hopkins University Press, 1973.

Ross, Edward A. *Social Control: A Survey of the Foundation of Order.* 1901. Reprint. New York: Johnson Reprint/Harcourt Brace Jovanovich, 1970.

Rothman, D. J. *The Discovery of the Asylum: Social Order and Disorder in the New Republic.* Boston: Little, Brown, 1971.

Rowe, Colin, and Fred Koeter. *Collage City.* Cambridge: The MIT Press, 1978.

Rutledge, Albert J. *Anatomy of a Park: The Essentials of Recreation Area Planning and Design.* New York: McGraw-Hill, 1971.

Saarinen, Eliel. *The City: Its Growth, Its Decay, Its Future.* New York: Reinhold, 1943.

Schlesinger, Arthur Meier. *Political and Social Growth of the American People, 1865–1940.* New York: Macmillan, 1941.

Schmitt, Peter. *Back to Nature: The Arcadian Myth in Urban America.* New York: Oxford University Press, 1969.

Schwendinger, Julia and Herman. *The Sociologists of the Chair.* New York: Basic Books, 1974.

Scientific American. *Cities.* New York: Alfred A. Knopf, 1965.

Scott, Mel. *American City Planning Since 1890.* Berkeley: University of California Press, 1969.

Sennett, Richard. *The Fall of Public Man.* New York: Alfred A. Knopf, 1977.

Sexby, J. J. *The Municipal Parks, Gardens and Open Spaces of London: Their History and Associations.* London: Elliot Stock, 1898.

Seymour, Whitney North, Jr., ed. *Small Urban Spaces.* New York: New York University Press, 1969.

Shepard, Paul. *Man in the Landscape: A Historic View of the Esthetics of Nature.* New York: Knopf, 1967.

Shurtleff, Arthur A. *Future Parks, Playgrounds and Parkways.* Boston: Boston Park Department, November 1925.

Simon, Jacques, and Marguerite Rouard. *Children's Playspaces.* New York: Overlook Press, 1977.

Smithson, Alison and Peter. *Urban Structuring.* New York: Reinhold, 1967.

Sommer, Robert. *Tight Spaces: Hard Architecture and How to Humanize It.* Englewood Cliffs, N.J.: Prentice-Hall, 1974.

Sparrow, W. J. *Count Rumford of Woburn, Mass.* New York: Thomas Y. Crowell, 1964.

Spear, Allan H. *Black Chicago: The Making of a New Ghetto, 1890–1920.* Chicago: The University of Chicago Press, 1967.

Steiner, Jesse F. *Americans at Play.* New York: McGraw-Hill, 1933.

Stevenson, Elizabeth. *Park Maker: A Life of Frederick Law Olmsted.* New York: Macmillan, 1977.

Still, Bayrd. *Urban America: A History With Documents.* Boston: Little, Brown, 1974.

Stinchcombe, Arthur L. *Theoretical Methods in Social History.* Chicago: The University of Chicago National Opinion Research Center, 1978.

Strauss, Anselm L., ed. *The American City.* Chicago: Aldine, 1968.

Street, David, and Associates. *Handbook of Contemporary Urban Life.* San Francisco: Jossey-Bass Publishers, 1978.

Suttles, Gerald D. *The Social Order of the Slum.* Chicago: The University of Chicago Press, 1968.

Sutton, S. B., ed. *Civilizing American Cities: A Selection of Frederick Law Olmsted's Writings on City Landscapes.* Cambridge: The MIT Press, 1971.

Swanberg, W. A. *Citizen Hearst.* New York: Scribner's, 1961.

Taylor, Lisa, ed. *Urban Open Spaces.* Washington, D.C.: Cooper-Hewitt Museum, The Smithsonian's National Museum of Design, 1979.

Tebbel, John. *The Life and Good Times of William Randolph Hearst.* New York: Dutton, 1952.

Tobey, George B., Jr. *A History of Landscape Architecture: The Relationship of People to Environment.* New York: American Elsevier, 1973.

Tunnard, Christopher. *Gardens in Modern Landscape.* New York: Scribner's, 1950.

Wade, Richard. *The Urban Frontier.* Chicago: The University of Chicago Press, 1959.

Warner, Sam Bass. *Streetcar Suburbs: The Process of Growth in Boston, 1870–1900.* Cambridge: Harvard University Press, 1962.

Weaver, Robert B. *Amusements and Sports in American Life.* Chicago: The University of Chicago Press, 1939.

Weir, L. H., ed. *Parks—A Manual of Municipal and County Parks,* Vols. 1 and 2. New York: A. S. Barnes, 1928.

Western News Company. *The Parks and Property Interests of Chicago.* Chicago: Western News Company, 1898.

Whitaker, Ben and Kenneth Brown. *Parks for People.* New York: Schocken, 1971.

White, Morton and Lucia. *The Intellectual Versus the City, From Thomas Jefferson to Frank Lloyd Wright.* Cambridge: Harvard University Press, 1962.

Whyte, William H. *The Last Landscape.* Garden City, N.Y.: Doubleday Anchor, 1970.

Whyte, William H. *The Social Life of Small Urban Places.* New York: The Conservation Foundation, 1980.

Wiebe, Robert H. *Businessmen and Reform: A Study of the Progressive Movement.* Cambridge: Harvard University Press, 1962.

Wiebe, Robert H. *The Search for Order: 1877–1900.* New York: Hill and Wang, 1967.

Wiebenson, D. *The Picturesque Garden in France.* Princeton, N.J.: Princeton University Press, 1977.

Wiemer, David L. *Private Funds for Parks and Recreation.* Long Island City, N.Y.: Playground Corporation of America, 1969.

Wille, Lois. *Forever Open, Clear and Free: The Historic Struggle for Chicago's Lakefront.* Chicago: Henry Regnery, 1972.

Williams, Raymond. *The Country and the City.* London: Chatto and Windus, 1973.

Wilson, K. *Golden Gate Park, The Park of 1000 Vistas.* Caldwell, Ind.: Caxton Printers Ltd., 1947.

Wingo, Lowdon, Jr., ed. *Cities and Space: The Future Use of Urban Land.* Baltimore, Md.: Johns Hopkins University Press, 1963.

Writers' Program, Works Projects Administration. *New Orleans City Park: Its First Fifty Years.* Washington, D.C.: WPA, 1941.

Writers' Program, Works Projects Administration. *San Francisco: The Bay and Its Cities.* New York: Hastings House, 1940.

Wurman, Richard Saul, Alan Levy, and Joel Katz. *The Nature of Recreation: A Handbook in Honor of Frederick Law Olmsted, Using Examples From His Own Work.* Cambridge: The MIT Press, 1972.

Periodicals

American Park and Outdoor Art Association. Vols. 1–7. 1897–1903. The following articles were cited in text:

"The Billboard Nuisance." Vol. 5, part 2 (1901), pp. 30–32.

Eliot, Charles W. "Popular Utilization of Public Reservations." Vol. 6, part 2 (1903), pp. 6–14.

Hall, Mrs. Herman J. "Park Inconsistencies." Vol. 7, part 4 (May 1904), pp. 19–20.

Holden, L. E. "Parks as Investors and Educators." First Report of the American Park and Outdoor Art Association. Vol. 1 (1897), pp. 42–50.

Olmsted, Frederick Law. "Public Advertising." Vol. 4, part 1 (1900), pp. 3–11.

Olmsted, J. C. "The True Purpose of a Large Public Park." First Report. Vol. 1 (1897), pp. 11–17.

"Report of the Committee on Park Census for 1901." Vol. 5, part 1 (1901), pp. 3–9.

Simonds, O. C. "Appreciation of Natural Beauty." Second Report. Vol. 2 (1898), pp. 75–80.

Garden and Forest. Vols. 5–10. 1892–1897. The following articles were cited in the text:

Macmillan, William. "The Care of Urban Parks." Vol. 8 (February 27, 1895), pp. 82–83.

Sargent, C. S. "The Proposed Speedway in Central Park." Vol. 5 (March 9, 1892), p. 109.

Sargent, C. S. Editorial Comment. Vol 5 (April 20, 1892).

Sargent, C. S. "Military Parades in Central Park." Vol. 6 (June 7, 1893), p. 241.

Sargent, C. S. "Tender Bedding Plants in Public Parks." Vol. 6 (September 6, 1893), pp. 371–372.

Sargent, C. S. "Work for the Municipal Art Society." Vol. 7 (January 10, 1894), pp. 11–12.

Sargent, C. S. "Playgrounds and Parks." Vol. 7 (June 6, 1894), pp. 221–222.

Sargent, C. S. "The Use of Color in Our Parks." Vol. 7 (July 18, 1894), pp. 281–282.

Sargent, C. S. "Keep Off the Grass." Vol. 7 (July 25, 1894), p. 291.

Sargent, C. S. "Park Boards and Their Professional Advisers." Vol. 7 (November 21, 1894), pp. 461–462.

Sargent, C. S. "Parks, Parkways, and Pleasure Grounds." Vol. 8 (May 15, 1895), p. 192.

Sargent, C. S. "The Architectural Attack on Rural Parks." Vol. 8 (September 4, 1895), p. 351.

Sargent, C. S. "The Need of an Efficient Park Service." Vol. 9 (May 6, 1896), p. 181.

Sargent, C. S. "Parklands and Their Boundaries." Vol. 9 (October 21, 1896), pp. 421–422.

Park International. July 1920–November/December 1921. The following articles were cited in the text:

"Andrew Jackson Downing, Father of American Parks." July 1920, pp. 43–48.

Attwell, E. T. "Playgrounds for Colored America." November 1920, pp. 217–224.

Bennett, Edward. "Grant Park, the Frontispiece of Chicago." November 1920, pp. 205–216.

Editorial Notes. "Field and Community Houses." September 1920, pp. 168–170.

Editorial Notes. "Night Riders to the Rescue of Park Scenery." January 1921, pp. 72–76.

Editorial Notes. May 1921, pp. 272–273.

Editorial Notes. "Tax Free Areas." July 1920, pp. 71–72.

Farrier, Edna. "Utilizing the City's Waste Spaces for Recreation." May 1921, pp. 248–253.

Gerry, Belinda. "The Spider Web Motif in Park Design." September 1920, pp. 163–166.

Herding, Franz. "Block Interior Parks." March 1921, pp. 117–125.

Measured drawings of display posts, road signs, sign and lantern brackets. July 1920, pp. 83–86.

Oliver, Judith. "Newspapers Vital to Parks." November 1920, pp. 263–265.

"Park Architecture: Field Houses." September 1920, pp. 128–137.

Peaselee, Horace. "Park Architecture: Bathing Establishments." July 1920, pp. 25–35.

"Villes et Villages Francais àpres la Guerre." Translated by Leon Rosenthal as "Open Spaces." September 1920, pp. 187–190.

Walker, Howard. "Memorials in Parks: Flagpoles." January 1921, pp. 53–56.

Parks and Recreation. Vols. 2–48. April 1918–December 1965. Vols. 1–11. January 1966–June 1976. The following articles were cited in the text:

Beckert, Wilhelm, ed. "Maintenance Mart." Editorial Comment. Vol. 42 (April 1959), pp. 202–204.

Bell, J. Haslett. "A Typical Neighborhood Park." Vol. 9 (July-August 1926), pp. 601–603.

Boyd, Mary Maxine. "Parks for All Seasons . . . and for All People." Vol. 5 (May 1970), pp. 22–23, 59–51.

Brauer, Donald G. "Park Planning for the Future." Vol. 7 (November 1972), p. 14.

Brown, V. K. (superintendent of playgrounds and sports, South Park Commissioners, Chicago). "What Shall We Do with This New Leisure?" Vol. 17 (May 1934), p. 363.

Brown, V. K. "The Place of Parks in a World at War." Vol. 26 (March-April 1943), pp. 150–155.

Cabot, John B. "Architecture in Parks: Only Changes in Expression." Vol. 42 (April 1959), pp. 154–157.

Corwin, E. F. "Rebirth of a Park." Vol. 7 (October 1972), pp. 17–18.

Crass, Harvey S. "Parks—Now and 25 Years Hence." Vol. 31 (December 1948), pp. 710–712.

Davenport, Edward C. "New Ideas for Making the Playground Attractive." Vol. 34 (October 1951), pp. 19–20.

"Designing Parks for Children." Vol. 42 (June 1959), pp. 272–273, 281.

Desy, Jean. "The Human Value of Parks." Vol. 35 (October 1952), p. 9.

Dineen, C. R. "Parks and Planning." Vol. 29 (November-December 1946), pp. 360–363.

Fisk, A. A. "Parks, A Social Asset." Vol. 6 (May-June 1923), pp. 391, 398.

French, Jere Stuart. "The Decline and Deterioration of the American City Parks." Vol. 5 (August 1970), p. 41.

Hare, Herbert. "Trend of Park History: Development in America through Four General Periods." Vol. 5 (1921–1922), pp. 61–63.

Keyser, C. P. "Parks and Cities." Vol. 20 (February 1937), pp. 263–266.

La Gasse, Alfred B. "Design of Park and Recreation Areas of Approximately 10 Acres." Vol. 38 (April 1955), pp. 4–6.

Lawwill, J. R. "A Philosophy for Park Structures." Vol. 31 (August 1948), pp. 427–428.

"Louisville Convention Proceedings." Vol. 4 (October 1920), pp. 38–92.

MacDonald, Keith A. "Color in Parks and Playgrounds." Vol. 39 (May 1956), pp. 5–6.

Mackintosh, D. L. "Are Our Public Parks Edifying?" Vol. 3 (July 1920), pp. 40–41.

McFarland, Horace J. "Parks and the Public." Vol. 6 (September-October 1922), pp. 12–14.

Meeds, C. H. "Should Playgrounds Be Landscaped?" Vol. 7 (September-October 1923), pp. 71–77.

Morrison, R. C. "Rugged Individualism and Community Beautification." Vol. 17 (July 1934), p. 387.

Moses, Robert. "Recipe for Better Parks." Vol. 48 (November 1965), pp. 660–661.

Mott, William Penn, Jr. "Dress Up Your Play Areas with Inexpensive Play Structures." Vol. 39 (May 1956), pp. 4–5.

Mott, William Penn, Jr. "Magic Key to Your Park's Story." Vol. 42 (May 1959), pp. 220–221.

"New Ideas for Making the Playground Attractive." Vol. 34 (October 1951), pp. 1–20.

Olmsted, Frederick Law. " Parks as War Memorials." Vol. 2 (July 1919), pp. 23–31.

"The Park That Children Built." Vol. 41 (September 1958), pp. 376–377, 390.

"The Public Dance Hall: The Problem as Dealt with by San Francisco's Committee." Vol. 7 (July-August 1924), pp. 589–602.

Smergalski, Theodore J. (supervisor of playgrounds, West Chicago Park). "The Relation of Supervision to Play and Recreation." Vol. 1 (July 1918), pp. 13–17.

Thompson, Hans A. "Seattle's Over-the-Freeway Park." Vol. 7 (June 1972), pp. 36–38.

Warner, Dave. "Totlots." Vol. 5 (July 1970), pp. 32–33, 57.

Weir, L. H. "Parks and Their Use," part 2. Vol. 24 (June 1941), pp. 448–451.

Weir, L. H. "Historical Background of the Recreation Movement in America." Vol. 29 (July-August 1946), pp. 238–243.

Wirth, Conrad L. "Related Park and Recreational Problems." Vol. 20 (December 1936), pp. 171–170.

Wyman, Phelps. "Without Views, No Parks." Vol. 8 (March-April 1925), pp. 359–361.

Recreation. Vols. 35–58. April 1941–October 1965. The following articles from *Recreation* were cited in the text:

Baker, Richard. "Public Relations in Recreation." Vol. 50 (October 1957), pp. 300–302.

Berger, Graenum. "Human Problems of Old Age." Vol. 39 (October 1945), pp. 373–374, 386–387.

Braucher, Howard. "A National Recreation Magazine Established Thirty-Five Years Ago." Vol. 36 (April 1942), pp. 1–2.

Bucher, Charles A. "Family Recreation: Foe of Juvenile Delinquency." Vol. 50 (February 1957), pp. 46–48.

Cummings, Carlos E., M.D. "How the Museum Serves in Wartime." Vol. 36 (July 1942), pp. 222–224.

Eckersberg, Alfred K. "Planning, Acquiring, and Building Chicago Parks." Vol. 49 (October 1956), pp. 392–393.

"Facilities Available to Colored Citizens." Vol. 35 (October 1941), pp. 439–442, 473–474.

Harbo, R. T. "Recreation Has a Job to Do." Vol. 38 (July 1944), pp. 201–204.

Hjelte, George. "City Parks . . . Amenity or Necessity?" Vol. 53 (May 1960), pp. 212–214.

Hutchins, Heriot C. "An Approach to Recreation." Vol. 43 (September 1949), pp. 271–275.

"In the Field . . . John W. Faust." Vol. 42 (October 1948), pp. 327–329.

Jansson, Florence. "Give Them Something to Do." Vol. 38 (January 1945), pp. 525–526, 550.

Moses, Robert. "The Moses Recipe for Better Parks." Vol. 49 (May 1956), pp. 214–215.

Moses, Robert. "New York City after the War." Vol. 38 (October 1944), pp. 373, 389–390.

Neumeyer, Martin H. "Wartime Trends in Recreation." Vol. 39 (January 1945), pp. 532–539.

Nichols, Robert B. "New Concepts behind Designs in Modern Playgrounds." Vol. 48 (April 1955), pp. 154–157.

Norris, Ruth. "The Human Values in Recreation." Vol. 55 (November 1962), pp. 443–444, 478.

Overstreet, Harry. "Recreation: New Obligations—New Approaches." Vol. 38 (February 1945), pp. 585–589, 607.

"Philosophies upon Which We Built." Vol. 49 (June 1956), pp. 269.

Prezioso, Sal J. "My Philosophy of Recreation." Vol. 54 (December 1961), p. 509.

Solomon, Ben. "Preventive Recreation." Vol. 49 (March 1951), pp. 562–566.

Spencer, Evelyn. "The Wheel Has Turned Full Circle: The Relationship of Group Work, Recreation, and Mental Health." Vol. 44 (November 1950), pp. 311–314.

Sutton-Smith, B. and Paul Gump. "Games and Status Experience." Vol. 48 (April 1955), pp. 172–174.

Wegner, The Right Reverend Nicholas H. "Significance of Play." Vol. 48 (October 1955), p. 358.

Williams, A. "An Organization Is Born." Vol. 40 (June 1946), pp. 260–263.

Williams, Harold. "Can Recreation Have an Ulterior Motive?" Vol. 51 (September 1958), pp. 228–229.

"World at Play." Vol. 35 (June 1941), pp. 199–205, 207–209.

Wren, C. Gilbert, and D. L. Hanley. "Time On Their Hands." Vol. 35 (September 1941), pp. 361–366.

Other Periodicals, Pamphlets, Articles

Abramovitz, Moses. "The Nature and Significance of Kuznets Cycles." *Economic Development and Cultural Change*, vol. 9 (April 1961), pp. 519–533.

The American City, vol. 64 (1949). Published by American City Magazine Corp., New York.

The American City, vol. 89 (July 1974). Published by Buttenheim.

American Scenic and Historic Preservation Society. *Sixteenth Annual Report*, 1911.

Bacher, Mary Ann. "Adventure Playgrounds for Children." *New England Outdoors*, vol. 5 (February 1979), pp. 12–14.

Bailey, Peter. "'A Mingled Mass of Perfecty Legitimate Pleasures': The Victorian Middle Class and the Problem of Leisure." *Victorian Studies*, vol. 21 (Autumn 1977), pp. 7–28.

Barlow, Elizabeth. *Frederick Law Olmsted's New York*. New York: Praeger in association with the Whitney Museum, 1972.

Beatty, Russell. "Metamorphosis in Sand." *California Horticultural Journal*, vol. 31 (April 1970), pp. 41–46.

Berman, Marshall. " . . . or 'What Man Can Build.'" *Ramparts*, March 1975, pp. 34–58.

Beveridge, Charles. "Frederick Law Olmsted's Theory of Landscape Design." *Nineteenth Century*, vol. 3 (Summer 1977), pp. 38–45.

Black, Edwin. "Riding With the Rat Patrol." *The Chicago Guide*, vol. 20 (August 1971), pp. 12–18.

Blodgett, Geoffrey. "Frederick Law Olmsted: Landscape Architecture as Conservative Reform." *Journal of American History*, vol. 62 (March 1976), pp. 869–889.

Bornstein, Sam. "Rides." *Proceedings of the Second Annual Conference on Revenue Producing Facilities*, Wheeling, W. Va., March 11–15, 1962.

Bornstein, Sam. "Amusement Rides Manual and Survey." *Bulletin No. 29.* American Institute of Park Executives Management Circles, 1963.

Bray, Joann M. "Some Perceptual, Behavioral, and Schematic Complexities of Recreational Space." Master's thesis, University of Chicago, August 1969.

Bray, Paul M. "Preservation Helps New Parks Take Shape." *Kite,* December 6, 1978, p. 1.

Brown, V. K. "Now and Then in Our Park Systems." *American City,* April 1949, p. 75.

Brynolson, Grace. "Gasworks (ugh!) Reborn as a City Park." *Smithsonian Magazine,* November 1977, pp. 117–120.

Cancian, F. M. "Functional Analysis: Varieties of Functional Analysis." In *International Encyclopedia of the Social Sciences.* David L. Sills, ed. New York: Macmillan, 1968, pp. 21–43.

Carlson, Alver. "Last of the Open Lands." *Omnibus* (Chicago), vol. 4 (1967), pp. 27–29.

"Central Park." *Scribner's Monthly,* vol. 6 (September 1873), pp. 523–539.

"Central Park: Part II." *Scribner's Monthly,* vol. 6 (October 1873), pp. 673–691.

"Central Park: I. Grass on Manhattan." *The New Yorker,* September 13, 1941.

"Central Park: II. A Nasty Place." September 20, 1941.

"Central Park: III. What a Nice Municipal Park." September 27, 1941.

"Central Park File. Photos and Lithos pre-1900." Vertical files. New York: Museum of the City of New York.

"Chicago: The Land and the People." *Survey Graphic,* vol. 23 (October 1934), pp. 468–471, 520–525.

Committee of the Southern California Youth Association. *Handbook for Teen Center Operation.* Publication 57–119 (May 1958).

"Coney Island for Battered Souls." *New Republic,* November 23, 1921, pp. 372–374.

Cooper-Marcus, Clare (ed.). *People Places.* Berkeley: Department of Landscape Architecture, University of California, 1976.

Cranz, Galen. "The Beautiful and the Useful: Urban Parks in China." *Landscape,* vol. 23 (1979), pp. 3–10.

Cranz, Galen. "Changing Roles of Urban Parks: From Pleasure Garden to Open Space." *Landscape*, vol. 22 (1978), pp. 9–18.

Cranz, Galen. "The Sharon Building: The Transformation of Women's Place in Public Recreation." *Heresies 11*, vol. 3 (1981), pp. 77–79.

Cranz, Galen. "Women in Urban Parks." *Signs: Journal of Women in Culture and Society*, vol. 5, Suppl. Chicago: The University of Chicago Press, 1980, pp. 79–95.

Cranz, Galen. "Women and Urban Parks: Their Roles as Users and Suppliers of Park Services." In *Building for Women*, S. Keller, ed. Lexington, Mass.: Lexington Books, 1981, pp. 151–171.

Dotterer, Steve, and Galen Cranz. "The Picture Postcard: Its Development and Role in American Urbanization." *Journal of Popular Culture* (in press).

Duis, P. R., and G. E. Holt. "Chicago's Green Crown: The Parks." *Chicago*, August 1977, pp. 84–86.

Dumont, Donna, et al. "San Francisco's Park Policy in the Nineteenth Century: Goals versus Outcomes." Working Paper 342. Institute of Urban and Regional Development, University of California, Berkeley, 1981.

Eckbo, G. "Man and Land." Proceedings of the Sixty-fourth Annual Conference of the American Institute of Park Executives, September 1962.

Eckersberg, Alfred Kenneth. "A Study of the Proposed Consolidation of the Chicago Park District and the City of Chicago." Masters thesis. University of Chicago, September 1949.

Eliot, Charles W. "The Need of Conserving the Natural Beauty and Freedom of Nature in Modern Life." *National Geographic*, vol. 26 (1914), pp. 67–71.

Enid A. Haupt Conservatory. Bronx, New York: New York Botanical Garden. (Park pamphlet.)

Everett, Helen. "Social Control." In *Encyclopedia of the Social Sciences.* Edwin R. A. Seligman, ed. New York: Macmillan, 1962, pp. 344–349.

Fairbanks, K. J. "A Community Building for $40,000." *American City*, April 1949, p. 86.

Foreman, H. G. "Chicago's New Park Service." *Century Magazine*, vol. 69 (February 1905), pp. 610–620.

Funkhauser, G. Ray. "How Do You See the City?" *Psychology Today*, January 1969.

Gibson, Richard M. "Golden Gate Park." *Overland Monthly*, vol. 37 (March 1901), pp. 762–763.

Gitlin, Todd. "Domesticating Nature." *Theory and Society*, vol. 8 (1979), pp. 291–297.

Gold, Seymour M. "The State of Urban Parks." *Parks and Recreation*, vol. 11 (October 1976), pp. 13–19.

Gold, Seymour M. "Future Leisure Environments in Cities." Unpublished Manuscript, April 1977.

Gold, Seymour M. "Neighborhood Parks: The Nonuse Phenomenon." *Evaluation Quarterly*, vol. 1 (May 1977).

Gold, Seymour M. "Nonuse of Neighborhood Parks." *Journal of the American Institute of Planners*, vol. 38 (November 1972), pp. 369–378.

Gold, Seymour M. "Planning Neighborhood Parks for Use." *Ekistics 255* (February 1977), pp. 84–86.

Gold, Seymour M. "Social and Economic Benefits of Trees in Cities." *Journal of Forestry*, pp. 84–87.

Gold, Seymour M. "Social Benefits of Trees in Urban Environments." *International Journal of Environmental Studies*, vol. 10 (1977), pp. 85–90.

Gold, Seymour M. "Recreation Planning for Energy Conservation." *International Journal of Environmental Studies*, vol. 10 (1977), pp. 173–180.

Gold, Seymour M. "Recreation Planning: State of the Art." Paper presented as the Beatrix Farrand Lecture for the Department of Landscape Architecture. College of Environmental Design, University of California, Berkeley, May 26, 1977.

"The Great Exhibition and the Central Park." *Harper's Weekly*, vol. 24 (December 11, 1880), p. 786.

Hall, William Hammond. "Influence of Parks and Pleasure Grounds." *Overland Monthly*, vol. 11 (December 1873), pp. 527–535.

Halprin, L. "Landscapes Between Walls." *Architectural Forum*, vol. 3 (1959), pp. 148–153.

Haynes, Rowland. "How Much Space Does a City Need?" *American City*, vol. 16 (March 1917), pp. 241–243.

Hyatt, Alpheus. "The Next Stage in the Development of Public Parks." *Atlantic Monthly*, vol. 67 (February 1891), pp. 215–224.

"It Was a Real Gas." *Progressive Architecture*, November 1978, pp. 96–99.

Jones, S. C. "Central Park: Manhattan's Outdoors." *National Geographic*, December 1960, pp. 781–812.

Kates, R. W., and J. F. Wohlwill, eds. "Man's Response to the Physical Environment." *The Journal of Social Issues*, vol. 22 (October 1966), pp. 15–20.

Keith, John P., and John P. Milsop. "Park Space for Urban America." *Trends*, vol. 9 (April-June 1972), pp. 37–45.

Kinkead, Eugene and Russell Maloney. *New Yorker*, February 4, 1967.

Lancaster, Clay. "Central Park: 1851–1951." *Magazine of Art*, vol. 44 (April 1951).

Lindsay, John V. White Paper on Parks and Recreation. Issued by the Fusion Candidate for Mayor, October 8, 1965.

Love, Ruth Leeds. "The Fountains of Urban Life." *Urban Life*, vol. 2 (July 1973), pp. 161–209.

McGinnis, Bret J. "How Does Your Department Rate?" *Twentieth Annual Proceedings of the Great Lakes Park Training Institute.* Bloomington, Ind.: Indiana University, 1966.

McLaughlin, Charles. "Olmsted, the Man and the Artist." Gund lectures and exhibition series. Department of Landscape Architecture, Harvard Graduate School of Design, Cambridge, Mass., April 1979.

Mannus, M. "The New York I Know: II. Central Park." *The Reporter*, January 21, 1960, p. 22.

Martin, Edward S. "A Philosopher in Central Park." *Harper's Monthly*, February 1914.

Mawson, Thomas H. "Public Parks and Gardens: Their Design and Equipment." *Transactions of the Town Planning Conference.* October 1910. London: The Royal Institute of British Architects, 1911.

"The Metro Forest." *Natural History*, vol. 82 (November 1973), pp. 45–84.

Midwest Institute of Park Executives. *Midwinter Lecture Series.* Midwest Institute of Park Executives, 1948–1960.

Midwest Institute of Park Executives. *Proceedings of the Nineteenth Annual Educational Conference.* 1960.

Milgram, Stanley. "The Experience of Living in Cities." *Science,* vol. 167 (March 13, 1970), pp. 1461–1468.

Mitchell, J. G. "The Re-Greening of Urban America." *Audubon Society Magazine,* vol. 30 (March 1978), pp. 29–59.

Mosley, Kevin. "Our Parks, People Keep Out!" *Chicago Land Magazine,* vol. 7 (December 1969), pp. 40–44.

Moulton, F. L., et al. "Politics and the Parks." *The City Club Bulletin,* vol. 4, no. 16 (1911), pp. 103–105.

Moulton, F. L., et al. "Proposed West Side Playground Sites." *The City Club Bulletin,* vol. 4, no. 10 (1911), pp. 102–111.

National Recreation Association. *Recreation and Park Yearbook: A Review of Local and County Recreation and Park Developments 1900–1950.* New York: National Recreation Association, 1950. Yearbooks for 1951, 1956, 1961.

National Recreation Association. *The Role of the Federal Government in the Field of Public Recreation.* Publication No. 1–3. New York: National Recreation Association, 1953–1954.

Negrovida, Peter. "Open Lands: The Struggle for Open Space is an Uphill Fight All the Way." *Chicago,* vol. 5 (1968), pp. 95–100.

"New Help for the Nation's Unused City Parks." *Journal of the American Institute of Architects,* vol. 68 (February 1979), pp. 9, 12.

Nichols, Robert B. "New York City's Park Design Controversy." *Landscape Architecture,* vol. 53 (July 1963), pp. 285–287.

Noda, Pat, and Galen Cranz. "Park Images in Recent American Films." Unpublished manuscript. Department of Architecture, University of California, Berkeley, 1978.

Olmsted, Frederick L. "Public Parks and the Enlargement of Towns." *Journal of Social Science,* No. 3 (1871), pp. 1–36.

Olwig, Karen Fog, and Kenneth Olwig. "Underdevelopment and Development of 'Natural' Park Ideology." *Antipode,* vol. 2 (1979), pp. 16–25.

O'Shea, C. M. *Trees of Central Park: Map I.* New York: Greensward Foundation, 1976.

Owings, Loren C., ed. *Environmental Values, 1860 to 1972: A Guide to Information Sources.* Vol. 4. Detroit: Gale Research, 1976.

Parker, G. A. "Report of the Committee on Park Census, 1903." *American Park and Outdoor Art Association*, vol. 7 (1903), pp. 7–15.

Proceedings of the Second Annual Conference on Revenue-Producing Facilities for Governmental Parks, Recreation, and Ecological Parks. American Institute of Park Executives, Wheeling, W. Va., March 11–14, 1962.

Proceedings of the Sixty-third Annual Conference. American Institute of Park Executives, Rochester, N.Y., September 24–28, 1961.

Proceedings of the Sixty-seventh Annual Conference. American Institute of Park Executives, Milwaukee, Wisc., September 19–23, 1965, p. 6.

Proceedings of the Third Annual Conference on Revenue-Producing Facilities for Governmental Parks, Recreation and Ecological Parks. American Institute of Park Executives, Wheeling, W. Va., March 10–13, 1963. (Rebholz, Melvin J., "Entrance Fees for Municipal County and City Parks," pp. 69–73.)

"Profiles: Central Park: II. 'A Nasty Place.'" *New Yorker*, September 20, 1941.

"A Ramble in Central Park." *Harper's New Monthly Magazine*, vol. 59 (October 1879), pp. 689–701.

Rauch, John H. *Public Parks: Their Effects upon the Moral, Physical and Sanitary Conditions of the Inhabitants of Large Cities with Special Reference to the City of Chicago.* Chicago: S. C. Griggs, 1869.

"A Reporter at Large—This is a Funny Time." *New Yorker*, October 18, 1941.

Riis, Jacob A. "Playgrounds for City Schools." *Century*, no. 47 (September 1894), pp. 657–666.

Rosenzweig, Roy. "Middle-Class Parks and Working-Class Play: The Struggle over Recreational Space in Worcester, Massachusetts, 1870–1910." *Radical History Review*, no. 21 (Fall 1979), pp. 31–46.

Sackett, Wallie. "Chicago Park District." Unpublished manuscript. Chicago Historical Society, September 1938.

Sax, Joseph L. "Recreation Policy on the Federal Lands." The Horace M. Albright Conservation Lectureship XVII, Berkeley, California, May 10, 1978.

Schoenwald, R. L. "Training Urban Man." In *The Victorian City:*

A Body of Troubles. H. J. Dyos and Michael Wolff, eds. London and Boston: Routledge and Kegan Paul, 1973, pp. 669–692.

Sessoms, H. D. *Glossary of Recreation and Park Terms. Bulletin*, no. 95. Arlington, Va.: National Recreation and Park Association Management Aids, 1972.

Shaw, Clarence L., Jr. "The Conservatory of Golden Gate Park." *California Horticultural Journal*, vol. 31 (April 1970), pp. 65–68.

Sheehy, G. "Nanas in the Park." *The New Yorker*, June 3, 1968, pp. 18–21.

Shepherd, C. O. "How Safe Are Our Parks?" *American*, May 17, 1964.

Smithson, Robert. "Frederick Law Olmsted." *Art Forum*, vol. 11 (1973), pp. 62–68.

Starbuck, James C. *Theme Park: A Partially Annotated Bibliography of Articles about Modern Amusement Parks*. M. Vance, ed. No. 953. Monticello, Ill.: Council of Planning Librarians, 1976.

Tafuri, Manfredo. "American Regionalism: From the Conservationist Movement to the New Deal." Unpublished manuscript. MIT Lectures, Cambridge, April 29, 1975.

Tafuri, Manfredo. "Architecture and Cities in America between the Two Wars." Unpublished manuscript. MIT Lectures, Cambridge, April 30, 1975.

Tafuri, Manfredo. "American Architecture in the New Deal Age." Unpublished manuscript. MIT Lectures, Cambridge, May 1, 1975.

Tafuri, Manfredo. "Frederick Law Olmsted and the Origins of Planning in the United States." Unpublished manuscript. MIT Lectures, Cambridge, April 28, 1975.

Tribble, Ray L. "Trends in the Design of Community Centers." *Twentieth Annual Proceedings of the Great Lakes Park Training Institute*, Indiana University, Bloomington, 1966.

Trondsen, Norman. "Social Control in the Art Museum." *Urban Life and Culture*, vol. 5 (April 1976), pp. 105–119.

Violich, Francis. "The Planning Pioneers." *California Living Magazine*, February 26, 1968, pp. 29–35.

Wade, Richard C. "Problems and Possibilities in Urban History." Unpublished manuscript. The University of Chicago, 1969.

Whitney, Alan. "Moravksy Den at Pilsen Park." *Chicago*, vol. 2 (September 1955), pp. 44–47.

Wiener, Martin J. "Review of 'Social Control in Nineteenth Century Britain.'" *Journal of Social History*, vol. 12 (Winter 1978), pp. 315–321.

Will, Thomas E. "Public Parks and Playgrounds: A Symposium." *The Arena*, vol. 10 (July 1894), pp. 274–288.

Wilson, O. T. "Vandalism—How to Stop It." *American Institute of Park Executives, Bulletin*, no. 7, 1961.

Woodbridge, Sally B. "Industrial Metamorphosis." *Historic Preservation*, April-June 1978, pp. 37–41.

Newspapers

Abendpost (Chicago), July 26, 1893, through December 24, 1934.

Advance Register (Tulare, Calif.), July 4, 1959.

Ambler, J. C. *Scrapbooks*, Chicago Historical Society Archives. Vols. 58–62. (A collection of newspaper articles.)

Argonaut (San Francisco), May 14, 1948, January 25, 1969.

Argus (Fremont, Calif.), May 4, 1975.

Brooklyn New York Eagle, December 22, 1900, January 15, 1901.

Bulletin (San Francisco), November 3, 1900, through January 5, 1901.

California Herald, May 15, 1901, through August 2, 1964.

California Living Magazine, section of the Sunday *San Francisco Examiner and Chronicle*, November 7, 1976.

California Times (Los Angeles), March 19, 1901.

Chicago American, April 16, 1962, through May 26, 1968.

Chicago Globe, March 12, 1888.

Chicago Hebrew Institute Observer, November 11, 1912.

Chicago Jewish Chronicle, vol. 24, week of April 28, 1933.

Chicago Times Herald, October 15–22, 1900, December 24, 1900.

Chicago Tribune, November 7, 1948, through June 19, 1960.

Chicagoer Arbeiter Zeitung, May 11, 1880, through January 2, 1889.

City of Mexico Herald, December 20, 1900.

Contra Costa Times (Calif.), January 5, 1975.

Cue, July 14, 1945.

Daily Alta (San Francisco), July 19, 1850, through July 27, 1890.

Daily Commercial News (San Francisco), December 13, 1968.

Daily Jewish Courier (Chicago), October 9, 1908, July 3, 1919, April 26, 1923.

Daily News (Chicago), March 27, 1936, June 16, 1969.

Daily News (New York), April 19, 1867, February 18, 1969.

Denni Hlasatel (Chicago), July 6, 1875, through July 11, 1922.

Dziennik Chicagoski, December 22, 1890, through February 9, 1922.

Dziennik Zjednoczenia (Chicago), August 11, 1922, through October 25, 1926.

Dziennik Zwiagkowz (Chicago), February 1, 1877, through August 28, 1918.

Grass Valley Union (Grass Valley, Calif.), November 2, 1900.

Honolulu Republican, December 28, 1900.

Illinois Staats Zeitung (Chicago), July 7, 1862, through October 1, 1900.

Interocean, November 22, 1912, and March 15, 1914.

Mission District News (San Francisco), September 18, 1975, through January 15, 1976.

Monitor (San Francisco), July 16, 1954.

Narod Polski (Chicago), vol. 22, July 10, 1918.

Nation's Cities Weekly (Washington, D.C.), vol. 3, (May 5, 1980), pp. 1–12. Published by the National League of Cities.

News (New York), July 9, 1888, through November 18, 1946.

New York Herald, January 20, 1964.

New York Herald Tribune, June 21, 1925, through August 2, 1964.

New York Post, July 12, 1974, through September 11, 1974.

New York Sun, December 30, 1933.

New York Times, December 12, 1933, through May 12, 1975.

New York Times Magazine, part of the Sunday *New York Times*, December 24, 1922, through January 12, 1930.

New York World Telegram, January 2, 1934.

Oakland Engineer, July 16, 1901.

Oakland Telegraph, December 26, 1975.

Oakland Tribune, April 21, 1976.

People's World (San Francisco), August 28, 1965.

Philadelphia North American, February 7, 1901.

Portola District News (San Francisco), December 11, 1968.

Post (San Francisco), August 29, 1899, through July 18, 1901.

Progress (San Francisco), February 8, 1893, through April 30, 1976.

Record (Chicago), November 8, 1900.

Reporter (San Francisco), March 1, 1975, through July 27, 1975.

Sacramento Daily Union, February 19, 1869, through January 10, 1872.

San Bruno Herald, January 14, 1976.

San Francisco Call, November 16, 1886, through August 11, 1913.

San Francisco Chronicle, June 11, 1894, through March 17, 1929.

San Francisco Examiner, June 11, 1894, through March 17, 1929.

San Francisco Herald, March 13, 1854.

San Francisco News, August 10, 1901, and August 28, 1945, through July 9, 1965.

San Francisco Newsletter, November 17, 1900.

San Francisco Shopping News, "North Beach Hub, The Square That Isn't," September 10, 1960.

San Francisco Sunday Examiner and Chronicle, February 20, 1966, through March 16, 1980.

San Francisco Today, January 14, 1976, through May 19, 1976.

San Jose Herald, July 29, 1901.

San Mateo Times (San Mateo, Calif.), July 12, 1975, September 29, 1975.

Saturday Evening Post, September 25, 1954.

Seattle Times, Engstrom, K., "Lake Union Park—A Back to Nature Site," December 16, 1973, pp. 32–36.

Sonntagpost (Chicago), November 10, 1918, through April 22, 1926.

South Street Reporter, vol. 8, Winter 1974–1975.

Star (San Francisco), March 4, 1893, through April 12, 1901.

Sun Times (Chicago), June 25, 1868, through May 7, 1970.

Svornost (Chicago), May 30, 1892, through June 1, 1896.

Twin Peaks Sentinel (San Francisco, Calif.), December 30, 1965.

The Village Voice (New York), May 23, 1974, "The Park Rated R_x," p. 1, col. 3.

Zgoda (Chicago), June 20, 1901.

Government Documents

Bernert, E. "Local Community Fact Book." Chicago: Chicago Recreation Commission, 1938.

Boston, City Council. *Documents of the City of Boston for the Year 1890.* Document 15. Fifteenth Annual Report of the Board of Commissioners of the Department of Parks. Boston: City Council, 1890.

Buchard, Edward L., ed. *Leisure Time Directory 1938–1940.* Chicago: Chicago Recreation Commission, 1938–1940.

Buchard, Edward L., ed. *Leisure Time Directory 1942–1944.* Chicago: Chicago Recreation Commission, 1942–1944.

Chicago, Board of the West Chicago Park Commissioners. *The Municipal Code of the West Chicago Park Commissioners.* Chicago: The West Chicago Park Commissioners, 1903.

Chicago, Board of the West Chicago Park Commissioners. *The West Parks and Boulevards of Chicago.* Chicago: The West Chicago Park Commissioners, 1913.

Chicago, Bureau of Public Efficiency. *The Park Governments of Chicago.* Chicago: Chicago Bureau of Public Efficiency, 1911.

"Chicago Can Get Fifty Million Dollars for Nothing! How It Can Be Done by Building the South Shore Lake Front Park Lands." Chicago: Chicago Plan Commission, 1916.

Chicago, "City Planning in Race Relations." Chicago: Mayor's Committee on Race Relations, February 1944.

Chicago, Department of Planning. "Basic Policies for the Comprehensive Plan of Chicago." Chicago: City of Chicago, 1964.

Chicago, Park District. *Annual Reports* for the years 1935–1969.

Chicago, *Plan for a Boulevard to Connect the North and South Sides of the River on Michigan Avenue and Pine Street.* Chicago: The Commercial Club of Chicago, 1908.

Chicago, *Principles for Chicago's Recreation Plan: 1952.* Chicago: Chicago Recreation Commission, 1952.

Chicago, Report of the South Park Commissioners to the Board of

County Commissioners of Cook County. *Annual Reports*, 1869–1934.

Chicago, *Report of the Special Park Commission to the City Council of Chicago on the Subject of a Metropolitan Park System.* Chicago, 1904.

Chicago, West Chicago Park Commissioners. *Thirty-First Annual Report of the West Chicago Park Commissioners for the Year Ending December 31, 1899.*

Childhood and Government Project, *Wednesday's Child: Bearing the Costs of Post-War America.* Draft Report, University of California, Berkeley, June 27, 1977.

Foreman, H. G. *Recreation Needs of Chicago.* Chicago: Cook County Board, 1905.

Foster, F. J. "An Article on Small Parks Read Before the Chicago Society for School Extension." Chicago: Chicago Historical Society, 1902.

Halsey, Elizabeth. *The Development of Public Recreation in Metropolitan Chicago.* Chicago: Chicago Recreation Commission, 1940.

Illinois, Department of Economic Development. *Outdoor Recreation in Illinois.* State of Illinois, 1966.

Johnson, F. E. *The Mayors of Chicago: A Chronological List.* Chicago: Municipal Reference Library of Chicago, 1962.

Kessler, George E. *A City Plan for Dallas.* Dallas: Board of Commissioners, 1911.

Lohman, Joseph D. *Police and Minority Groups.* Chicago: Chicago Police Department, 1947.

Massachusetts, State Planning Board. *Park, Parkway and Recreational Area Study.* Boston: Massachusetts State Planning Board, 1941.

Matthews, Nathan, Jr. *The Investigation of the Boston Park Department.* Boston: Boston Municipal Printing Office, 1900.

National Recreation Association. *The Recreational Resources of the United States, Their Conservation, Development and Wise Use.* New York: National Recreation Service, 1953.

National Recreation Association. "The Role of the Federal Government in the Field of Public Recreation." New York: National Recreation Association, 1952.

New York Municipal Reports:

Lindsay, John V. *Parks and Recreation.* White paper issued by the Fusion Candidate for Mayor, October 8, 1965.

Lindsay, Nancy. *Small Parks Project: The Bronx.* City Parks Department #5, Summer 1975.

New York City, Borough of Brooklyn, Department of Parks. Annual Report 1915.

New York City, Borough of Manhattan, Department of Parks. Annual Reports 1912–1915.

New York City, Department of Parks. Minutes of the Board of Commissioners (titles vary), 1872–1931.

New York City, Department of Parks. Annual Reports 1871–1911.

New York City, Department of Parks. Annual Reports 1916–1966.

New York City, Department of Parks, Recreation and Cultural Affairs. Annual Reports for the Years 1967–1979.

New York City, Department of Parks. *Six Years of Park Progress.* New York, 1940.

New York City, Department of Parks. *Eight Years of Park Progress.* New York, 1941.

New York City, Department of Parks. *12 Years of Park Progress.* New York, 1945.

New York City, Department of Parks. *16 Years of Park Progress.* New York, 1949.

New York City, Department of Parks. *18 Years of Park Progress.* New York, 1952.

New York City, Department of Parks. *20 Years of Park Progress.* New York, 1954.

New York City, Department of Parks. *22 Years of Park Progress.* New York, 1956.

New York City, Department of Parks. *26 Years of Park Progress.* New York, 1960.

New York City, Department of Parks. *28 Years of Park Progress.* New York, 1962.

New York City, Department of Parks. Memorandum on 1935 Budget Request. Contains a graph showing variation in the city budgets and park department budgets from 1927 to 1935.

Park Association of New York City. Citizens' View of Their Parks. New York, 1962.

"Parks in New York City's Future." *Proceedings of the Third Annual Pratt Planning Conference.* New York: Planning Department, 1965.

New York City. *Report of the Bureau of Recreation.* 1912.

New York City. *West Side Improvement.* Published on the occasion of the opening, October 12, 1937.

New York State. *Documents of the Assembly.* 80th sess. Vol. 2, no. 131, 1857.

New York State. *Documents of the Senate.* Vol. 3, no. 82, 1853.

New York State. *Documents of the Senate.* 84th sess. Vol. 1, no. 18, 1861.

New York State. *Documents of the Senate.* Vol. 3, no. 26, 1884.

Olmsted, Frederick Law. *Pittsburgh.* Pittsburgh Commission of City Planning, 1910.

Olmsted, Frederick Law. *Pittsburgh.* Pittsburgh: Commission of City Planning, 1918.

Olmsted, Frederick Law, and J. Nolen. "Experts' Report on Civic Center." *Preliminary Report on the City Planning Commission of the City of Milwaukee.* Milwaukee: Phoenix Printing Co., 1911, pp. 19–24.

Olmsted, Frederick Law. *Conditions in Detroit 1915.* Detroit City Planning and Improvement Commission, 1915.

Rebholz, Melvin J. "Entrance Fees for Municipal, County, and City Parks." *Proceedings of the Third Annual Conference on Revenue Producing Facilities for Governmental Parks, Recreation and Ecological Parks.* Wheeling, W. Va.: American Institute of Park Executives, March 10–13, 1963, pp. 69–73.

"Recreation." *A Water Policy for the American People—The Report of the President's Water Resources Policy Commission.* Chapter 16. Washington, D.C.: Government Printing Office, 1950.

Report of the Lowell Historic Canal District Commission. Lt. Gov. Thomas P. O'Neill III, Chairman. Lowell, Mass.: Government Printing Office, 1977.

San Francisco Municipal Reports:

First Biennial Report of the San Francisco Park Commissioners, 1870–1871.

Second Biennial Report of the San Francisco Park Commissioners, 1872–1873.

Third Biennial Report of the San Francisco Park Commissioners, 1874–1875.

San Francisco, Board of Park Commissioners. Annual Report 1872–1924.

San Francisco, Board of Park Commissioners. Minutes 1896–1943.

San Francisco, Department of City Planning. *Recreation and Open-Space Programs.* 1972.

San Francisco, Department of City Planning. *Programs Recommended for Carrying Out the Improvement Plan for Recreation and Open Space.* 1972.

San Francisco, Department of City Planning. *Recreation and Open-Space Programs: Recommendation for Implementing the Recreation and Open-Space Element of the Comprehensive Plan of San Francisco.* July 1973.

San Francisco, Playground Commission. Reports 1912–1930.

San Francisco, Playground Commission. Minutes 1910–1948 (record books in McLaren Lodge).

San Francisco Recreation Department. *Recreation Bulletin,* 1925–1948.

San Francisco, Recreation and Park Department. Annual Reports 1950–1975.

San Francisco Recreation Department, miscellaneous publications:

Joseph Lee Week, July 25–31, 1948.

Randall, Josephine. *Challenge of Recreation and San Francisco's Answer.* 1935.

The Story of San Francisco's Teen Age Centers. 1947.

Supervised Recreation. 1939.

There Are No Strangers Here. 1947.

San Francisco, Recreation and Park Department. *The Develop-*

ment of Parks and Recreation Areas in San Francisco. Unpublished mimeograph, ca. 1954.

San Francisco, Recreation and Park Department. Memorandum from John J. Spring on "Revised Policies, Re Granting of Permits and Reservations." September 8, 1976.

San Francisco, Recreation and Park Department. *News Bulletin,* 1950–1954.

San Francisco, Recreation and Park Department. Plan for Action. Prepared by Blyth Zellerbach Committee, February 1971.

San Francisco, Recreation and Park Department. Report prepared under contract between Planning Research Corporation and the San Francisco Bureau of Government Research. February 1971.

San Francisco. Recreation and Park Department. Summer Act, 1963.

Seattle. *Annual Report for the City of Seattle.* 1912.

Shanes, Ethel. *Recreation and Delinquency.* Chicago: Chicago Recreation Commission, 1942.

Special Park Commission. *Report on Metropolitan Park System.* Minneapolis, 1905.

Suggested Goals in Park and Recreation Planning. Chicago: Chicago Park District, 1959.

Theobald, William F. *The Female in Public Recreation.* Ontario: Ontario Recreation Society, Ontario Ministry of Culture and Recreation, 1976.

U.S., Bureau of the Census. *Historical Statistics of the United States, Colonial Times to 1957, Continuation to 1962 and Revisions.* Washington, D.C.: Government Printing Office, 1965, p. 20.

U.S., Department of Housing and Urban Development. *Urban Recreation.* Prepared for the Nationwide Outdoor Recreation Plan by the Interdepartmental Work Group on Urban Recreation, HUD–401. Washington, D.C.: Government Printing Office, 1974.

U.S. Department of the Interior, National Park Service Special Study: the 1974 Summer Session. *Gateway National Recreation Area.* November 1975.

U.S., Department of the Interior, National Park Service. *Yosemite Summary of the Draft General Management Plan.* August 1978.

U.S., Government Printing Office. American Scenic and Historic Preservation Society. *Documents 61,* 1908; *60,* 1910; *73,* 1909; *58,*

1911; *59,* 1912; *59,* 1913; *57,* 1914; *65,* 1915; *57,* 1916; *51,* 1917; *62,* 1918; *102,* 1919; *117,* 1920; *92* and *93,* 1922; *109,* 1923; *92,* 1924; *108,* 1926.

U.S., Government Printing Office. Government Message on Juvenile Delinquency. *Documents 19* and *36,* 1945.

U.S., Government Printing Office. Government Message on State Park and Parkway System. *Document 82,* 1932.

U.S., Government Printing Office. International Sunshine Society Report. *Documents 55,* 1918; *132,* 1920.

U.S., Government Printing Office. Report of Brown Valley Park Commission. *Documents 9,* 1907; *36,* 1909; *4,* 1915; *7,* 1917; *42,* 1918; *61,* 1919; *46,* 1923; *108,* 1926.

U.S., Government Printing Office. Report of the Society for the Preservation of Scenic and Historic Places and Objects. *Documents 18,* 1900; *60,* 1903; *62,* 1904; *55,* 1907.

U.S., Government Printing Office. Report of the Superintendent of Public Works. *Documents 33,* 1904; *14,* 1907; *13,* 1908; *19,* 1909; *14,* 1912; *23,* 1913; *56,* 1914; *30,* 1915; *28,* 1916; *22,* 1917; *28,* 1943; *30,* 1944; *60,* 1945; *39,* 1946; *50,* 1947; *60,* 1948; *53,* 1949.

U.S., Government Printing Office. Report of the Urbanism Committee to the National Resources Committee. *Our Cities: Their Role in the National Economy.* 1937.

U.S., Government Printing Office. Society for Reformation of Juvenile Delinquents. *Annual Report, Documents 42,* 1913; *16,* 1908; *61,* 1910; *24,* 1916; *35,* 1917; *33,* 1918; *118,* 1919; *80,* 1922.

Works Progress Administration. *WPA Projects: Analysis of Projects Placed in Operation through June 30, 1937.* Washington, D.C.: Government Printing Office, 1937.

Index

(*Page numbers for material in figures are in italics.*)